CATLIN PUBLIC LIBRARY DISTRICT

3 1781 00019 1534

What others are saying about *Child-Friendly Divorce* and the Parenting Through Divorce Program:

LSTA FY 2005 GRANT

"*Child-Friendly Divorce* is a must read for therapists and those who are undergoing divorce.

Child-Friendly Divorce might sound like a contradiction in terms, but, using extensive legal experience and experience in counseling and dealing with those undergoing divorce, Diane Berry shows with an integrated approach with attention to psychological needs of parents and children, divorce can be made less traumatic.

Ideally Diane Berry would be personally available to every divorcing couple and their children, but the benefits of her wisdom in this wonderful book provide guidelines for both 'the head' and 'the heart' in a very practical and useful way."

–**Dr. Robert A. Dickens**, Psychiatrist

"As a social worker, I have been exposed to the negative effects on children when parents divorce and act in ways that are counter-productive to meeting their children's needs. The majority of parents who divorce want their children's needs to be met but simply do not have the knowledge on how best to do this. As a participant in Ms Berry's class, I found the information presented to be a unifying summary of the information I had gathered and learned in the past from multiple sources. Ms. Berry presents the tools necessary to help parents recognize what behaviors children commonly exhibit during a divorce, how to address them and tips for restructuring your relationship with your former spouse in a manner that can produce a smooth transition for both parents and children."

–**Dawn Tisler**, Juvenile Delinquency Social Worker

W9-CYB-302

A sampling of comments from participants court-ordered to attend Parenting Through Divorce:

"It taught me more than what I knew after being a mom for 14 years."

"I wasn't too happy to be attending this but am very glad I came."

"I really enjoyed it. [The program] really helped me focus on something in the midst of a chaotic life. I would suggest having more classes."

"A much needed course. There should be one similar prior to [getting] a marriage license. This should be nationwide. Outstanding instructor. Excellent ideas presented and offered own experiences. Stressed over and over the importance of focus on children."

"I have learned extremely useful information to help my children."

"I discovered mistakes that won't be repeated."

"Excellent, practical suggestions."

Timely and valuable."

I learned a lot and was reassured that I was doing a lot of good things already. Great examples and stories to help you relate [to] what your kids are feeling."

"I feel it was very helpful, especially the examples from Diane and [information regarding] handling children's behavior problems..."

"I think that it was a great experience. I have learned a lot from this."

Very helpful. I feel a lot better and a lot of my questions have been answered. I know what to look for, what to do and not to do with my kids."

CHILD
A Divorce(d) Therapist's Guide
FRIENDLY
to Helping Your Children Thrive
DIVORCE

DIANE M. BERRY, MSW, LCSW, JD

FIRST EDITION

Blue Waters Publications
Manitowoc, Wisconsin

CHILD-FRIENDLY DIVORCE

A Divorce(d) Therapist's Guide to Helping Your Children Thrive!

© 2004 by Diane M. Berry, MSW, LCSW, JD

Blue Waters Publications, LLC
P. O. Box 411
Manitowoc, WI 54221-0411
Contact@bluewaterspublications.com
http://www.bluewaterspublications.com

All rights reserved. No part of this book may be reproduced or transmitted in any form or by any means, electronic or mechanical, including photocopying, recording or by any information storage and retrieval system, without written permission from the author, except for the inclusion of brief quotations in a review.

While the case studies and examples described in this book are based on interviews and situations experienced by real persons, the names, professions, locations and other biographical details have been changed to preserve their privacy and anonymity. Unless otherwise noted, examples provided in the text do not reflect actual persons, living or dead. Any resemblance to actual persons is purely coincidental.

Printed in the United States of America
ISBN, print ed. 0-9742078-4-5
ISBN, PDF ed. 0-9742078-2-9
First Printing 2004

Cover Design by Dunn+Associates

Library of Congress Cataloging-in-Publication Data

(Provided by Quality Books, Inc.)

Berry, Diane M.
Child-friendly divorce : a divorce(d) therapist's guide to helping your children thrive! / Diane M. Berry.—1st ed.
    p.cm.
    LCCN 2003094176
    ISBN 0-9742078-4-5
    ISBN 0-9742078-2-9(PDF ed.)
    1. Children of divorced parents—Psychology.
    2. Divorced parents—Life skills guides.
    3. Divorce—Psychological aspects.
    4. Parenting, Part-time.
    I. Title.
HQ777.5.B495 2004   306.89
                QBI03-200519

Dedication

This book is dedicated to my daughter, Katie, for her inspiration and her wisdom. She has challenged me to be my best, as a parent and a therapist, and has enabled me to develop this information to share with others in similar situations.

Catlin Public Library District
101 Mapleleaf Dr.
P.O. Box 350
Catlin, IL 61817
(217) 427-2550

"One's mind, once stretched by a new idea, never regains its original dimensions."

~Oliver Wendell Holmes

Contents

Foreword

With divorce affecting the majority of families in one capacity or another, it is crucial to make use of all of the information available to us about how to make this life event easier on those most vulnerable family members, our children. Over the past few years, I have observed that the Parenting Through Divorce program has been and continues to be an instrumental and significant tool in helping my divorce clients understand the significance of their individual actions on their children of all ages, during the divorce process and afterwards.

As an attorney practicing mainly Family Law, I have personally seen the impact this program has in helping parents deal more appropriately with their emotions during an extremely painful and difficult time in their lives. The principles utilized in this program have also been helpful to me in counseling my clients in their divorce action.

I strongly believe that this program should be utilized in paternity cases as well as divorce cases, because it directly applies to any parent having difficulties in dealing with the other parent and the ultimate effect on their children.

What makes this program even more effective is the fact that Diane and Terry Berry have personally dealt with blended family issues and have developed constructive and appropriate ways to deal with the various challenges faced by families who have gone through divorce and/or entered into second family situations, and the effect it all has on the individuals and family as a whole.

Now, for the first time, the information shared in this valuable program is available in written form to an even wider audience. Read it and use it—for your benefit and that of your children.

Clare Bader, Family Law Attorney

Preface

A Note to the Reader

This is a challenging time to be a parent. Experiencing divorce adds yet one more challenge with which to cope. It is my hope that this text will help you to do so in a positive manner.

You will encounter stories of my own personal experiences, both divorce related and otherwise, as well as situations encountered by clients and families I have worked with. I provide these examples both to entertain and to teach. If you can benefit from their experiences, all the better. Real life examples provide both a flavor and format for applying theoretical suggestions to real life. Hopefully these will assist you, dear readers, in so doing. My work, whether practicing therapy, teaching a class or writing a book, is nothing if not accessible and usable.

There is not enough room in one manual to include everything you need to know about parenting and divorce. Therefore, Blue Waters Publications has developed supplemental articles and information which are available via our website and will continue to be updated as new information becomes available. Please feel free to contact us if you have questions that are not answered by any of these materials.

Diane M. Berry
Manitowoc, Wisconsin

About the Author

 Diane Berry has both personal and professional experience with her subject matter. Starting her professional career as a divorce attorney, she quickly realized that the part of her work she enjoyed the most was talking with her clients about the emotional issues and all the life changes divorce imposes on the players. After that, her role involved dealing with other lawyers and judges and often amounted to, in many cases, "dividing up the silverware!"

Berry returned to school to pursue a Master's Degree in Social Work (MSW) and had a daughter. Two years later, Berry's husband of nine years admitted he was involved in an affair and asked for a divorce. Her life was turned upside down as she returned to her home town, took a social work position as a child protective services worker and embarked on raising her daughter as a single parent.

Several years later, Berry married a man with two teen-aged sons, and has now been a step-parent for thirteen years. Additionally, she and her husband, who is also a therapist, have two children together and have personally dealt with many of the issues with which her clients are struggling. It is this combination of both personal and professional experience that makes her work, and this book, different from any other divorce reference guide.

In her work as a therapist with individuals, couples and families experiencing divorce, Berry saw many caring, well-intentioned parents doing and saying things that were emotionally damaging to their children. This led Berry to develop a four hour educational workshop, entitled Parenting Through Divorce, which became the basis for her book, *Child-Friendly Divorce*.

Berry has also been a Divorce Mediator for Manitowoc County since 1991, meeting with divorcing parents referred by the court system to assist them in working out agreements regarding legal custody and physical placement issues. The majority of the couples Berry works with are able to reach a mediated agreement on these important issues, thereby avoiding a court decision dictating how children will divide their time. In this context, Berry has done an extensive amount of writing, crafting technical legal agreements that rarely get challenged or altered by the parties or attorneys involved.

Berry lives with her husband, three children and two dogs and divides her time between Manitowoc, Wisconsin, the northwoods of Wisconsin and Taos, New Mexico.

A Note on Gender

To avoid long and awkward phrasing within sentences, the publisher has chosen to randomly alternate the use of male and female pronouns, in referring to both children and parents, to give acknowledgment to persons of both genders.

Acknowledgments

I have not attempted to cite in the text all the authorities and sources consulted in the preparation of this manual. To do so would require more space than is available. The list would include departments of the federal government, libraries, periodicals, Web sources, and many individuals.

Scores of people contributed to this volume, including many fine parents who have attended the Parenting Through Divorce class and took the risk of sharing their stories with me and other class members. You have helped me share this information with others but, more importantly, you have helped others deal with situations they face in a positive manner because they had your example to emulate. I thank and respect you.

Special thanks go to Dr. Robert A. Dickens, Attorney Clare Bader and Social Worker Dawn Tisler for their kind words about this work, Kathi and Hobie for the cover and interior design, Tom Cleereman for website design, Dan Poynter for the publishing "poynters" and my friend and right hand Lisa Klein for *all* that she did to make this book possible. Thanks also go to Family Court Commissioner Lorene Mozinski and Circuit Court Judge Darryl Deets for their continued support of my work and this program. Additionally I owe a debt of gratitude to my parents, Betty and the late Jerry Ebert, for instilling in me a love of the written word, my family for tolerating my unavailability and absentmindedness when writing and to Bill Schlei, for being a cooperative and amicable co-parent. I sincerely thank all of these fine people.

I also want to extend a very special thank you to my husband Terry, for keeping the home fires burning, allowing me to escape to the northwoods of Wisconsin to complete this manuscript. You are also my gentlest but swiftest editor. I could not have done this without your assistance and support and remain eternally grateful.

Disclaimer

This book is designed to provide information about the subject matter covered. It is sold with the understanding that the publisher and author are not engaged in rendering legal, accounting, therapy or other professional services. If legal, therapeutic or other expert assistance is required, the services of a competent professional should be sought.

It is not the purpose of this manual to reprint all the information that is otherwise available to parents on this subject matter, but to complement, amplify and supplement other texts. For more information, please see the many references in the Appendices.

Every effort has been made to make this book as complete and accurate as possible. However, it may contain mistakes, both typographical and in content. Therefore, this text should be used only as a general guide and not as the ultimate source of parenting information. Further, this manual contains information on parenting during divorce that is current only up to the printing date.

The purpose of this manual is to educate, inform and entertain. The author and Blue Waters Publications shall have neither liability nor responsibility to any person or entity with respect to any loss or damage caused or alleged to be caused directly or indirectly by the information contained in this book.

If you do not wish to be bound by the above disclaimer, you may return this book to the publisher for a full refund.

"What the caterpillar calls the end of the world, the master calls a butterfly."

~Richard Bach

INTRODUCTION

DIVIDING UP THE SILVERWARE

*A Personal and Professional Perspective
on Divorce*

We've all seen the dismal numbers: over 50 percent of first marriages and 60 percent of second marriages end in divorce. One third of all children under the age of 18 live with only one parent. One million children must cope with parental divorce each year.[1]

With the majority of our children being affected by this type of trauma at some point in their lives, it is imperative that parents begin to look not only at how divorce affects their children, but, even more importantly, what they can do about it. This has been a mission in my life for the past ten years.

Beginning my professional career as a family law attorney, I had the opportunity to observe some of the devastation that can occur when parents divorce, even before I became a parent myself. The bitterness and hostility between previously loving, caring persons is too often directed at, or at the very least observed, by the most innocent of victims, their children.

As a fledgling attorney, I quickly realized that I had some aptitude for the part of the job that almost every divorce attorney detests—dealing with the emotional upsets and crises that are a necessary part of the process of breaking apart a marriage. If fact, I discovered that the part of that job that I most enjoyed was the first appointment, when I would spend approximately an hour and a half to two hours with a new client, listening to all that was happening in their lives; the problems and the pain, the hopes and the fears. Then, together, we would figure out what, if anything, they wanted to do about it. After that, my job as an attorney seemed to revolve around dividing up the silverware and an excessive amount of contact with judges and other attorneys, which I enjoyed significantly less.

As a part of my work, I accepted Guardian ad Litem appointments for the county in which I worked. For these appointments, I was hired by the county to represent or act on behalf of children involved in either a divorce or custody proceeding, or as victims in child abuse or neglect investigations.

It was in doing this work that I realized that it was the social workers that were able to do my favorite part of my job, all the time. Their work focused on those emotional issues and transitions that I most enjoyed. When I discovered this, I decided to go back to graduate school to obtain a Master's Degree in Social Work (MSW).

About the time that I made that decision, two other momentous occasions occurred in my life. I became pregnant with our first child and my husband of seven years was transferred to Madison as part of his employment. This worked out extremely well for me as there was a graduate school at the University of Wisconsin Madison with a terrific Social Work program.

Shortly after our daughter, Katie, was born, I eagerly began taking courses toward my ultimate professional goal—the MSW. By the time Katie was 18 months old, I had completed two courses toward my degree.

Then, one week to the day before my 30th birthday, my husband Bill came home very late one rainy Friday night and uttered words I will never forget, "*I am in love with the most wonderful woman in the world and I want a divorce.*" I understood, even at that moment, that these words would forever change my life. I just didn't completely understand how.

My entire world, as I knew it, ended at that moment in time. We were Catholic and had been married in the Church. When we said our vows, I had married for life.

I knew we had been having some problems. The adjustment to parenthood after eight years of marriage, with only ourselves to worry about, had not been an easy one. I also knew that Bill felt that my primary focus, after all that time alone together, had become our daughter—because, of course it had! He was somewhat resentful of this fact. We had spoken with our priest and had begun seeing a counselor at my insistence. Still, I was stunned by his announcement!

I was not aware of Bill's affair, at least consciously, although several weeks prior to that evening I had driven Bill's lunch across town to him at his place of employment to drop it off in his car at his request. While doing so, I happened to spot his wallet sitting on the dashboard. To this day, I am not sure what made me look. But I opened it up and looked inside, only to find an individual picture of the woman he later confessed to being in love with.

When I confronted Bill about the photograph, he told me she had just had them done and had given one to everyone that worked in their department. But this was not the type of photograph you give to female friends. It was not X-rated, by any means, just slightly seductive. Nonetheless, I believed him—mostly because I wanted to, I expect. I can tell you that upon hearing his announcement I was shocked!

And nothing in my personal, educational or professional experience as an attorney or as a social worker prepared me for the emotional roller coaster I was about to experience.

It is this process that I want to share with you. Bill and I separated rather quickly; the next day, in fact, at my insistence. My reasoning was that if he was set on continuing his relationship with "Sandy", and he was, I did not want him living with me. I was not about to make it easy for him to continue his relationship with her. He had to make a choice.

And so he did. I suspect he had assumed I would just go along with his plan to live in our home with me and our daughter until he decided to move out. But in response to my ultimatum, he moved out the next day and began living with a friend.

As we had only recently moved to Madison and, as I had been quite occupied being pregnant and having a baby for much of the 18 months we had lived there, most of the people who comprised our social group were persons employed by the same company for which Bill worked. Unfortunately, the woman he had become involved with was also employed by this entity, in his department, so it quickly became extremely uncomfortable for me to have much contact with anyone who could be considered part of my initial support system. As a result, I began looking elsewhere in an attempt to establish a life for myself and my daughter.

I was employed at that time as a part time Assistant District Attorney in a neighboring county, prosecuting traffic and juvenile offenses in an attempt to pay for my schooling and contribute to the family income. My heart wasn't in it, but I did it. Being an attorney was what I could do to earn the highest part-time income.

I struggled with the position, however, viewing myself as more of a social worker than a prosecutor, especially with the juveniles. I found myself leaning toward counseling and community service for the majority, which pleased them and their attorneys immensely.

This posed a dilemma, however. I now needed a full-time job to support myself and my daughter, yet I had a difficult time trying to convince myself that I should apply for legal positions. I knew, however, that was how I would be able to earn the most comfortable income.

Also, I knew it was doubtful that I would be able to obtain a social work position in the Madison area. While I had been working toward my Master's Degree, I had applied for a number of such positions as they became available. I felt that with my law and undergraduate degrees, there were a number of Bachelor level social work positions for which I was qualified. Madison, however, is a college town and over-run with social workers. Most of the applicants with whom I was competing for these positions typically already had their Master's Degrees. So now I was under qualified!

Shortly after Bill's Friday night announcement, briefly able to focus on what I needed most at that time, I made the decision to move home. Bill and I had both grown up in the same small town of 33,000 people in Northeastern Wisconsin. Both of our families of origin still resided there, so Katie could be near both extended families.

This was also where my true support system was: my family, my friends, my future. As soon as I made the decision to move, two miracles happened, affirming my belief that I was headed in the right direction and that I had not been abandoned by any spiritual connection or guidance.

The very next weekend, Katie and I traveled to Manitowoc to look for a place to live. My mother, a local realtor who does not typically deal with any rental properties, had only that week sold a home to a young couple who would be surrendering the perfect two bedroom house they had been renting. It was located four blocks from my parents' home.

Manitowoc is a community of families. At that time at least, there were few rental properties in the city at all, much less homes that were available for rent. The fact that my mother was made aware of this property becoming available, only a day or two before my need for it, could only be a miracle!

The house was perfect. It had two bedrooms, a great location, in a nice neighborhood and reasonable, affordable rent. I couldn't have asked for more if I had scripted this event myself!

The second miracle was a little more complex. As I stated previously, during our time there, I had been applying for social work positions in Madison. Aside from the trouble with my qualifications, I had this credibility problem: no one in Madison believed that a lawyer really wanted to be a social worker!

In Manitowoc, for whatever reason, they believed me. I sent my resume to the Manitowoc County Human Services Department which, coincidentally, happened to be interviewing candidates to fill a social work position in the Child Protective Services Unit, which was exactly where I wanted to work. I was told they had already interviewed approximately 50 candidates, but just hadn't found the right person. I was the last person to be interviewed and was asked to stay for a written test and second interview the same day, late on a Friday afternoon.

After spending the weekend with my parents, I went "home" and received two telephone messages that next Monday. The first told me I had the house. The second told me I had the job. I took these messages as signs that I was moving in the right direction; affirmation that I sorely needed at the time.

The way it worked out, approximately one and one half months after Bill's Friday night announcement, our daughter and I moved up to Manitowoc, about three hours north of Madison, and I began putting my shattered life back together. This involved an, at times, complicated schedule, arranging visits between Katie and Bill, transportation arrangements, child care planning and the myriad of details that any single parent juggles every day. It was a busy time, but also a time of much growth and healing.

I eventually was the one to actually file for divorce once I was established in Manitowoc. I had always been the "responsible" one in our relationship so I was not sure Bill would do so and I didn't want to be hanging on forever. I wanted to move on with my life. Being an attorney, I also knew that I wanted jurisdiction for any matters concerning the placement and custody of my daughter to be in Manitowoc County, not in Madison.

Our divorce proceeded uneventfully from that point on, until the day arrived when both Bill and I appeared in court to affirm that our marriage was, indeed, irretrievably broken. We had been able to work things out between ourselves so the final hearing became just a formality putting an end to our lives together. In fact, the day, several months before, when we had actually separated our home and possessions as I was moving my things up to Manitowoc, felt more like the day of our true divorce than that of our court hearing. That was almost a non-event.

In the short time of twenty minutes, Bill and I both testified, the judge said his piece and our sacred connection to each other was legally and permanently severed. Except that we would always be connected through our daughter.

While I was employed at Manitowoc County, I met the man who would eventually become my second husband and my life partner, both personally and professionally. Terry was a family therapist with the County, working with families whose adolescents were having some trouble, either in school or in the community. He was also divorced, having been left by his wife of ten years when their sons were eight and nine years old. We connected immediately.

Terry's sons were 17 and 18 when we started dating. Katie was just three, so we had children at opposite ends of the age spectrum. This made life quite interesting, especially as I had never parented teenagers or boys before!

It is this journey that I want to share with you; our struggles with many of the issues that separated, divorcing and single parents deal with. I have experienced them as a lawyer, a divorce mediator, a social worker, a therapist and, now, as a divorced and remarried parent. I have much information about what can make things easier, and what can only hurt the situation and your children. I can help.

In fact, in 1995 I finally graduated from the University of Wisconsin at Milwaukee with a Master's Degree in Social Work and a specialization in Marriage and Family Therapy. I had attended classes on a part-time basis over the previous four years and during the pregnancies of my two youngest children. All three of my children were present at my graduation, as was my husband and one of my stepsons.

I then began my career as a therapist, working primarily with persons suffering with depression, anxiety, stress. I also found myself working with a number of clients faced with significant life changes, such as divorce or stepfamily adjustment, that were causing them some difficulty.

When dealing with clients experiencing divorce, I encountered what I found to be a strange phenomenon. I found myself working with many persons, couples and families, who were good, well-intentioned, intelligent, caring parents who were unwittingly doing and saying things to their children as they were in the throes of the divorce, that were harmful to the very persons they wanted most to protect and shelter from all of that: their children.

Many had already endured much sadness and unhappiness. Most often I would work individually with these clients, helping to educate them about how their actions were affecting their children, but was frustrated at the seeming enormity of this problem and the slow process of reaching only one parent at a time.

At the point of that realization, I developed a program that I have called "Parenting Through Divorce." It was designed as an informal class to educate parents about how to best handle some of the more common situations faced during the typical divorce. I initially offered the program on a voluntary basis, approximately twice per year, to parents who were willing to hear what I had to say.

In 1998, the Family Court Commissioner in our County heard of the program and attended one of the classes. She determined that what I was sharing was valuable information for divorcing parents and made the program mandatory for all parents experiencing divorce in Manitowoc County. It has also been ordered for some couples who are long past their divorce (you'll hear more about them in Chapter 9) and for some couples who have never been married, but who have a child together.

At its inception, this program was offered to persons responding to notices in the local newspaper on a completely voluntary basis. Initially, I would hear from persons in a wide variety of different situations. I would, of course, get the people in the middle of a divorce, who were concerned about how their children were being affected and what they could do about it. I would also see persons who had been divorced for a number of years, who were still having trouble dealing with their children's other parent on matters regarding the children. The people I admired the most were those persons thinking about filing for divorce, but wanted to know before they made that decision, how their children were likely to be affected. That's dedication!

I am still running this program. Since it has been made mandatory for all divorcing parents in our county, however, most of the persons coming through the class are in the process of a current divorce. The state of Wisconsin requires a 120 waiting period between the day divorce papers are first filed with the court and the day a final hearing may be held of the matter. Most persons attending the class are in the window of this waiting period; in the throes of the divorce, as it were.

Additionally, while at first offering the program twice a year was sufficient to handle the demand in our small community, over the past twelve months I have taught the class 18 times! It was booked to capacity, approximately 15 persons, each time. The group is now regularly offered 24 times per year (12 times by me and 12 times by another therapist that I trained to do the program) in our county of approximately 85,000 people. Persons register for the class 3-4 months in advance. These facts really bring home the enormity of divorce and its effect on our families and society! The majority of our families and children today are being affected by this phenomenon, this crisis we call divorce.

While these numbers may depress and disappoint you, the material that follows will not. What I would like to share, by means of the printed word, is how to help yourselves and your children through the process of divorce; how to make this crisis of life as easy and manageable as possible for all involved. In many cases, people find they are able to use this experience as an opportunity for growth and development, both for themselves and for their children. After all, our goal as parents is not to prevent our children from experiencing any stress. They will need to learn how to handle stress as they will certainly experience it as adults. We certainly do!

Rather, our goal for our children is to keep the stress they face as manageable and moderate as possible; keep it to a level they can overcome, whether it is caused by parental divorce or some other stressor occurring in their lives. This is called resilience and this is what I can teach you!

You will notice as you traverse the chapters that follow, that each begins with an example of the issue presented in the chapter to follow. Some are examples of the right way to handle the issue; some illustrate methods that could benefit from some improvement. It will be easy to tell which is which.

Each is designed to illustrate common events and

circumstances experienced by children whose parents are experiencing divorce and my hope is to help you step into the shoes of your own children to view the experience from their perspective. The examples should make it easier for you to do so.

At the end of each chapter and, occasionally at other appropriate places within the text, you will find quotations from famous, not-so-famous or anonymous persons that I have chosen to illustrate the principles espoused in the chapter or section. Pause and give yourself a moment or two to reflect on the wisdom and significance of the quotation as they, along with the examples provided and the summaries discussed below, can lead to a deeper understanding of the information and attitudes being shared within the text itself.

Each chapter also ends with a one- to two-page summary of the most important points espoused in the chapter. The purpose of these summaries is to facilitate review of the material and to make it easier to access the information presented. Take a few moments as you complete each chapter to skim over the summary to determine how you can best use the information to help your children adapt.

On that note, let's begin.

"When one door of happiness closes, another opens; but often we look so long at the closed door that we do not see the one which has been opened for us."~

~Helen Keller

CHAPTER 1

SURVIVING THE TRAUMA OF DIVORCE

What Happens to the Children?

Jamie spent the first seven years of his life in his family's four bedroom home on five acres of land on the outskirts of the city. He helped his parents by caring for his dog and two cats and, as often as he could, from morning until night, he was outside playing in the woods and meadows surrounding his home. Jamie also had many friends living nearby and, with his grandparents living only a short walk away, through the woods, he was a regular impromptu visitor at their home.

When his parents divorced, Jamie was forced to leave his former life behind. The family had to sell the home and Jamie went to live with his mother in a second story apartment in the city. The only play area he had, other than his tiny bedroom, was a city park several blocks away where he was able to persuade his exhausted mother to take him twice a week. He lost his home, his friends, his school, his grandparents—everything secure and familiar to him. Eventually, his mother noticed he wasn't doing his chores, he was fighting with his peers and, when he brought home his next report card, his grades had all dropped. All are common seven year old reactions to separation and divorce.

Divorce is a trauma for children. Make no mistake about this. It means a loss of their family as they know it. Most children have a number of mixed feelings that they struggle with in coming to terms with parental divorce. But what parents will see from their children is highly dependent on their ages and levels of development.

There are a number of emotions that are common to children of all ages when a divorce happens. While what you see will vary depending on age, your child will most likely feel some variation of these feelings. Knowing what to do about it can make the difference between handling them positively and creating further distance in your relationship with your child.

Anger is a common reaction in children of divorce. You may observe angry behavior from your child, but whether or not your child will tell you it is *you* they are angry with, is largely dependent on the age and developmental level of the child. For some age groups, showing or verbalizing anger directly toward a parent is simply too terrifying, especially at this time when kids are often afraid of being abandoned by the very parent they depend on for their own sense of security.

As parents, we also want to remember that anger is what we call a secondary emotion. This is also good for us to remember as persons experiencing divorce and dealing with our own negative emotions, but we will talk more about this in Chapter Three. Whenever we, or our children, feel anger, we have felt something else first; most typically some variation of hurt, fear or frustration. Often, it is a combination of all three emotions that is affecting us.

A simple example of this that adults can relate to is that of being cut-off by another driver while driving down the road. The first reaction we may be aware of is typically anger. We ask, "How dare he? Who does he think he is?" or some such thing. But if we step back a little further, we realize that our first reaction and realization was truly one of fear: "Oh no, I'm going to have an accident!" The emotion of fear preceded that of anger.

In a situation of parental divorce, kids most commonly feel both hurt and fear or anxiety. They see their family disintegrating before their very eyes and, on some level, realize that family is necessary for their survival. In fact, they often see it as more necessary than it truly is (i.e. some age groups believe that an intact family is crucial for their survival, which is obviously not the case.) This leads to a very deep fear about their very survival. However, while it is certainly not recommended as a positive parenting technique, a divorce, when coupled with sensitive parenting, can produce healthy, well-adjusted children.

Many children of divorce also internalize some blame for the divorce, feeling that something *they* did somehow caused their parents to divorce. This leads to feelings of guilt and hurt that can also manifest as anger (i.e. "Dad left because I was bad.") But whether or not your children will show you their anger, again, depends on their developmental level.

It is not uncommon for children experiencing divorce to feel betrayed and personally rejected by the parent that decided to leave. They internalize the parent's rejection of the other parent as a rejection of themselves (i.e. "Mommy doesn't want/love me anymore.")

Most children also feel profoundly sad when a divorce is imminent. These children typically report feeling a deep sense of loss at the change their families are experiencing.

Finally, often, before a divorce happens there has often been a considerable amount of tension in a family. This tension can manifest as a significant amount of conflict, arguing and bickering, or it can take the form of silence, so thick if feels as if you could cut it with a knife. In either case, children in these families often feel a sense of relief when one parent moves out of the family home and the decision to divorce has been made.

I have heard from many parents in my classes that their children seem more relaxed and comfortable since they have separated, and are doing better both socially and in school. It is not that these children want their parents to divorce, but they typically want and need significant relationships with both parents and find that it is better and easier to see them separately.

While the emotions described above are common to children in divorcing families, therapists working with these children and researchers studying them find that age *does* affect a child's reaction to divorce. Each age group appears to have its own unique set of difficulties to work through, directly related to the level of emotional development the child has experienced.

It is how these age groups and developmental stages differ in reaction to personal divorce that will encompass the remainder of this chapter. We will explore what the typical emotions are and what they most often look like in terms of behavioral changes. If parents know what to look for, they are in a better position to help their children make a positive adjustment.

Some of the ideas that will be shared with you are the results of scientific research studies looking at the effects of divorce on children. For the two youngest groups discussed, however, there has been a limited amount of hard research completed, in part because they are so young. Therefore, most of the information regarding these youngest victims of divorce will be based on case study information and reactions observed by or reported to me, in addition to data from other resources on divorce and child development.

By the end of this chapter, we will have explored and established the emotional and behavioral basis for what parents are seeing from their children at this difficult and upsetting time. These reactions will be separated by age and developmental level. Then, in the two chapters immediately following, we will explore what parents can do to help children through this adjustment process and encourage them to thrive in spite of it.

It is the awareness of this process, and what to do about it that I seek to share in this book, for parents of children of all ages. For every age group, there are a number of things parents can do to increase the likelihood of their children's positive adjustment to their divorce. It is my goal to help you to help your children succeed in this task.

The Reaction of the Littlest Ones~Infants(Ages 0-12 months)

Though he had been on a regular eating and sleeping schedule for several months, six month old Kyle began waking and crying in the middle of the night when his parents separated. Inconsolable for

*what seemed an interminable length of time, he would eventually fall
into an exhausted, but restless sleep.*

Babies have a limited number of options in reacting to any
given situation. We see this as they respond to parental divorce as
well. Infants are affected by divorce and separation, as they are by
many stressors they may face, largely because of the changes in
the care they receive.

When parents are experiencing a divorce, or any
emotionally troubling situation, they are distracted and less
emotionally available to their children. Cries are not responded
to as quickly; babies are not picked up and held as soon or as
often when they cry. A parent is normally less focused on the
baby as their focus is on the emotional difficulties they are
currently experiencing.

Babies realize this; they sense it. Any parent will tell you
that a baby can sense tension in the parent or in the home.
When mom or dad becomes distracted and less attentive, the
baby reacts.

Babies reacting to divorce are really responding to the
upset and tension transmitted to them by their parents. The
parent may be worried, preoccupied, anxious or distressed. The
care they are providing may just not be up to the same standard
as before the separation. The infant's routine may be somewhat
disrupted. All of these events can lead to the reactions we will
discuss below.

How babies react to separation and divorce is easy for
parents to miss because, due to their rather limited options,
their reactions are similar to their normal behaviors. The only
differences may be in the timing and quantity of these behaviors. They are doing essentially the same things they have
always done; they are just doing them more often or at particular times.

Parents in my classes regularly admit that they had not
realized how much their baby was affected by their divorce, or
connected their actions to the situation, until we discussed
these reactions in class because they are so easy to dismiss as
normal behavior.

Because of this extremely limited repertoire of behaviors,

babies are limited in their responses to these transitions and changes in routine to:

❀ Increased crying and upsetness,

❀ Being more fretful, in general,

❀ Eating problems and

❀ Digestive disturbances.

These babies may cry more often, more easily, or for longer periods of time when hungry, uncomfortable or at any time of transition. They also typically wake earlier from naps and have a harder time getting to sleep at night. They may also have more digestive problems, resulting in more vomiting and diarrhea than is typical for them. This can also lead to more frequent upset tummies, which can also increase crying and decrease sleep. Because these symptoms are so commonly seen in these little ones of such limited ability, however, it is easy to chalk them up to situational causes, such as a flu bug, teething or some inconsequential malady, rather than an emotional reaction to divorce.

Parental awareness of these reactions can enable us to deal more effectively and constructively with the child's reactions, and set the stage for a more successful adjustment to the new family situation. Increased attention and nurturing, in addition to other factors we will discuss later, can help children begin adapting successfully to these changes. Attributing a child's crying and digestive troubles to teething will not promote the same positive adjustment in the child.

The Toddler Reaction~(Ages 1-2 1/2)

Andrew was an easy-going child who seldom cried or became upset. However, the week after his parents separated, he began kicking at his mother as she was getting him ready for a visit with his dad, then threw himself to the carpet, screaming and pounding his fists on the floor.

Similar to Infants, Toddlers have little comprehension of

what is happening in the family when a separation or divorce is experienced. Reactions observed by parents are actually the toddler's response to stress in their homes and to the sudden disappearance of one of their parents. As any parent of a toddler will confirm they, also, react strongly to any changes or upsets in their routine.

Toddlers typically respond to separation, more than divorce, due to their rather limited understanding of the complicated concepts of marriage and divorce. What they are reacting to is the fact that they see only one parent at a time, which is typically a change for a toddler, and the fact that they may not see a parent for a week or more at a time, which is also most often unusual for a toddler in an intact family.

An exception to this occurs if one parent is frequently absent from the family for a week or more, something that often occurs due to employment responsibilities, such as working as an over-the-road trucker or in traveling sales. If that has been the situation in your family, you may notice little actual reaction at the time of separation or divorce. Your child may only begin to react when he is older and begins to comprehend the significance of the family situation.

This raises another important point. Even if your child is a toddler when you experience your divorce, and goes through the normal toddler reactions to this family change, she will most likely re-experience the divorce as she achieves each subsequent developmental level. Thus, when she becomes a preschooler, you may notice her exhibiting some of the reactive behaviors that a preschooler would typically exhibit if parents are experiencing a divorce at that stage of her life, though, most likely, to a lesser extent. What the child is doing is mastering the tasks of that developmental stage, which requires that she incorporate the divorce as part of her life and family experience. But not to worry—this is normal and the child should not experience the symptoms to the same degree as if the divorce were happening at that moment, but at a milder level.

Toddlers respond to this family stress in much the same way they react to any stress in their lives. We know stressed toddlers frequently exhibit aggressive behaviors. Toddlers of divorce are no exception. Those experiencing divorce stress often react with aggression and increased irritability. As they are also wont to do, toddlers may express their distress by means of temper tantrums. Again, they are expressing the feelings of hurt, fear, frustration and insecurity. Their choices for expressing these strong negative emotions are extremely limited.

It is easy with this age group, as well, to attribute these actions to normal toddler behavior. Again, what you want to pay attention to is timing and frequency. If you had encountered an occasional temper tantrum before the separation, but since the breakup you experience them every other day, this is a good indication that the increase is divorce-related. Similarly, if you have always had a reasonably complacent, mild-mannered child and, since the separation, the day care center reports to you weekly on his aggressive behaviors, the indication is there. What you want to do is become aware that this is an emotional reaction to the family situation and start taking steps to help your child make a positive adjustment to the divorce.

Also common to this age group is regression to earlier forms of behavior. If he had given up bottles, pacifiers or security blankets, you may notice your toddler again persistently requesting these items. Or, if she had been making progress in toilet training, you may notice changes in those behaviors as well.

Parents would do well to accommodate these small regressions. It will hurt nothing and will help immeasurably to allow the child to go back to using a security blanket or pacifier for a few extra months or even several years. The request, or demand, is the toddler's way of telling you they are feeling insecure at this time and indicating to you what they need to best comfort themselves. The pacifier or blanket represents security for her and can help her adjust to the changes in her family. Let her tell you what she needs.

Before I moved my 18 month old daughter, Katie, up to our new Manitowoc home, we had begun experimenting with toilet training. The potty chair had its place in the bathroom and, while she was not even close to being completely trained, she knew what it was and could talk about what it was for.

After we moved to Manitowoc, the chair took its place in the bathroom, but Katie would no longer acknowledge its existence. When asked about it, she appeared not to know what it was and would not discuss it, but would get distracted and focus on something else, such as the rubber duckie in the bathtub. This was her way of telling me that she could not take on a new developmental task at the same time she was adjusting to our new family. Within six months, however, she was again acknowledging the chair and talking about what it was for. Katie was three, however, before she was completely potty trained. This delay or regression has resulted in no long term problems for her; it merely set her back for a time in the normal progress of development. This is the most typical type of a regression.

This raises another important issue: that of how long children's divorce-related problems continue. A number of authorities report that these changes last anywhere from a few weeks to a few months.[1] In my experience, both personally and professionally, these divorce-related changes typically last quite a bit longer than that. It is not unusual for children's symptoms to last for up to two years after the separation, typically with no long term effects on the child's eventual adjustment or development. The divorce will always be a part of their life experience, and a part of the person they become, but taking two years to adjust or overcome symptoms does not get in the way of the child's successful adjustment to the event.

Other regressions we noticed in our family related to the bottle and the pacifier. At the point of the separation, Katie liked to have a bottle at bedtime and to use a pacifier occasionally when she napped. After the separation, she requested or demanded a bottle with every meal, and wanted to keep the pacifier with her throughout the day. We accommodated these requests, again understanding her need for added security during this stressful time. I remember wishing I had something that would as easily soothe me!

Rather than fight her on this issue, we trusted her process and, sure enough, when she felt more secure, she didn't need these comforting techniques anymore. If parents struggle against what the child knows he needs, they can short-circuit or prevent a successful adjustment to the divorce. Listen to your children. They speak volumes if parents only allow themselves to listen and to hear them.

Another common way for this need for security to present itself, both for the Toddlers and for the next oldest group, the Preschoolers, is through asking to sleep with a parent. I am not an advocate of the "family bed" concept that some professionals espouse, whereby a child sleeps with both parents all night every night, until she is viewed as old enough and ready to have their own bed and sleep alone, often not until they enter school. I believe this encourages dependency in children where none need exist. In addition, such a practice often prevents all three (or more) persons in the bed from getting a good night's sleep, as sleeping young children often seem to be made up primarily of knees and elbows, and prefer to sleep sideways, much to the chagrin of exhausted parents!

However, at times in their lives when children need additional security, they will often ask to sleep with a parent. This is not necessarily a harmful situation when viewed as a time-limited symptom of divorce adjustment. Frequently, when children are not getting enough attention or nurturing during waking hours, or just feel the need for additional closeness, sleeping with a parent can help them find that nurturing and security at night. A parent experiencing divorce often welcomes the company as well, and has room for an extra body in the bed.

It is best if the child falls asleep in her own bed, however, and then crawls in with the parent if she wakes during the night. This way, the child remains accustomed to self-soothing at bedtime but knows she can seek comfort during the night if she needs to. Letting the child fall asleep in your bed can prolong this process and also lead to a greater dependency on the parent.

We experienced this phenomenon in our family through a non-divorce related circumstance. When our youngest daughter, Meghan Rose, was three, I took a job that required me to work 40 hours per week. As a result, I was often starting my workday before she woke in the morning. Previous to this, she had only known me to work 10-15 hours a week or attend graduate school, for about the same number of hours, and most often, when I was not at home with her, her father was.

This new arrangement required Meghan to attend a day care center starting about 7:30 a.m. each week day, from which I would retrieve her most days around 4:30 p.m. With those hours and without consent, Meghan had started a full time job as well. The first month, we noticed that Meghan was more withdrawn than usual. We expected a change such as this and understood its origin.

Then, in the second month, something rather extraordinary began to occur. Nearly every night, Meghan would wander into our bedroom in the middle of the night and crawl into bed between us, most often snuggling up to me. We understood then that she needed more nurturing and cuddling with her mother and was taking it upon herself to get that need met, accomplishing this via her nocturnal visits.

About a year later, I was able to leave that job and my schedule improved, so I was able to spend more waking hours nurturing my daughter. The nocturnal visits dropped off. I asked her one day why she didn't join us in the middle of the night anymore and Meghan very wisely replied, "I don't need to anymore."

Meghan is ten now and we still notice that occasionally, in times of stress, such as the beginning of a new school year, she will wander into our room for several nights and sleep between us. Interestingly, she is our most independent child, and the one who, controlling for age, does the most to meet her own needs and take care of herself. She knows what she needs and how to get it. Oh, the wisdom of children—if parents can only trust and accept it!

Preschoolers React~(Ages 3-5 1/2)

Previously well-adjusted to her child care provider, when her parents separated, three year old Taylor began to cling to her father's leg, crying, "Don't leave me, Daddy. I'll be good!" whenever he would drop her off.

Preschoolers are the youngest group to be included in the scientific studies discussed earlier. They tend to show the most dramatic changes in behavior and typically have a poor grasp of what is happening in the family. Developmentally, they are more advanced than their younger siblings in that they are understand "mom" and "dad" to a greater degree, but they still do not grasp the complex concepts of marriage and divorce.

Due to their developmental level, preschoolers typically become bewildered and frightened for a number of reasons. This anxiety about the world at large, especially any change, is often expressed in ways that most parents find aversive: clinging, whining, temper tantrums, irritability and increased aggressiveness. These are normal divorce reactions from this age group as well. While these may not be entirely new behaviors for these children, parents are likely to see an increased number of these symptoms and an increase in their intensity in reaction to separation and divorce.

But something else is operating here as well, complicating divorce adjustment in this age group. Developmentally, preschoolers tend to perceive their parents as a single unit: "mom and dad." Therefore, when one leaves or moves out of the home, the child becomes convinced the other parent will somehow leave them as well. This is a normal, developmentally appropriate reaction for children in this age group.

Parents in divorcing families typically hear these fearful preschoolers ask, "When you die, who will take care of me?" or, upon going to bed, "Will you be here when I wake up in the morning?" These questions are especially likely to come at transition times, when you are dropping them off at daycare (i.e. "Are you going to pick me up tonight?") putting them down for a nap, or at bedtime. These are times when anxiety is increased, due to the impending separation from the parent, and because the transition, itself, raises the level of emotion. We will discuss transition times and their effects further in Chapter Seven.

Even routine separations can become traumatic. Bedtimes often become more difficult because your preschooler is afraid he will wake to an empty house. He may also wake up crying more often during the night for this same reason. The calmer and more reassuring you can be at these times, the more quickly the child will adjust.

Another factor affecting a preschooler's adjustment to

divorce is their very normal but overwhelming self-centered-ness. Preschoolers share the common perception that the world revolves around them. For this reason, preschoolers, more than any other age group, though all will do this to some extent, are likely to believe that the divorce happened because of something they did or didn't do: "I was bad," "I was too noisy," etc. How heartbreaking it must be for a young child to carry this weight, believing that they were the cause of the family break-up!

All children, no matter their age, need to hear that they were not the cause of the divorce and that the divorce is just between their parents. These little ones need to hear it most of all. Do not assume if you are not hearing these fears from them that they are not having them. In the absence of affirming infor-mation, children's imaginations run wild. Your silent child may just be certain she caused the divorce and feel too overwhelmed and ashamed to mention it to anyone! How tragic for a child to carry that weight around. Tell her *now* that it is not her fault!

Because of the anxiety common to this age group, which is then exacerbated by the separation or divorce, preschoolers also tend to lose their most recently acquired skills. Similar to the Toddlers just discussed, they may regress to younger, more immature behavior. Parents may notice more frequent lapses in toilet training. Preschoolers may also return to security blankets or old toys, or revert to thumb-sucking behavior in spite of having previously kicked the habit. Parents may also notice more frequent masturbation in their children as this, also, is a comforting and soothing behavior. Again, these regressions last anywhere from a few months to two years.

The good news about these littlest ones to be studied in any detail, is that in a follow-up study that looked at the long term adjustment of all age groups, from Preschoolers through Teens, this group showed the most positive adjustment to the divorce ten years later. They were doing better, even when compared to their own older siblings raised in the same family setting![2]

This result initially puzzled the researchers as these little ones typically had no memory of when the family was intact and living together, and they were more vulnerable than their older siblings at the time of the separation. Why, then, were they better adjusted ten years later?

The answer to this important question is powerful information for parents of children of all ages! The critical factor in the lives of these little ones seemed to be that, because they were the littlest at the time of the divorce, they tended to receive better care throughout the years immediately following the divorce than did their older siblings, who were more able to care for themselves and often left to do so. The Preschoolers received more "TLC" from parents, grandparents, other extended family members, child care providers and older siblings—everyone in their lives—while their older siblings were left to fend more for themselves. That fact, alone, helped these little ones to look much better than their own siblings as long as ten years after the divorce!

This is a powerful piece of information for parents of all children. The more you give to your children now, while the divorce is happening and when they need it, the better they, too, will look in ten years.

So make it a point to give all of your children the extra care you may be saving for only your youngest child. That will help them adjust to the family trauma as well. The more nurturing a child receives when experiencing a traumatic event, such as parental divorce, the better and more easily he will be able to adjust to it.

We must remember that our goal as parents is not to prevent or protect our children from experiencing any stress in their lives. We are not here to completely shelter them from hard times. After all, we know they will face stress as adults and, if our experience is any indicator, it will not be a small amount.

Rather, our goal as parents is to keep the stress facing our children moderate enough that they can succeed in spite of it; moderate enough that they can overcome it. This fosters a resiliency in children that enables them to handle progressively greater stressors, within limits and appropriate to their ages. To that end, if we can provide the appropriate assistance and support in times of stress, we can not only enhance their long term adjustment to our divorce, but help them to learn a skill that will assist them for the rest of their lives.

School Age Children~(6-8 years)

The example of seven year old Jamie at the beginning of this chapter is quite typical of this age group.

School age children tend to be the most openly grief stricken of all age groups when reacting to parental divorce, especially boys. In fact, it is at this age that we start to notice a difference between boys and girls, which will be discussed thoroughly in Chapter Three. But all children of this age tend to yearn intensely for the parent they see less often and show the greatest amount of loss and despair of all ages. Further, more than any other group, these children tend to believe their intact family is absolutely vital to their very survival; that they cannot live with a divorced family.

These are also the children that will likely prompt telephone calls from teachers. Many will have difficulty concentrating in school or relating to their peers, especially those from intact families, due to the very deep despair they are experiencing. They just can't seem to distract themselves from the problems and changes happening at home to focus on school work. Parents are likely to hear from the school that their child is daydreaming during class, fighting with peers on the playground, and not completing or not handing in (even completed) assignments.

School age children are also extremely susceptible to feelings of abandonment and rejection. Specific to this age group is the concern or worry that they will be replaced in the absent parent's affections by another child. They reason, "Dad will find another seven year old boy to love so he won't need me anymore."

While all children have a difficult time with parental conflict, these children feel it most acutely. Many feel a very desperate loyalty at this age to both parents and can feel they are literally being pulled apart if parents engage in a conflictual discussion in their presence. While it is always best to raise issues that could result in conflict when children are not around, if it happens unexpectedly, *shut it down at once* and take it up another time, especially if you have a 6-8 year old child within hearing distance.

Anger is common among children of divorce and the school age child is no exception. However, most will *not* tell they are angry with you about the divorce. Sharing strong negative emotions directed toward a parent is simply too frightening at this age, given the depths of the loss and despair they are experiencing. What they will do, however, is show it to you indirectly: they will fight with peers, act aggressively with siblings, refuse to do chores, and fail to complete their homework. If you notice any of these behaviors from your previously calm and conscientious school age child, he may be telling you he is angry about the divorce. You can then use that awareness in ways we will discuss in succeeding chapters to help him adjust.

Pre-Adolescents~(9-12 year olds)

"You're a loser; I hate you!" eleven year old Jenna screams at her mother as they engage in yet another battle over homework. Jenna is convinced that her mother is being selfish in choosing to divorce her father and seeks every opportunity to share this opinion with her.

Children in this age group are grappling with the issues of identity and values, even when their parents are not divorcing at this time in their lives. This is one of the major developmental tasks of this age group. Pre-Adolescents typically rely heavily on their parents' identity and values to define their own.

A parental divorce at this stage in their lives means the world, as they know it, has ended! This leads to their struggle; grappling with the issues of who they are and what they believe in, with no stable resource to look to for help in answering those questions. Pre-adolescents dealing with a divorce typically experience a shaken sense of identity and a shaken sense of right and wrong, leading most typically to frustration and anger.

In fact, anger is the most distinguishing reaction for a significant number of 9-12 year olds. Many exhibit an intense anger, directed at one or both parents, usually whoever they blame for the divorce. This may be the parent who left the home, filed papers or had an affair. These are the children who *will* tell you how angry they are with you, loudly and clearly, because, according to their pre-adolescent reasoning, differences can always be worked out. Therefore, they reason, you could reconcile, if you only tried hard enough. And if you are not reconciling, it means you are not trying, so you are selfish and care about no one but yourself! They also typically accuse parents of being indifferent to children's needs. As with the other age groups, all of this emotion dissipates in time, especially if parents are aware of what is happening and can assist the child in working through it. This will be discussed in greater depth in the next two chapters.

We also want to remember, here, our previous discussion of anger as a secondary emotion. Whenever we feel anger we, or in this case, our children, have felt something else first. In a familial divorce it is most typically fear and hurt. Remembering that these are the emotions fueling your pre-adolescent's anger can assist you both accepting it and in helping them to work through it.

Pre-adolescents also typically express their distress in the form of somatic complaints "I have a headache." "My stomach hurts." "I don't feel good." "I don't want to go to school today." All of these are common refrains when you have a 9-12 year old in the house.

However, do not let them skip school with these kinds of complaints, absent a solid medical reason such as a fever, vomiting, diarrhea, or a doctor's excuse. If you are in doubt about whether your daughter should stay at home, call or take her to a doctor. But if there is no medical reason for her to stay home, send her to school.

Why the hard line approach against skipping school? After all, they are going through a rough time, right?

Stability is the answer. School is the same today as it was last week, as it was last month, as it was last year. It is a solid six to eight hours a day when children know what is likely to happen and what is expected of them. It is, for the most part, predictable, stable, solid, and unchanging—the exact opposite of home and family at this time.

Home is chaotic and changing at this point. It may be in

a different location; perhaps half of the furniture is gone or leaving; many other changes are in the offing. The last thing your child needs is to spend more time than usual in an unstable, chaotic situation. School offers a short vacation from these changes. It offers the very stable environment that your pre-adolescent child needs right now.

Also, letting them stay home, when in the past you would not have even considered it, gives your child the message that all of the rules are changing and unstable as well. This contributes to their feeling of chaos, even though they will swear to you that it does not.

Because these children are old enough to care for themselves in many ways, they are often a relief for parents, who focus more on the younger children who require more hands-on care. As a result, however, the nine to twelve year olds tend to feel lost in the shuffle, as well as hurt, rejected, unimportant and powerless. This makes them especially susceptible to being swept into a bitter and open alliance with one parent against the other, if one of the parents is inclined to encourage such a union. The child is most likely to align with the parent who was left or hurt most in the divorce. This type of alliance makes the pre-adolescent feel needed, powerful and important, positive alternatives in their minds, for the time being, to feeling unimportant and unnecessary.

All parents should know that such alliances are unhealthy and emotionally damaging for the child, who is the product of *both* parents, including the "bad" or maligned one. Alliances such as this usually do not last longer than six months to a year, unless fueled by a hurt, angry parent. Children involved in such an arrangement most often feel guilt, anguish and regret once they get some distance on the divorce, and often deeply resent the parent that encouraged such an alliance. Therefore, even if a parent is willing to ignore the harm caused to children by this tactic, it most often backfires as a means of developing a close relationship with a child.

Teenagers React~(13-17 years)

"I don't feel like trying out for the football team this year. It just

doesn't matter to me anymore," 15 year old Erik says to his mother as she drives him to school. In the past month, he has also stopped hanging out with friends he has had for the past five years, stating that he prefers to stay at home watching television.

It was in 1969 that Dr. Elisabeth Kubler-Ross wrote her landmark work about the grief experience, *On Death and Dying* (MacMillan Publishing, 1970). For some years, she had been working as a physician and treating terminally ill patients. Observing the ill from the point of their diagnosis through the time of their death, she identified five stages that persons diagnosed with a terminal illness experienced in coming to terms with the illness, which came to be known as the grieving process.

Upon initially being apprised of their fate, and the likelihood of recovery, most patients would react with *Denial*. This was often exhibited by statements such as, "I'm not going to die," "They'll find a cure," and "I'm going to beat this." It was marked both by a state of numbness or shock at the findings, and a refusal to accept the finality and inevitability of the result.

After the denial stage, came the *Anger* at their fate. Now realizing what would likely happen, many would rail, "This isn't fair!" and "Why did this have to happen to me!" Bitterness and resentment often accompanied this stage.

Following the anger, came a *Bargaining* stage. Patients attempted to bargain for a more promising outcome, often turning to God as the object of their pleas. Statements such as, "I will do anything if you only make me well," "I will be the best Christian (Catholic, Jew, etc.) in the world if you only make me well," "I will go to Church every Sunday," and the like are not uncommon at this stage. Patients seem not to understand the futility of their requests because they have not yet reached the stage of accepting their illness and its likely outcome.

When the bargaining subsided, *Depression and Withdrawal* took over. Along with the depressed mood and melancholy, this stage also included the beginning of the withdrawal from persons, places and things in which the patient had previously been invested. Things that used to matter a great deal do not provoke the same reactions as they formerly did at this point.

This pulling away from things that used to be important to the patient is the beginning of the final stage, *Acceptance*. At this point, the patient begins to accept her fate and may find some peace in it, if she lives long enough to accomplish this. She may even begin to verbalize this to others and to plan for "after I am gone."

Persons may cycle through the stages several times before achieving Acceptance, and can get stuck in one stage or several. The most typical sticking places are Anger and Depression, because they are painful to move through. The temptation is to "stuff" or medicate these uncomfortable feelings, rather than to face them. But everyone experiencing this type of loss begins with some level of Denial and, if they work through the entire process, ends with Acceptance.

Some years later, it was discovered that persons experienced this same process whenever they faced any significant loss in their lives. Researchers discovered that it did not matter whether the loss was their own life, as in the patients with whom Dr. Kubler-Ross worked, or if it was the loss of a parent, child, sibling or spouse, the loss incurred through divorce or the loss of a home or job they loved. Even the loss of a pet could initiate the grieving process.

This is the process you are going through, as well, as you come to terms with the end of your marriage, regardless of whether you wanted or chose to divorce or that decision was forced upon you. It is also the process your teen aged children are experiencing as they react and adjust to the divorce.

From teens, we tend to see a deep sense of loss, as well as the grief, sadness and anger typical in the grief process. Also common are the feelings of emptiness, chronic fatigue and difficulty concentrating that we often see with depression. Again, you will most commonly see these in stages, but knowing what to expect can help you to help your teen cope with these feelings and to express them. They may be tempted, as are adults experiencing losses, to stuff them down deep in an attempt to ignore them or to feel better, thinking they will never be seen or heard from again. This is a mistake. These feelings do not go away, they just go into hibernation. Then they jump up and bite you when you least expect it, such as when you have another, even a minor, unrelated loss. Just like you, your teen must work through these feelings in order to heal them and adjust to the divorce.

The danger in having your teen not work through these feelings of grief and loss is that they will pretend everything is fine, but will actually not make the adjustment at all. What happens eventually, however, is that years later they will still be suffering the effects of the divorce and attempting to squelch the feelings.

The same is true for you. No matter which role you played in the decision to divorce, you are experiencing a significant change or loss in your life. Therefore you must work through this process as well in order to be fully adjusted to your divorce.

A young man I know experienced this phenomenon, though he was not yet a teen at the time of the divorce. When his parents divorced, Patrick was a happy, athletic and popular nine year old kid. After the separation, his grief-stricken father moved him and his brother up to a small town in northern Wisconsin in an attempt to make a new life for himself. Patrick had a difficult time making friends in this new location, which was not very welcoming to outsiders. At school, he found that the social groups were already formed and he was at the bottom of the social order.

Patrick became sullen and withdrawn. Much of this behavior lasted into his high school years when, after a move to yet another town, he finally began to make friends. But he was still not dealing with his feelings of loss. Patrick is now 32 years old and has only in the last two years begun to become aware of the effect of his parents' divorce on his life. Now he is beginning to deal with his grief. But what of the years he lost?

The other phenomenon unique to teens whose parents are experiencing divorce is to question their ability to maintain a long term relationship. They see their parents as role models and authorities on the issue of relationships. When we get into relationships as adults, we often find ourselves modeling our parents' roles and relationship behavior.

Teens witnessing a family divorce observe their parents unable to make a relationship last forever. Often, there is little indication to the children that a divorce is being considered until the decision is made. In their minds, there is a strong relationship and often the couple and family is still spending quality time together. Then, out of the blue, a separation occurs and one partner leaves.

When this happens, the teen is likely to question whether and how they can ever trust a member of the opposite sex to be committed to them for a long term relationship. Researcher and author Judith Wallerstein discusses this phenomenon in her work, *The Unexpected Legacy of Divorce*, as one of the most difficult issues facing teens whose parents have divorced.[3]

This is something both of my stepsons have struggled with. When I met them, the boys were 17 and 18. Both popular, socially active teens, they would spend weekends watching movies and eating pizza with a large group of friends. But neither became involved in a serious long term relationship until they were in their mid-twenties. It has only been in recent years that they have truly been able to invest themselves in a one-on-one relationship.

Their experience was similar to that described above. They came from a family that spent a significant amount of time together. There were family camping trips, dad coached Little League, and family time was happy and companionable. To all outward appearances, they were a family that worked well together. One day, when the boys were eight and nine, they learned their mother was leaving the family and filing for divorce. She immediately traveled to Europe and they did not see her for more than six months. She was literally "here today and gone tomorrow."

Hearing this, it is easy to understand that my stepsons would question their ability to maintain a relationship. One can also understand, given this experience, why they might have some difficulty trusting a woman to make a long term commitment to them. In discussing this phenomenon with them, both admitted having doubts along these lines that made them quite cautious about being in a serious relationship. Even in less traumatic cases, however, this extreme caution and difficulty trusting remains one of the most common symptoms experienced by teens in divorced families.

It is often puzzling to parents why teens are so affected by parental divorce when most seem not to want much contact with their parents or families and don't spend much time at home. We want to remember, however, that while teens need their time away from home and family, they also need a safe haven to return to.

Teens move away from their families and achieve independence by taking several steps forward, then a step back. They venture out and try something new, such as a new job or a new group of friends, and then retreat to their safe haven, home, to regroup. A short time later, they venture out again, perhaps investigating a new hobby or interest, then, again, come home to their safe haven. The family is the safe haven to which they can retreat when necessary and upon which they rely emotionally when they venture outward.

If the home becomes disorganized and chaotic, as typically happens in a divorce, and if parents become less available to the teen, adolescents lose their safe haven and feel left adrift, abandoned. It's as if they are thrown out into the world before they are ready. When that happens, teens can become unable to accomplish the true task of their teenage years—figuring out who they are and what they stand for. It is during these years that they must make a number of important decisions: what kind of work they want to do for the next 40-50 years of their lives, what kind of relationship and family they want to have, what their values are and how they will follow them. When teens are not able to accomplish these tasks, they can end up, in their later years, frustrated and empty, leaving work and family to complete the task of searching for themselves, causing disruption to yet another family.

They may find themselves jumping from job to job and relationship to relationship, not having had the ability to investigate these identity and values issues in their teenage years. Patrick, in the example previously given in this chapter, was greatly affected by his parents' divorce and this was apparent in his long term adjustment as well. Now 32 years old, he is currently between relationships again and is also still unemployed and trying to decide what kind of a career or degree he would like to have.

When teens act out their distress at parental divorce, they typically do so in one of three typical ways. In the first, like the younger children, they may regress to earlier patterns of behavior. They may abandon same age friends, teen interests and adolescent activities and behave as they did when they were much younger. They may take to hanging around with 11 and 12 year olds, playing games and engaging in activities they enjoyed back when they were that age.

It is often comforting for these teens to not have to take on the typical risks of adolescence; to not put themselves on the line. Most have to use everything they've got just to cope with the changes in their families and have nothing left for their age-related tasks. In addition, the period of time to which these teens regress was also typically a "safer" time in their lives: perhaps their parents' marriage was in better shape so the family was more cohesive and content. There was no change occurring, as there is today, so it is comforting to take themselves back to that time.

The second way teens act out their distress at parental divorce is to become far older than their years. They may be immersed in the role of family protector and provider, again at the expense of their adolescent years and tasks. They may take on one or two part time jobs, in addition to school, in order to contribute to the family income; they may take on a major role in keeping the family functioning, such as taking responsibility for meal preparation, caring for younger siblings, managing the household. While it is appropriate for them to help out, these children are truly taking on adult roles and, again, sacrificing their teen age years.

The third way teens often express upset over divorce is even more dangerous. At this age they can express their anger and internal conflicts in dangerous ways not typically available to their younger siblings. These teens may become involved in precocious sexual activity, alcohol and drug use, delinquent behavior or gang activity. Teens usually choose this latter path when faced with some combination of anger, lax supervision, loss of their safe haven and exposure to parents' sexual behavior. This will be discussed further in Chapter 10.

As with their younger siblings, these behavior problems are most often transient, but they can become permanent patterns if the home environment after the divorce does not stabilize. However, even if the behavior problems are not permanent, due to the serious, lifelong ramifications that can arise from some of the choices teens are mature enough to make, the behavior can have permanent consequences, such as an unwanted pregnancy, criminal charges, disease and death.

While teens can work their way out of these behavior patterns in time, and often without outside help, because of the harmful consequences, if your teen is exhibiting any of the behaviors in this third and last category, I would run, not walk, to the nearest professional for help. A good start may be contacting the school and getting the school counselor or social worker involved. But that may not be enough. You may want get your child involved with a therapist to help them sort out their feelings before any of the more negative consequences result.

Young Adults~(18+)

Six months away from achieving her lifelong goal of graduating with a Master's Degree in Archeology, 24 year old Michelle quit school, broke up with her fiancé and joined the Peace Corps. In response to her separated and incredulous parents, Michelle snaps, "Well, you two walked away from it all. Why shouldn't I?"

While it surprises many people, young adults are significantly affected by parental divorce as well. Often exhibiting a typical grief reaction like their teenaged siblings in working through this experience, most young adults are quite shaken when parents divorce, even though they are often out of the family home and well-focused on a life of their own. What divorce does to this group, however, is something similar to what it does to adolescents: it causes them to question not only their ability to engage in and maintain a long term relationship, but also the choices and assumptions upon which they are basing the life they are busy establishing.

Because they are further along in the process of developing this independent life, most young adults have already made some choices for themselves based on values typically inherited from their parents. They are more committed to these choices than teens, who are just thinking about or experimenting with them, and, as a result, often have a more intense and negative emotional reaction toward parents.

This makes sense if we remember that we learn how to be in relationships with others by watching what our parents and those closest to us do in those types of situations. We make decisions about who we are and what we stand for by spending years unconsciously observing our parents operate in relationship to society and each other. When, in the midst of creating a life based on similar principles and tenets, one of our chief role models for how to "do" this kind of life decides he has had enough and is running off to join a commune or to live the life of a teenager, it cannot help but cause us to question our own choices.

This questioning, and the underlying uncertainty to which it invariably leads, often results in anger at whichever parent is making the choice to leave or to throw off the values the adult child has adopted. This makes sense when we, again, look at anger as a secondary emotion. It is easy to understand the frustration, uncertainty and fear caused by this drastic change in the role model upon whom we have based many of our values and life decisions. It is from these underlying feelings that the anger flows, and it can last until such time as the adult child takes time to re-evaluate his choices and come to terms with his parent's defection.

Duration of Problem Behaviors

We have already discussed how long parents can expect children's behavior changes to last, but often the duration of children's problems coincides approximately with the amount of time parents take to regain their emotional equilibrium and again, become able to provide nurturing and support. Cessation of parental conflict, as partners get some emotional distance from the marriage and tensions begin to subside, is another factor that enables children of all ages to stabilize.

A number of families regain their equilibrium enough so children are back at a functioning level within the first year after the divorce, though it is common for younger children to take longer to recover. It is not uncommon for this process to take up to two years. Regaining equilibrium is easier for children who were well adjusted before the divorce and who have had successes in meeting the challenge of previous stressors, school and the like, as they have a wide variety of resources they can call upon to accomplish this. Again, this speaks to the resilience factor. This resiliency can allow them to resume healthy functioning even faster than their families.

A recent study reported that 18 months following the separation, 25 percent of all children studied were still showing symptoms in response to the divorce.[4] Some of the most common reactions noticed included depression, withdrawal, anxiety, poor self-esteem and the like. Three and a half years later, in a follow-up study, 37 percent of the same children were found to be functioning poorly. Researchers were puzzled by these results: why were more children doing poorly five years after the separation than at 18 months?

What they found upon examining these families more closely is that the children who were still struggling were those whose families had not regained their equilibrium after the divorce, but had become stalled in a chronic state of stress, instability and transition. These families continued to struggle with bitter battles over custody and placement, parents were unavailable or uninvolved, or had become overwhelmed or emotionally unstable. Children experienced a chaotic, out of control home life, characterized by poor supervision and discipline, or outright abandonment. Multiple changes, often involving moves, changes of school and multiple partners for parents, can also contribute to these delayed behavioral changes. What these children were facing was a state of chronic stress and the continuous demands made on them to adapt and readapt, far exceeded their capacity to do so and overwhelmed their natural resilience.

That's the bad news. The good news is, there is much parents can do to prevent these reactions and to make this adjustment easier on their children! Just having this information available to you and developing an awareness of your child's probable reactions helps you to help him.

In my class, at this point, we go around the room and have parents talk about which of the preceding symptoms they have noticed in their own children since the separation. Parents will typically have picked up something during our discussion and most do report some change they have observed in their children that they are now able to connect to the divorce.

Take a few minutes now that you have finished the chapter to go back over the sections pertaining to the age group and developmental level of your own child. I have also included a two page summary of these changes at the end of the chapter to make it easier to do a continuing evaluation of your child's behavior. Refer back to it periodically as your divorce proceeds.

Think, also, about what you have seen from your children in the past weeks or months. How does what you have seen compare with the typical reactions you have just read? This chapter is certainly not an exhaustive list—just a listing of the most typical reactions seen from children experiencing divorce. If you've noticed something not included in the list, but you believe it has only started since the separation or divorce happened, more power to you! This awareness of your child's struggle can assist and empower you in dealing with it—and in helping them to do so as well.

If you have noticed no changes in your child's behavior, don't be too quick to pat yourself on the back. That does not mean that your child is having no difficulty with the divorce. Read on! We will discuss this in greater detail in Chapter Two.

Also, when we gather for the second session of our class, most often scheduled one week after the first, I begin by asking parents if they've noticed anything in their children in the week between the sessions that they can *now* connect to the changes in the family. Invariably, armed with the information you've just read and given the opportunity to observe and interact with their children, a number of parents do become aware of ways in which their children have, in fact, been affected by the divorce that they had not previously connected with this life experience.

Spend some time interacting with your children and observing them with these guidelines in mind. Remember, the more you are aware of how they are being affected, the better your ability and position to help them make a positive adjustment to the divorce.

"I am an old man and have known a great many troubles—but most of them never happened."

~Mark Twain

How Children Are Affected By Divorce

Studies find that age and level of development does affect children's initial reaction to divorce. Each age group appears to have its own unique set of difficulties to work through.

Infants (0-12 months)—Are affected by divorce largely because of the upset and tension transmitted to them by parents, disruptions in routine and lapses in care due to parents' distress. They tend to exhibit:

____ Increased fretfulness ____ Digestive difficulties
____ Eating difficulties ____ Increased spitting up

Toddlers (1-2 1/2 years)—In response to stress in their homes, tend to:

____ Become more irritable or irritable more frequently,
____ Have more temper tantrums,
____ Show more aggressive behavior,
____ Regress to earlier forms of behavior.

Preschoolers (3-5 1/2 years)—Show the most dramatic behavior changes of any group studied. They also tend to:

____ Become bewildered and frightened,
____ Feel terrified of abandonment,
____ Feel responsible for the divorce,
____ Have difficulty with routine separations,
____ Be anxious, clingy and whiny,
____ Lose their most recently acquired behaviors,
____ Regress to earlier forms of behavior.

School Age Children (6-8 years)—Especially boys:

____ Are the most openly grief-stricken,
____ Feel intense loss and despair,
____ Yearn for their absent or less-seen parent,
____ Believe the intact family is vital to their survival,
____ Have difficulty relating to peers,
____ Experience difficulty concentrating in school,
____ Feel personally abandoned and rejected,
____ Worry they will be replaced by the parent,

(School Age Children, cont'd)

____ Feel strong loyalty to both parents,

____ Have a rough time with parental conflict,

____ Express their anger indirectly—hitting peers/siblings, refusing to do chores, homework.

Pre-Adolescents (9-12 years)—Struggle with identity and values issues:

____ Experience a shaken sense of identity,

____ Experience a shaken sense of right and wrong,

____ Accuse parents of selfishness,

____ Can be swept into bitter, open alliance with one parent,

____ Intense anger at one or both parents,

____ Express somatic complaints: headache, stomach ache,

____ Feel guilty if involved in an alliance and resent the parent they were aligned with.

Adolescents (13-17 years)—A typical grief reaction:

____ Denial ____ Anger ____ Bargaining ____ Depression

____ Acceptance ____ Deep sense of loss

____ Difficulty concentrating

____ Feelings of emptiness ____ Chronic fatigue

____ Question own future & ability to maintain relationship

Development can get derailed as they:

____ Regress to younger behaviors,

____ Become a "mini-adult", or

____ Express distress in dangerous, risky behaviors.

Young Adults (18+)—Grief and anger reaction:

____ Denial ____ Anger ____ Bargaining ____ Depression

____ Acceptance

____ Question their own values, beliefs, life choices,

____ Express frustration, uncertainty and fear regarding choices they have made,

____ Question own future & ability to maintain relationship.

"When we long for life without difficulties, remind us that oaks grow strong in contrary wind and diamonds are made under pressure."

~Peter Marshall

CHAPTER 2

APPLYING THE QUICK FIXES

*How to Help Your Children Cope
with the Immediate Crisis*

Thirteen year old Ryan and fifteen year old Sean's parents had mutually decided to end their 15 year marriage. The boys were told of the decision in the living room of the home that the family had shared for the past twelve years, and given information about how their lives would change in the near future. They learned that both parents would be sharing the home until Dad made arrangements for a place of his own. They were consulted and had the opportunity to provide input regarding the time they would spend with each parent and the schedule of their school and extracurricular activities was taken into account. No changes were made until the boys were out of school for the summer, so they would have time to get used to the new arrangements before school began again in the fall.

When they had questions, Ryan and Sean felt comfortable talking with their parents and asking for additional information because they had seen them working together discussing the divorce and the coming changes in the family. When Ryan tested the new arrangements and his limits by shoplifting a pack of baseball cards, his parents sat down together with him to discuss the problem, reinforce the limits and, jointly with Ryan, decide how to further handle the situation. The *boys were left with the feeling that, even though their parents no longer wanted to be together, they were loved and of primary importance to both of them. The remainder of the divorce and the family's adjustment proceeded without incident.*

We learned in Chapter One that parental divorce is a crisis for children, regardless of the family involved or what it has experienced previously. No matter the situation, divorce raises issues and presents challenges that are difficult to deal with, especially for the children involved. Parents can set the stage for a positive adjustment to their divorce very early in the process. Starting off right, helping children to handle the crisis successfully from the first moment they are made aware of it, can help set the stage for children's successful long-term adjustment to your divorce.

In Chapter Two, we will discuss some ways to make these early moments easier for your children and for you as well. Many of these techniques are also helpful on a long term basis.

Telling Your Children About the Divorce

Whenever possible, it is a good idea for both parents to sit down together with children to tell them about the divorce. They will be reassured by seeing the two of you able to work and talk cooperatively together for their benefit, despite any conflict existing between you. They will also be less likely and less able to deny the reality of the decision.

In addition, both spouses will benefit from knowing exactly what and how the children were told. Obviously, telling children about the divorce together is not recommended for relationships where domestic violence has been an issue, or if you are fairly certain it will lead to an argument.

Tell All Children Together

Ideally, all children should be given the information together and at the same time. While parents must consider age and developmental differences in determining what they will say, the initial announcement of the divorce should be presented to all children together. A child hearing about a parental divorce from an older sibling may temporarily or permanently lose the ability to trust the parent to share important information with him.

Of course, depending on the age differences among your children, you may need and want to have a more extensive discussion with older children after younger children are in bed. At that time, you can give the older siblings more detailed information, which may be inappropriate for the littlest ones. In this manner, you can attend to the specific needs of all children.

Wait to have this discussion until the decision is definite and try to give children about two weeks before one of you moves out. Children need some time to adjust to the idea of divorce, but not too much time to fuel the naturally overwhelming hopes for reconciliation. Further, the longer the anticipation of a separation hangs on, the more difficult it can be for all family members involved.

Handling the Hope for Reconciliation

I also want to briefly discuss the concept of reconciliation. I don't think I'm exaggerating when I say that it is the most fervent hope, wish and dream of 99 percent of children of divorced or divorcing parents that their parents will reconcile. Even if you are exploring reconciliation, do not tell the children unless and until you are pretty sure it will happen because the only thing worse than losing your family once, is losing your family two, three or four times. This puts children in that state of chronic stress that we discussed in Chapter One from which it is difficult to stabilize and recover.

In talking with my stepsons about this phenomenon, both assured me that they were hoping for their parents to reunite, even at 17 and 18 when I came to know them. At this point, their parents had been divorced for nearly ten years and their mother had been remarried for nine! Further, with Katie, the effects of this reconciliation hope were truly startling!

As I've shared with you, Katie was 18 months old when her father and I separated. We did not explore reconciliation: Bill was otherwise engaged and by the time that romance had ended, I had started a new life for myself and our daughter. Nonetheless, in the beginning of her second grade school year,

Katie began coming home talking about when her dad and I would "get back together!"

The first two times I heard her say this, I just let it pass. After all, she hadn't heard that from me; I was happily remarried with two additional children. Further, her dad had just remarried the previous summer, so I was fairly certain she hadn't heard it from him, either.

The third time she started a sentence with, "When you and my dad get back together," I realized this issue was not going away and I would have to deal with it. I calmly and in my best assertive parent tone informed Katie that her dad and I would not be reconciling, as I was happily married to Terry and her dad and Anne had just gotten married as well. Without missing a beat, Katie came back with, "Well, it happened for Stephanie's parents, it will happen for you too."

Instantly the muddy waters cleared and I understood what had happened. At her school each year, the three classes of each grade are mixed up and redistributed so that each child has an opportunity to be in class with and get to know all of the other children in the grade. That fall, for the first time, Katie was in class with Stephanie, whose parents had been married, then divorced and were now remarried. Her recent exposure to this family was sufficient to establish in Katie's mind that this was the natural order of life. According to her second grade reasoning, couples married, divorced, and then remarried at some later point in time.

I quickly, yet diplomatically, I hope, disabused her of this notion and we continued on with a rather uneventful second grade year. She did become best friends with Stephanie, however, and some part of me was sure it was because Stephanie had what Katie coveted: her intact family. Still, it was with a heavy heart that I learned two years later that Stephanie's parents had again divorced. Apparently, the problems that had come between them the first time they were together remained in spite of the intervening years and experiences.

Tell Them in a Comfortable Setting

The discussion you have with your children should take place in an environment where they can be comfortable and relaxed. Your home is typically the best setting. They should be told about the decision in a warm, loving and calm manner. Parents should not use this time to hammer out agreements or negotiate unresolved issues. Your entire focus should be on the children and what they need from you at this moment. Children should be encouraged and feel free to ask questions and talk about their feelings without fear of hurting or angering you. They will benefit if parents can honestly tell them that the divorce has been carefully considered and is necessary to solve a serious problem.

What to Say

Most children need to find or hear some reason for the divorce. Without one, their imaginations often run rampant with reasons and fears that are usually far worse than the truth, and often involve themselves as part of their reasoning ("It's my fault. I caused an argument.")

In addressing this, be honest but keep explanations simple. Tell your kids the basic reason(s) for your decision, but use caution. Never, even indirectly, hold a child responsible for the divorce.

I recently had a gentleman get up and walk out of my class when I stated this, after he said to me, "I'm getting divorced for the second time and both divorces were *caused* by the kids." (Emphasis emphatically his). I explained to him, and continue to maintain, that while children can certainly complicate your life, and can change it a great deal, they do not, under any circumstance, cause divorce, which is an adult relationship issue.

If there are changes in the relationship after the arrival of, or as a result of the children, it is the responsibility of the adults in the family to attempt to work those out. It is *not* appropriate to blame the children for this change. They did not ask to be born. Perhaps this gentleman's second divorce would not have occurred if he had accepted some responsibility for the first one. As we will discuss later in Chapter 10, any relationship is a complicated interaction between two persons and each bears some responsibility for the outcome.

What Not to Say

In talking with your children, do not give specific details about a parent's "bad behavior." And do not, under any circumstance, badmouth the other parent. A child needs to respect and love both of his parents. Attacking the character of the other parent interferes with that process or, worse yet, triggers the child to come to the aid of the maligned parent. A child can literally feel torn apart by parents hurling insults at each other, even when they are speaking only to the child and outside of each other's presence.

Further, a child is a combination of your genes and those of the other parent. If you refer to that person as "the jerk" or a "pathological liar," children can internalize these characteristics as part of their own makeup, as well, and start behaving accordingly. What a tragic and life-changing consequence of divorce. Do not be a part of this.

It is crucial that you do not get into an argument with each other, about the reasons for divorce or any other issue, when talking with your children about the divorce. This can undo all the good you are attempting to accomplish by talking with them together. It may be helpful to practice together what you will tell the children before the time comes. If you are fairly sure you cannot pull this off without arguing, please refer to Chapter Nine to work on your relationship with the other parent before attempting this conversation.

What children need to hear is something simple and general, such as "Mommy and Daddy aren't happy living together anymore, so we're going to live separately now. But we will both always be your Mommy and Daddy."

If the decision belongs to one, but not both of you, the deciding parent must own that choice. "Mommy isn't happy living with Daddy so she's going to live somewhere else. But I will always be your Mommy and we will see each other often."

Don't pretend the choice is mutual if it is not. Kids will figure this out and will find it hard to trust you after an untruthful statement. They need for you to be honest and trustworthy, especially now.

Children do not need, and should not be told, that a

parent has been involved in a sexual relationship or an affair. But when a new partner does come on the scene, it is best children hear about this directly from the parent involved. See Chapter 10 for a more extensive discussion of new relationships.

Reassure Them Often

Be sure to provide plenty of reassurances about your continued love and concern for children throughout this discussion. The following statements are important to share with your children on a very regular basis:

- ❀ Divorce is just between parents; the divorce has nothing to do with kids,

- ❀ It is not your fault; you are not responsible for the divorce,

- ❀ Parents don't divorce children,

- ❀ We will both always be your Mommy and Daddy,

- ❀ We will both always love you.

It is important for children to come away from this discussion and the experience of their parents' separation and divorce with an understanding of two main ideas: 1) they still have two parents and 2) the divorce is not their fault. Only when they hear, understand and believe these points from parents will they be able to positively and successfully adjust to the divorce.

Why is it so important to say these things out loud? After all, your children know you and know that you love them, right? Yes. However, in the midst of a family crisis such as a divorce, children's imaginations often run away with them. It does not take much for a child to jump from the fact that her misbehavior in school led to an argument between her parents to the conclusion that she caused the conflict that resulted in the separation that occurred a week later. Children have a very simplistic view of relationships—it doesn't take much for them to accept total responsibility for the end of the marriage.

You must prevent this. The only way to do so is by verbally saying the contrary to your children. It is my belief that children cannot hear these statements often enough! Although I did have a woman in one of my classes that shared that whenever she would say these things to her two daughters, ages 12 and 14, they would respond with, "Yeah, yeah, Mom, we know!" I would hazard a guess that these two probably did know that there were, indeed, loved by both parents and not feeling responsible for the divorce. Absent that kind of affirmation, however, please tell your children these things often and with feeling.

Talking With Your Kids About the Divorce

Whenever you have an announcement to make to your children, about such events as a move to a new home or a change in how or when they will spend time with each of you, do the best you can to follow the guidelines listed above. If you can manage it, make the announcement together, to all children at once, in an environment that is comfortable and familiar to them.

Wait until any decision is definite and tell them roughly one to two weeks before the change is set to occur. This will give them some time to prepare themselves for the change, but not so long that they begin to ruminate about it.

Give Details That Concern Kids

Give them as many details about the future as you can. Children need concrete information about how the divorce, or any impending change, will affect them personally. They are very self-centered creatures and this will be their main concern. Think from your child's perspective, "How will this change my life?"

A recent attendee of my class shared with me a classic story of his four year old daughter's very appropriate self-concern. When her parents announced they would be divorcing she thought for a minute, then asked, "But who will get the swing set?" You can see the concern here: where will I be able to play?

Do You Have Any Questions?

End all of these conversations and announcements the same way: "Do you have any questions?" They will promptly, and often vehemently, respond, "No!" This is because children rarely have questions at a time when parents have the time and focus to deal with them, or when you are sitting down looking at them eyeball to eyeball. But you have still done something wonderful and extremely valuable here. You have left the door open for future discussions by sending them the message, "This is something I want to talk with you about and it is OK for you to ask me about it." Then sit back and wait for the questions to come.

And they will come; probably when you least expect and are the least prepared for them. A prime time for kids to open these discussions is when you are driving them in a car to an extracurricular activity or school function. As we will learn in Chapter Six, as your kids get older you may spend much of your extra time with them driving them from one important activity to the next. This fact affords them the opportunity to ask you all those questions that are burning in their minds. So, all is not lost.

Why is driving in a car such a terrific time for you children to come up with those questions? Think about it. You are not looking directly at them, but staring straight ahead and hopefully focused on something else, such as the road. At least until the question is asked.

Your child can feel like he's under a microscope when you are looking at him, waiting for the questions to come. You are watching him intently for any signs of reaction or distress. This can be quite disconcerting for a child.

When you are driving, not only are you looking and focused elsewhere, but perhaps it is dark outside, providing an added measure of security.

Therefore, even in the event that you are able to glance over to get a quick look at him as, or after, the question is asked, there is little for you to see. Your child may even be sitting in a back seat so it is virtually impossible for you to scrutinize his face for signs of possible distress.

Use "Divorce-English" When Talking With Kids

You will also want to tune in to any questions that are, or could be, divorce-related. Often children want information about the divorce, but are not comfortable coming out directly and asking it. So, they may ask a seemingly innocuous question without even mentioning the divorce issues, hoping to get at least a part of the information they are seeking. As a parent, you will want to put "divorce-English" on any questions your children ask you, especially at those safe times. Those of you who play pool or billiards know what I mean.

For the rest of you, I will give an example. Say you are driving your almost-sixteen-year old son to basketball practice one school night in November. It is dark, he is feeling safe, and he asks you, "Are we gonna have a graduation party when I graduate from high school?"

You are surprised at this question. For one thing, it is two years before you need to be having this conversation. For another, it relates to nothing the two of you have discussed in the recent past. Those are two clues that there is possibly a divorce-related issue under the surface. With this type of questions, it could easily be, "Can you and my dad (mom) be in the same room with each other without mortally embarrassing me *if* we have a graduation party when I graduate from high school?" He is testing out his options ahead of time.

How you respond is important. While you only have half of the control of this situation, the part you do have is crucial. Take comfort in the fact that either the other parent will be similarly questioned, or you are already seen as the more rational of the two of you. You will want to say something reassuring, but honest, at this point. "Honey, your dad (mom) and I will work together on this. We will both want to celebrate that big accomplishment of yours."

You will want to reassure him, even if you are quite certain you will be the only one planning to "work together." See Chapter Nine if you feel that is the case. Notice that you have not made any specific promises, such as a party for 300 at an exclusive club, but you are reassuring, nonetheless. This is truly what your child needs at this time. Do not commit to specifics at this point: it is too early and you at least want to give the other parent the opportunity to have some input. Or you should-even if you are quite certain they will not take you up on that offer. Also see Chapters Seven and Nine if this is an issue for you.

Helping Children Cope

As we have just learned in Chapter One, your children are likely to show some kind of changed behavior in the weeks and months immediately following your separation. The behavior changes you notice in your children are symptoms of their distress and reflect their anxiety and fears about what is happening in their lives. Some parents, however, notice no behavior changes in their children. If that is the case in your family, please do not assume that this means your children are not being affected by the divorce.

Current research shows that most parents are unaware that their children actually are affected by their divorce, and of the extent of their children's difficulties. Several years ago, a colleague of mine happened to catch a television show that was highlighting a therapy program being offered for parents and children experiencing divorce that addressed this very issue. Video segments were shown of intelligent, caring, well-meaning parents who were in the process of divorce, reporting that their children were having no difficulties adjusting to the divorce and that, to the contrary, they were handling the change quite well. Video clips were then shown of the children of these very parents, in tears, describing some of the struggles they were having with the changes occurring in their families. Needless to say their parents were stunned.

I can tell you from my experience these parents were not unusual. For a variety of reasons, the parents I have seen, also, are often completely out of touch with the difficulties with which their children are struggling. Many are too completely overwhelmed by the divorce process, both the legal and emotional, to be in tune with their children's experiences. Further, often our children, in an attempt to take care of us, put up a front that everything is fine, even when their hearts are breaking.

The ideas that follow are suggestions that are helpful whether or not you notice any changes in your children's behavior, or whether, in fact, they are having difficulty adjusting to your divorce. These techniques will just help them adjust more easily, no matter where they are in the process.

Reassure Your Children

Try to allay at least some of your children's fears about the divorce as quickly as you can. You will want to reassure them frequently of your love and concern. Tell them often that you love them and give them extra hugs and kisses. Strive to get your family life stabilized and back to some semblance of normalcy as quickly as possible so children can relax and feel safe in the new family situation. Predictability will be important in their adjustment; they need to know, as much as you can tell them, what will happen and when. Don't make too many changes to the rules and limits—kids get stability out of knowing what to expect in their families. We will discuss this in greater detail in Chapter Three.

To the extent that you can, set up a schedule with their absent parent so they not only see that parent frequently and regularly, but will also know when that will happen. Children need to be able to predict some of what will happen in their lives, and typically need some time to prepare themselves for any transition. Don't make these new arrangements more difficult by springing them on your children.

By the time Katie was about five, I had developed the habit of keeping a calendar on the wall near the telephone. I would mark off the weekends and days she would be with her dad with a big "X" on the calendar. Truthfully, I did this more so that I would remember and be able to plan for these times, but I also explained to her what the "X's" meant so that she could be aware of these times and prepare herself as well.

One day she came to me shortly after arriving home from her father's house and said, "I really like how you always let me know where I'm going to be." She was telling me, in her five year old way, that she, too, needed time to prepare herself for these transitions. This is something I have attempted to remember throughout this process and incorporate in all arrangements I have made that concern her.

This is also a useful piece of information for children of all ages. I don't think Katie is unique in needing this preparation time, even at the age of five. I also think she may have appreciated it earlier, but perhaps lacked the words to express it until that age.

Help Them Understand and Express Their Feelings

Children also often need help understanding and expressing their confused feelings. This is not surprising when you think about it. It's hard enough for an adult to navigate the rocky waters of divorce, with mixed feelings about the loss of the love relationship, fear about an unknown future and the like. For a child, who understands little about the experience and has no control over it, this process can be extremely confusing.

It is an important part of the process on coping with and adjusting to their parents' divorce for children to express the emotions they are experiencing at this time, rather than to stuff them down deep, only to have them arise and haunt them or explode years later. If not expressed at this point in their lives, these emotions and experiences can haunt children for the rest of their lives, and profoundly affect their future relationships.

I have a friend, John, who was divorced in the 1970's. Back then, much less was known about how people were affected by divorce and even less was known about how divorce affected children. In his grief, John moved up into the woods of northern Wisconsin with his two young sons and, in the throes of dealing with his own emotional pain, did not attend to the emotions experienced by his boys. While their physical needs were competently and adequately met, their emotional wounds went largely untended.

John's eldest son, Patrick, is now 33 and, two years ago, accepted a one year teaching position overseas. He did a wonderful job keeping in touch with his father via email from his new home (perhaps even better than when he was in college in a nearby state!). John shared with me one of the first communications Patrick sent, as it was profound in the statement it made about his adjustment to his parents' divorce. He wrote, "I've met a number of other teachers here from the states. One of the girls is a child of divorce, just like me."

Patrick's parents had divorced when he was nine. Here he was, some 24 years after the fact, still identifying himself by this life experience! Now that we know the damage that divorce can do to children if left unchecked, you can do much better for yours than was done for Patrick. Reading this book is a great start!

So, how do you help your children express these feelings? There are a number of options. And do remember, there is a difference between feelings and actions. Feelings are always acceptable. They may not be pleasant or healthy or fun, but they are OK. The behavior, such as punching someone in the mouth, may not be. Do not hesitate to set limits on inappropriate actions.

Often your child's feelings will be obvious. You can make them even more overt and call the child's attention to them to assist her in understanding what is happening. Say, for example, your teenage daughter slams down the stairs in the morning and it is quite clear to all observers that she is in a lousy mood. She sets the juice on the counter with a loud "bang!" and snarls at her younger siblings quite ferociously. You want to let her know how she is coming across.

"You're pretty angry this morning," you observe, in as neutral a tone as you can muster. As tempting as it is, if you snarl back at her, the opportunity is lost. Don't worry about guessing the wrong feeling. If you are incorrect, she will most likely correct you with unrestrained delight. But that's OK, because the point is not to be right. Just pick a feeling and go for it. In the meantime, you have opened up a conversation, a dialogue between the two of you that would not have happened otherwise. She's opened the door, just a crack, into her emotional reality. Once inside, you can effect change.

"I'm *not* angry; I'm frustrated! Nothing's going right today!" she snarls again. Here's your opportunity to be sympathetic, empathic and to teach her something about handling that difficult emotion, all at the same time.

With a soft, nurturing voice, you respond genuinely, "I'm sorry you're having a hard time, honey. Is there anything I can do to help?" Usually there isn't, but if there is, it is often something pretty easy for a parent to do, such as making her lunch, helping with her homework, doing some of her laundry, that is likely to make her feel quite loved and cared for, rather than attacked and dismissed like snapping at her would accomplish. Empathy is a much more effective option.

Another good choice is to offer a suggestion about what works for you when you are frustrated. You are then teaching your child how to manage stress and difficulty —a life skill she will probably use extensively in her future. You could say, "You know, when I feel that way, I like to take five minutes and have a cup of hot chocolate (or run around the block or take a hot bath, something that actually *has* worked for you in the past.) If you've not used any of these choices, give some of them a try— you might be pleasantly surprised. Even if she chooses not to do it, you've assisted her in labeling her emotions and planted the seeds of other options that she can think about and perhaps try out at a later time. And remember, you've opened up that discussion that you would never have had otherwise.

Encourage Preschoolers to Express Feelings Indirectly

The one exception to helping make your children's feelings more overt by helping to label them is with preschoolers and younger children. It is terrifying for three to five year old children to acknowledge and admit that they have strong negative emotions, such as fear and anger, that are directed at one or both parents. For these young ones, this is not a helpful solution and can cause more harm than good.

The good news, however, is that children this age are often very transparent in their play. You can use this to your advantage.

For instance, your preschooler is obviously very angry this morning and is playing with her doll. You casually observe, "Your dolly seems really angry this morning. What could she be so upset about?" In most cases, you will very quickly get a complete and accurate description about what is upsetting your child.

Another technique is to use drawing to pull these emotions out. Ask your young child to draw a picture of how he is feeling today and to "use lots of color for the different feelings." Once the drawing is completed, it is external to the child and becomes safe to talk about as it is no longer a part of them. At that point you say, "Tell me about your picture. What does all this blue mean here? How about the red?"

"Well," responds your child, "the red is a whole lot of mad and the blue means really, really sad." Bingo! You've helped your child express his feelings in a safe, effective and appropriate manner. Mission accomplished!

With younger children, there is another technique that can be used to reassure them. As we have learned, young children have a tendency to personalize and "awfulize" life events, making them worse than they really need be. They may concoct very creative and clever scenarios in their heads about how they are responsible for their parents' divorce, yet be too frightened or ashamed to talk with you about it. Answering questions they have not asked can deal quite effectively with this tendency.

For example, your child broke your favorite vase, at which time you and her other parent got into a heated argument about a lack of supervision, and sometime later, for a variety of reasons, you decided to divorce. Your child witnesses the event, the argument and later is made aware of your decision. She assumes that she is responsible for the divorce. You do not know this because she is too ashamed of the role she assumes she played in the scenario to even mention it to you.

But you can deal with this, whether or not something similar has happened in your family, by making several generic comments to reassure your child, such as, "A lot of kids think that it was something they did that caused their parents to divorce. But divorce isn't about children. It is just between parents."

Making a number of similar statements to your children while they are adjusting to your divorce can help them absolve themselves of any alleged responsibility for it. Further, as children feel more reassured in this regard, they may also open up to the point of discussing some of their feelings about the divorce with you.

Encourage Older Children to Express Feelings on Paper

Older children can benefit from expressing their feelings on paper in a wide variety of ways. Remember, the goal, again, is to encourage them to get these feelings out, to regurgitate them as it were, while they are fresh, and not to carry them around for the next twenty or thirty years. Journaling is one effective technique for accomplishing this, and one that I often recommend for adults experiencing divorce, as well, no matter whether the choice to divorce was theirs or their partner's. It is a useful exercise to record these feelings on paper and process, or put meaning to them. If a blank, white page is daunting to your child (or you), you can suggest she complete the following sentence:

"Today is _____ and I feel _____ because _____."

For example, "Today is Friday and I feel scared because my dad just moved out of our house."

Feeling is expressed and your (and their) mission is accomplished. More often than not, however, they may find that just that one sentence is enough to spur them on to write a whole page about the experience of a parent moving out, or whatever the event is that is leading to their primary feeling today.

Writing letters is another good technique to suggest to your older child. It is often quite therapeutic for them to write a letter to the parent or parents with whom they are upset or angry. The goal, again, is just to get the feelings out. These letters, in most cases, are not sent to the party to whom they are addressed. The mere writing of it, and regurgitating the feelings, is the entire goal. Sharing the feelings with the parent inciting them is not the purpose. If the child feels that there is something they do want to share with that parent, she should probably write another draft, toned down to a more appropriate expression of emotion, to share.

There is another type of letter that can help you or your child express emotion: the goodbye letter. In this case, the theme can be "Goodbye to my family as it used to be," "Goodbye to my home," or anything similar. In writing this type of letter, your child would start out identifying the things he is most going to miss about the family the way it used to be, i.e. Good bye to family vacations at the cabin, games of "Clue," bonfires in the backyard, cookouts, birthday parties, etc. He can then wrap up the letter with the things he is not going to miss and is, thus, bidding "Good riddance" to. There are some of these in every family, especially those in which a divorce is occurring: Good riddance to the arguments, silence during meals, crying every holiday and so on.

This is a good technique for parents experiencing divorce as well to assist in processing and working through the experience. Start your letter with the things you will miss, such as "our beautiful home", and finish it as a "good riddance" letter, listing the things you will not miss, such as "Good riddance to my mother in law, with whom I will never have to spend another holiday!" Humor does help you come to terms with difficult events, even with a divorce not of your choosing.

Many older children may enjoy expressing their feelings in the form of short stories, poetry, songs and song lyrics, as well. Just because you have never known your child to engage in these behaviors, does not mean they don't, or won't, if it is suggested to them in their time of need.

Several years ago, we lost our family dog, Duncan, very suddenly. Katie was 13 at the time and took his loss very hard as she was quite close to him. She moped around the house for several days, but would not talk about it. Finally, I took a clue from what I have been telling divorcing parents about helping their children for quite a few years and suggested that she write a poem about Duncan. She mumbled something and disappeared. I wasn't sure where she'd gone off to, but about a half hour later, she came down from her bedroom with five verses of the most wonderful poem I'd ever read—all about Duncan. I didn't know that she had it in her! I'd never known her to write a poem before, not even in school. I was impressed.

So impressed, in fact, that I emailed it to the woman in Houston, TX who had helped us adopt Duncan, as we had obtained him through the Wheaten Rescue Program (he was a Soft-Coated Wheaten Terrier). She was also impressed and posted it on the program's website as "A Tribute to Duncan."

Katie was thrilled, but more importantly she was healing. Almost immediately I noticed her dealing with Duncan's death in a different way. She could talk about him and she could, for the most part, function again. Writing the poem had done the trick for her, helping her come to terms with a significant loss. It could work for your children, in dealing with your divorce or any other loss in their lives, as well.

Of course, there are other ways to express feelings on paper. Drawing, water color painting, just about anything your creative child can come up with will help. However, it's up to you to set them on the right track and to help them understand how important it is to do this.

Help Children Get Involved with Outside Activities

Just as sending your children to school everyday provides them with a break from all of the changes they are currently experiencing in the home and family, keeping them involved in all of their usual extracurricular activities will provide a vacation from the changes as well. Therefore, you want to insist that they make it to basketball practice, dance class, debate club, or whatever activities they were involved in before the separation. Remember, this will be an hour or two that is pretty much the same for them after this momentous event in their lives as it was before. It is a period of time when they know what is expected of them and none of it has anything to do with separation, divorce or loss. It will be a vacation from change and provide some stability in their lives; it will be good for them.

Occasionally you will encounter some resistance from your child who will prefer to sit at home and wallow in his misery or take care of you. Do not allow this to happen. One agreement I make with my children at the beginning of each school year is that they may choose their extracurricular activities for the year, but then they are committed for the entire school year. They will not drop out of basketball in mid-season or quit dance class before the recital. They understand that their team or class is depending on them to be there and to follow through with their commitment. Next year, if they want to make a different choice, i.e. to give up dance class and take up basketball instead, they may do so. But for this school year, they are committed to the activity.

The same is true for summer choices. If there is a program in which your child participates every summer, keep them involved for stability reasons. Once committed, expect them to follow through until the program ends. This, also, will give them a break from home during the summer months.

If your child has not been involved in any extracurricular activities up to this point, this is an excellent time to get him involved in one or several. Not only does it provide him with a temporary escape from the changes at home, it also provides him with a support system and other caring adults that can be there for him in a way that, perhaps you cannot, as you are an interested party. It can do him a world of good to have this external focus, even if you are not noticing any changes in his behavior. In addition, he can be learning life skills, in the form of stress management techniques and sports that can foster his resilience and also help him in the future.

Distract a Ruminating Child

Some children get focused on a problem or issue and find it difficult to distract themselves with more positive opportunities. If you find that your child is expressing the same feelings over and over again, and you notice that the more misery he expresses, the more miserable he seems to feel, he may need some help to redirect his attention to some positive and interesting activities that will give him a break from his grief.

Often a child gets so caught up in his grief and misery that it is difficult to break out of that thought pattern and focus on something more positive. This is a child that you want to encourage to "call Tommy and see if he wants to do something," or "come help me plant some tulip bulbs in our new garden." Most children will respond positively to slight pressure from you and will discover that once they are active and doing something, their misery dissipates.

In time, they will be able to do this for themselves, but in the early throes of divorce, many children need assistance from parents in accomplishing this. Pay attention when your child is talking about her negative feelings. While she does need to process this experience, if it seems unending or excessive to you, or if she seems to spend little time on positive activities, it may be time for you to step in.

Enlist Family, Teachers and Adult Friends to Help Your Child

Most children experiencing divorce are hesitant to talk to their parents about their feelings for fear of offending or hurting them. Children are typically very aware of difficulties experienced by their parents at this time. Further, if they have anything to say about their other parent, they feel they are being disloyal to that parent sharing those thoughts and feelings with the other parent. For this reason, I always recommend to parents that they enlist the aid of any other trustworthy adults in their children's lives to be available as support persons for them.

The school is a wonderful resource, available free of charge to any parent of a school age child. Divorcing parents should run, not walk, to their children's school and let the appropriate people there know what is happening in the family. There are any number of teachers, counselors, social workers, parent aides, coaches, scout leaders and the like, who are already familiar to your children through the school system. These wonderful people are available to be one more caring adult in the lives of your children and who can provide emotional support during this time of stress and change.

Whether or not you are noticing any behavior changes at home, or hearing about them from school personnel, inform the school what is happening. You can even ask the counselor or social worker to invite your child into their office several times for a quick game of checkers to just touch base with your child. Again, it is a relatively safe opportunity for your child to open up as no one is staring at him eyeball to eyeball. And, he does not have to worry about offending dad by talking to mom or vice versa. Utilize this valuable resource for the benefit of your child. The counselor can also get back to you if there are concerns that your child has, or that the school has about your child.

In the same manner, invite other interested adults to be there for your child. Tip off the scout leaders, coaches, dance teachers and anyone else who has contact with your child. In addition, if your son or daughter has a close friend and seems reasonably comfortable with one or both of that child's parents, you may want to invite the parent to check in with your child on a regular or occasional basis. Just have them let your child know, if they are willing, that if she ever needs someone to talk to, they are available. Again, think in terms of building a support system for your child, for times when you cannot fill that role.

Use Children's Books on Divorce to Help Your Child Cope

At the end of this book, in Appendix C, I have included a number of books for children about divorce. When possible, I separated them by age-appropriateness. This is by no means an exhaustive list, but these are some of the better volumes that I am familiar with. Make these books available to your children to help them get the information they need to handle this change.

I am a firm believer in self-help reading. We can learn much about how someone else has handled a similar situation and learn to re-frame or think differently about a problem we are facing. Then we are always free to heed the advice given, or to take what fits and leave what does not.

Even as adults, there is much we can learn from self-help books. For that reason, I have included an adult reading list in Appendix B which includes books about divorce, personal growth and divorce-related issues.

Younger children, even those with the ability to read, tend to enjoy reading books such as these with a parent. Bedtime is often a good time to do this. One of the women in my Parenting Through Divorce class shared that, early in the divorce process, she and her four year old daughter had read a chapter a night from R. A. Gardner's *Boy's and Girl's Book About Divorce* (Bantam, 1971). She reported that it raised a number of issues that she would not have thought to discuss with her daughter and that her daughter seemed to enjoy this time as well. She also indicated that the reading seemed to open the door for discussions between them that she felt would not have occurred otherwise.

Older children will not want to have anything to do with reading with you and, typically, will not want to even let you know they are interested in, or curious about, the information. However, I can promise you that if you stop at the library or book store for a supply and make the books available to them, perhaps by leaving them lying unattended on the coffee table in the living room, I can guarantee you will find that they have been moved when you return. Remember, they are interested; they just don't want you to know it because that might trigger questions they may not be ready to answer.

Getting Your Child a Pet to Love Can Be Therapeutic

I offer this suggestion, both here and in my classes, with an extreme caution: consider this option only if your children are old enough to help care for a pet at this time. Remember, whether or not you chose to divorce, you are going through an extremely stressful time right now. Any change we experience in our lives is a stress for our bodies and our minds to adapt to. Divorce is certainly a major change, even when it is positive.

Take care of yourself, practice good stress management and give yourself a good six months before taking on anything else for which you will need to be responsible. Refer to Chapter 4 for more thoughts and techniques on taking care of yourself at this time.

However, if your children are of school age, and capable of feeding, watering, walking, grooming and cleaning up after a pet, it can be a wonderfully therapeutic experience for them to have another living creature to love and care for at this stressful time in their lives. Nurturing another living being has a way of breaking us out of our own misery in a way few other activities can do.

Children May Benefit from Talking with a Therapist

Many children survive their parent's divorce every day without seeing a therapist. But it can be a valuable experience to have a neutral professional to bounce your thoughts and feelings off of, in addition to the interested, caring adults in your life that can be at once well-meaning and sometimes destructive. Caring family members may have thoughts about why the divorce happened that they have trouble hiding, even from a child.

In addition, if you have any indication that your child is suicidal, seriously depressed, or engaging in any of the risky acting out behaviors discussed in Chapter One, I would run, not walk, to the nearest therapist that specializes in working with children and divorce-related issues. These matters are simply too important to be left to non-professionals when the stakes are that high.

Bolster Self-Esteem

In Chapter 12, we will cover self-esteem in some detail, but a few thoughts on that subject are appropriate here as well. Most people in a family in which a divorce is occurring can use some work on their self-esteem, adults and children alike. As a family is breaking up, things are said and done that are damaging to us emotionally. Therefore, even if your children are showing no changes in their behavior, doing a few simple things to build their self-esteem can only help them.

One of the most basic and low-cost things parents can do is offer ample, but genuine praise and encouragement, appropriate to both the child and the situation. Sending some time individually with each child everyday your children are with you is helpful, as is providing opportunities to do things your child does well. Encouraging your child to learn a new skill at this time can give provide a distraction, as well as giving them a sense of accomplishment. Having your child teach you something they know but you don't can lead to positive feelings as well.

These ideas and others are covered in greater depth in Chapter 12.

Dealing With Denial

We have already discussed denial in the context of the grieving process in Chapter One. I want to expand on that discussion a little at this time. Denial is actually a healthy psychological mechanism that our brain provides for us, to prevent us from feeling emotional pain on a constant basis.

Think for a moment about a painful experience or loss that you have had previously in your life. While you were in the acute stages of dealing with that situation, did you ever temporarily "forget" for short periods of time that you were experiencing that loss? That is a part of denial and is perfectly healthy and normal.

I remember when my father died, I would often wake in the morning and for the first ten minutes of my day, I would occasionally forget that he was gone. I would get up and go about my morning routine and some ten minutes later, "remember" that my father had died. The realization of this loss would settle into me like a heavy weight settling onto my shoulders; a familiar albatross. Then I would continue my day, now acutely aware of my pain.

This temporary memory lapse was my brain, protecting me from becoming overwhelmed with my grief. This is normal and nothing to worry about unless it occurs on a long term basis. Typically denial like this lasts six months or less.

The same type of thing happens to children whose families are experiencing divorce. They may temporarily "forget" that their parents are getting divorced. This may become apparent to you as they go to set the table for dinner and set the same number of place settings that you all needed before the separation. Or, they may begin to talk excitedly about the summer vacation you always take up at your in-laws cabin.

At times like this, you want to very gently remind them of the divorce. You can use gentle humor, such as, "We have fewer dishes to wash now," or "Not all of us will be taking that vacation this year." The point is not to embarrass or ridicule them, but to help them to remember the divorce. You can also mention other ways life has changed since the divorce began.

Gently encouraging your child to talk with you about the

divorce and how she feels is helpful at these times as well. But do not push if your child is not ready or willing to talk. Remember, it is enough to just open the door to the possibility of future conversations.

Sharing some of your own feelings and, perhaps, a few of your tears, can be appropriate here as well. But remember to save the bulk of your feelings, tears and talking for your adult support system which we will discuss in Chapter Three. Do not overwhelm your children with your emotions. The point of sharing it with them here is to normalize their reactions, demonstrate how these feelings can be expressed and to acknowledge what you will miss about your family as it was, which can validate their reactions.

Finally, it is always a good idea to provide plenty of reassurances of your love. Spend a little extra time with your children each day they are with you. It is also helpful at this time to encourage and invite the other parent to give them extra time and attention also.

When Kids Withdraw

It is not unusual for children to withdraw from or lose interest in things they had been involved with prior to the divorce. Remember, this, also, is part of the typical grieving process. What this might look like in your child is sitting on the couch in front of the television or hibernating in his bedroom with the headphones on. He may make comments such as, "I don 't want to go to basketball," "I don't want to go to Jamie's house," or "I just want to stay home today; I don't feel like doing anything." What is a parent to do?

First, you want to remember that your kids will need time to mourn their losses, just as adults do. You can help them through this by recognizing what is happening for them and helping them to understand it as well. In addition, a little extra love and attention, support and sensitivity go a long way toward helping them through the withdrawal.

Letting kids talk about how they are feeling, while being an attentive audience, can make this easier as well. As long as they are talking, good things are happening; they are processing those feelings. You may need to step in to distract them temporarily and help them to move on, but often they will do this themselves, once given the opportunity to talk.

Secondly, do what you can to stabilize the home environment as quickly as possible. Given that this is discussed in detail in Chapter Three, we will not go into it in depth here. Just know that you want to provide as much predictability and structure as you can as quickly as you can manage it.

Whatever you do, absent a concrete medical reason, do not let your child skip school because they are depressed or upset. Remember, school is the same today as it was yesterday as it was last week and represents stability to your children, as well as giving them a break from dealing with all of the change that is going on at home right now. Home may be in a different place, with only half the furniture. It is probably a pretty chaotic place at this point. School, and other structured activities kids are involved in as well, such as basketball, scouts, dance class, gymnastics, etc., provides much the same function as denia—a necessary break from all the change. If they do not have a fever, vomiting, diarrhea or a doctor's excuse, send them to school!

In this chapter, we learned some things parents can do to help their children in the immediate crisis of the separation and early divorce process. Further, we explored a number of ways parents could help their children process this experience, even when, as is common in many families, they notice no changes in their children's behavior. We acknowledge that most parents are not aware of the amount of distress their divorce is causing their children.

Therefore, whether or not you've noticed changes in your child's behavior, take a look at the checklist on the following pages and try some of these simple techniques. In a separate notebook, you may want to list those that you try and make a note of your child's response. This will be good information to look back on and discuss with your child as you both get some distance from the divorce.

Applying the Quick(er) Fixes:

1. Telling Your Children About the Divorce:

❀ Talk to them together, if possible

❀ Tell all the children at the same time

❀ Talk in a comfortable setting

❀ Share some simple reason for the divorce

❀ Don't mention reconciliation until you are sure it will happen

❀ Say only positive things about each other

❀ Give as many details about their future as you have

❀ Reassure children that:
~Parents don't divorce children
~They are not responsible for the divorce

❀ Leave the door open for future questions with "Do you have any questions?"

❀ Tune in to any questions that could be divorce related

2. Helping Kids Cope Even if you Notice No Behavioral Changes

❀ Allay their fears as quickly as possible:
~Stabilize family life quickly
~Reassure them of your love and concern
~Set up a schedule for placement times

❀ Label children's confusing feelings~Suggest appropriate ways to express them

❀ Encourage preschoolers to express feelings indirectly:
   ~Telling a story about a toy or doll
   ~Drawing pictures of feelings
   ~Answering questions they are not asking

❀ Encourage older children to express feelings on paper:
   ~Journaling
   ~Today is ____ and I feel ____ because_____.
   ~Writing letters to parents
   ~Writing goodbye letters
   ~Writing poems or song lyrics
   ~Drawing, painting, etc.

❀ Distract a ruminating child

❀ Get your kids involved with outside activities and people

❀ Enlist the help of family, teachers, and adult friends to provide children with extra support.

❀ Provide children's books on divorce to help them cope and get more information.

❀ Get a pet for your child to care for if age permits

❀ Enlist the aid of a counselor or therapist.

❀ Do anything to help bolster self-esteem.

3. Dealing With Denial

❀ Talk realistically to children about the divorce

❀ Gently encourage your children to talk

❀ Share some of your feelings and fears

❀ Reassure children of your love

❀ Spend extra time with your child

❀ Encourage their other parent to spend extra time with them also

4. When Kids Withdraw

❀ Understand they need time to mourn their losses

❀ Listen to them

❀ Stabilize the home environment

❀ Send them to school!

"Avoiding danger is no safer in the long run than outright exposure. Life is either a daring adventure, or nothing."

~Helen Keller

CHAPTER 3

SETTING THEM UP FOR SUCCESS

*How to Assist Children's Long Term
Adjustment to Divorce*

Though her mother had to increase her work hours after the separation, thirteen year old Jessica knew what to expect. Mom, Jessica and her older brother Tyler had sat down and developed a plan for who would be responsible for what chores and decided what the rules of their new household would be. Jess knew that she was to come right home after school and begin her homework. Tyler would start dinner and, just before Mom got home, Jess would set the table. During dinner her family would connect with each other, discussing the events of their days and talking about plans for the evening and the remainder of the week. Jess also knew that bedtime was at 10 p.m. and that she was responsible for helping Mom with the dishes. Feeling confident that she knew what to expect most days when she got home, Jess continued to earn good grades in school and both family and teachers remarked that she seemed to adjust easily to the changes in her family.

There is much parents can do to foster children's long term adjustment to any major change in the family. If relationships with parents are close, nurturing, supportive and dependable, they can buffer children from many of the blows inflicted upon them by stressors in their lives. Divorce is no exception.

We must also remember that our goal as parents is not to prevent or protect our children from experiencing any stress, but to help make the stressors our children face moderate enough so they can tolerate and overcome them. This fosters the resilience that they need and we, as parents, seek to help them achieve.

There are four key ways to do this that will be discussed in this chapter. These involve building good relationships with your children, developing open communication with them, stabilizing the home environment and limiting the amount of change in children's lives. The third, stability, is by far the most crucial to their long term adjustment for reasons that will be explained in this chapter!

Build Good Relationships with Your Children

The first key is building good relationships with your children. The quality of children's relationships with their parents is so important that if these relationships are close, nurturing, supportive and dependable, they can buffer children from many blows inflicted on them by stressors. We will discuss, in this section, some ways to build such relationships with your children, or to enhance the positive relationships you have already built with them.

This is by no means an exhaustive list. There are many things you do each day to build or strengthen your relationships with your children. But these are some ideas of where to start, especially useful when you are feeling overwhelmed by dealing with a divorce and fresh out of creative ideas for connecting with your children. Use them as a springboard of sorts to develop or identify what works best for you and your family. I also invite you to contact me at the numbers at the end of this book or at my website (*www.bluewaterspublications.com*) to share with me and readers of future editions of this book any techniques you have discovered or developed that have worked well in enhancing your relationships with your children.

You will notice that a number of the suggestions I offer

you throughout this book come from ideas offered by members of my Parenting Through Divorce class or parents I have worked with in therapy. I don't pretend to have all the answers and enjoy sharing helpful ideas contributed by others. This is just a starting point. If there is something you have done that you feel has helped your child adapt, please let me know so that I can share it with readers of future editions of this work.

Spend Time Alone with Your Children

It is important to set aside time every day that your children are with you to spend time with them individually. Now, before those of you with more than one child start to think I am asking you to add hours to an already-too-long day, read on!

In arriving home after work with your three children in tow, keep one child with you in the kitchen as you begin to prepare dinner. Be sure to ask him about his day as you are getting the meal together. He will relish the private conversation the two of you are able to have, absent interruptions from his siblings, and will most likely thrive on having the floor, launching into humorous antics or heartfelt confessions that would have remained secret in the presence of the other children.

Next, keep another child with you as you clean up after dinner, perhaps soliciting her assistance. Quickly begin to ask about her day. She, too, will appreciate your undivided attention and will, more than likely, open up as her sibling did, sharing secrets that would have remained unvoiced in the absence of this time alone with you.

Private time with the third child can wait until closer to bedtime. Perhaps you will linger several additional minutes when tucking her into bed, or read a story with her and discuss it afterwards. However it happens, on most days there will be time to squeeze in these brief interludes with your children and still accomplish your many required tasks.

Be sure to alternate what you do with whom, unless there is a good reason not to do so (i.e. one child loves to cook with you or, God forbid, do the dishes!). Children will come to depend on you to spend these private moments with them and you may find them "saving" special revelations to be shared with you at these times. You are assisting them to express their feelings, rather than keeping them bottled up inside, to infect them like a toxin, and you are helping to teach them how to do this for themselves. Again, you are teaching them life skills, not just divorce adjustment; helping them to learn to talk about their feelings and providing a safe environment in which to do so.

Show Children Empathy and Respect

Let your children know that you understand their pain and their fears. Have respect for these feelings and respect for your child's right as a person to have some privacy and some feelings she chooses not to share with you.

Respect other rights your children have as well. Absent clear evidence that they are involved in harmful or dangerous behavior, don't rifle through their personal belongings or property. Treat them with the respect that you want from them.

The most effective way to teach your children to respect others is to model it for them in how they are treated. Children watch what we do far more closely than what we say and our model for how to behave stays with them far longer that what we tell them about how to act.

Reassure Your Children

Provide plenty of reassurances to your children of your love, coupled with plenty of hugs and affectionate comments. "Catch them being good," is a familiar parenting phrase that is even more important in a divorce setting when children's self-esteem has already taken a beating and the world can seem pretty bleak at times.[1]

If all children hear from you is what they are doing wrong, they will stop listening. Give them something to listen, and look forward, to. Nurture them with your words as well as with your hugs.

Be Interested in Their Activities

Show an interest in your children's activities, friends, school lives and current interests. Attend open houses at school and basketball games enthusiastically and without complaint. Tell your children what you enjoyed about each event. Even if you had a miserable experience, you should be able to come up with something positive!

See this as an opportunity to build a new, stronger relationship with your child, now that there is no distraction from a primary intimate relationship. You may never have this opportunity again. Make the most of it.

Support Your Child's Relationship with Their Other Parent

Continue to support your child's contacts with their other parent. Be encouraging and enthusiastic when they will be spending time with that person, rather than seeing it as taking something away from you or as a threat to your relationship with your child. The more you can encourage and affirm her time with her other parent, the better your child will adjust to your divorce.

Be aware of how you can subtly convey these feelings ("You don't want to go over there and miss...") or how you can make them regret the time they spend with that person, (i.e. by planning all the fun activities at your household for the times your child is supposed to be at their other home). You are putting your child in the middle by acting in this manner—to his own detriment. The only person you are hurting is your child. You must stop this at once!

Build Your Own Support System

Reach out to other adults for support. Single parents with social support generally relate better to their children and tend to be happier and more positively adjusted than those who do not have this support. This is just common sense when you think about it. If we are feeling better and more fulfilled ourselves, all of our relationships are bound to be more positive!

We will talk more about stress management in Chapter Four, but for now, just know that you will be a better parent by taking time out for yourself. Further, as we will discuss in

Chapter Ten, part of adjusting to a divorce involves talking to other adults, our support system, about what we are experiencing so that we can move through and beyond it. This practice will help both you and your child, as long as you are not using *them* as your support system! Find one or, better yet, several adults to depend on for your emotional support. Your children will be better for it.

Create an Atmosphere of Open Communication with Your Child

Closely connected with the task of building good relationships with your children is that of creating an atmosphere of open communication with your children or enhancing the good communication which you already have. You may already enjoy frequent heart-to-heart talks with your child. If you do, that's great, and you are already well on the way to helping them successfully adjust to your divorce as you have established yourself as a person to whom they turn for support. You are part of their crucial support system.

Perhaps, however, over the last year or so, as your marriage was breaking down, you have had little time to focus on seeking your child out for these types of intimate conversations. So you currently have no pattern of easy conversation about life's trials and tribulations. But don't despair; all is not lost.

You have already laid the groundwork for changing this pattern. Back in Chapter Two we discussed how you were going to tell your children about the divorce and leave the door open for them to come to you with any questions they might have. In doing that work, you have begun to establish yourself as someone to whom your child can turn, especially with questions about the divorce. All it takes now is a little fine tuning. There are a number of ways to continue your progress. The ideas that follow are some suggestions about how to accomplish this

Listen to Your Child

One of the most effective techniques to enhance the communication process in any setting is listening. Your relationship with your children is no exception. I am talking about *really* listening here—not the kind of listening I do when my son is regaling me with the latest episode of his favorite television action show. My eyes glaze over as I mentally organize my grocery list and wait for him to finish. You know what I mean. We all do this.

I am talking now about active listening. This requires you to focus and pay attention to what your child is really saying— and to not be also thinking about your latest project at work or your grocery list. Be fully in the present moment, thinking about nothing other than what your child is telling you.

Another part of this technique involves eye contact. Look directly at your child as he is talking to you. We all know from other relationships, and from being on both the giving and receiving ends of the communication process throughout our lives, the kind of difference this makes in whether or not we feel we are being heard. Any wife who has ever attempted to talk to her husband while he is staring blankly at a television screen can attest to the importance of eye contact.

In this day and age of families being busier than they have ever been, running literally from one activity to the next, your children know this as well. Turn off the television, put down the newspaper and look at your children when they are talking to you. I can promise you they *will* notice the difference!

Other components of active listening include asking questions, giving feedback, reflecting feelings and restatement of content. You needn't necessarily use all of these in every conversation, but if you play it by ear, you will use those most appropriate for each discussion.

Asking appropriate questions of your children as they are talking to you affirms not only that you are listening, but also that you are interested in what they have to say. Giving feedback, or responding in some manner to what they have said, sends the same message.

Reflecting feelings is nothing more than identifying what your child may be feeling based on their statements or behavior, and sharing your observations with them (i.e. "You seem to be really scared about what's going to happen in our family.") If you guess wrong, they will tell you, as we discussed in Chapter Two. The goal here is merely to get them to share these feelings with you, to get them talking and to further establish yourself as a support person for them.

Restating the content of what your children are telling you is a good tool to check the accuracy of your interpretation of their statements. After a long explanation of plans for an evening with friends, you may want to clarify that you've understood them correctly. Restating them could sound like this, "So, you're saying you're all going over to Chuck's house to watch a movie, then you'll meet other friends at the pizza place and afterwards, just you and Chuck are coming over here to play video games?" If you repeat what they say, word for word, this technique can sound a little artificial. Modify and summarize some of what they have said to convey your genuine interest in their statements and achieve a smoother flow to your comments. You may need to practice this technique a little in front of a mirror to get comfortable with it, but it does work and it's certainly worth it in the difference it can make with your child.

Put Yourself in Your Child's Place

As you talk and listen to your children, try to put yourself in their places so you can understand the feelings that lie beneath the words. Then, you can reflect these back to them. Imagine what you might be feeling if you were in their places and use that information to interpret what you are actually hearing from them. Check out your interpretations to make sure they are accurate.

Tune Into Divorce Related Questions

As we discussed in Chapter 2, tune into any questions that are, or could be, divorce related. Try to hear what they are not asking. Make every effort to answer their questions patiently and honestly, giving them the respect they deserve and, thereby, encouraging them to come to you again in the future.

Put "divorce-English" on even seemingly unrelated questions because the child may not be ready to ask for the information they truly need. Also, be open for these questions to come at inopportune times, as you are driving them in the car or mutually engaged in a joint activity. See Chapter Two for a more complete discussion of this technique.

Accept Their Feelings

Allow your children to have their own thoughts, feelings and opinions about the divorce and life, in general, and work to accept them. This includes their anger, which you will now be able to recognize as a secondary emotion. Look for the underlying feeling and accept and respond to that. In most cases, the anger will then take care of itself.

Another important point about feelings—they aren't right or wrong, good or bad. They just are. All people, children and adults, have them. They are part of our human experience.

What may not be acceptable is how the feelings are expressed. The behavior that accompanies our feelings, such as expressing anger by yelling at parents or hitting a sibling, is definitely *not* appropriate. Also, while we cannot eliminate feelings from our existence, we can have some effect on the extent of negative emotion we are willing to endure.

Use Emotional Regulation to Help Yourself and Your Child

What I am referring to is a cognitive behavioral technique I frequently use in therapy to help people change their thinking process to cope with, and reduce, all types of negative emotions—anger, fear, grief, jealousy, sadness, frustration and the like. While there are minor differences in application, techniques similar to this are taught by many therapists and have a number of different names, but most are based on work pioneered by Aaron Beck and Albert Ellis. For the sake of simplicity, and for reasons that will become obvious, I call it the Event, Thought, Feeling Process. It is easy to learn but does require practice.[2]

The basic premise is that any event, anything that happens in our lives, is neither good nor bad, but neutral. We give it meaning by the thoughts we have about it. These thoughts give rise to our feelings and these feelings, in many ways, direct the actions we choose to take in response to the event.

The process can be diagrammed as follows:

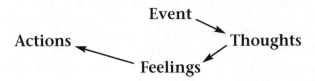

By way of illustration, we will walk through the process with the simple example of a rainstorm. A rainstorm is neither good nor bad, but neutral; it just *is*. Any meaning it has for us comes from the thoughts we allow ourselves to have about it.

Assume for example, you are a farmer, and you planted your crops a month ago, but nothing is sprouting because there has been no rain. The ground is so dry it has developed large, deep cracks. You need a good crop this year because last year there was a drought. If this crop doesn't save you, the bank will foreclose and take the farm, which has been in your family for five generations. It is important to you to be able to pass it on to your children as well. You are pondering these heavy thoughts, and your very existence, as you stare out the window of your farmhouse one day when suddenly the skies open up and it begins to rain.

You will have some pretty predictable thoughts about this neutral event, the rainstorm. You may think:

❀ Thank God—now I will have a good crop.

❀ The bank won't take the farm.

❀ I will be able to pass the farm on to my children,

❀ I won't have to look for another job."

Your feelings will flow directly from these thoughts. Given the probable thoughts listed above, you will most likely feel very relieved, excited, hopeful, happy and at peace.

If you are like most of us, you will also act in accordance with your feelings. Others will probably be able to guess some of the feelings you are experiencing just from observing you. You may be grinning from ear to ear as you watch the rain fall. You might be on the phone with your banker, saying, "Looks like you're not going to get it this year!" You may be on the phone with a friend asking, "Do you want to do something today? It's raining so I can't plow." Or, you may express your pleasure and relief by dancing out in the cornfield in the rain! But we will be able to tell, just by looking at you, that you are experiencing some pretty positive emotions.

If, however, instead of being our farmer, you are the single parent of four children under the age five, who had been planning a picnic at the beach for this very day, you may have quite a different reaction to this turn of events. You know that the kids have been looking forward to this picnic for more than a month and are so excited that they jumped out of bed this morning and right into their swimming suits. Then they chased each other around the house, collecting and blowing up all the beach toys they could find. They are now loaded in the mini-van and you are headed out the back door with the picnic basket over your arm, when the same neutral event occurs—the skies open up and rain begins to fall.

Your thoughts about this event will most likely be very different from those of our farmer. You might have thoughts such as the following:

❀ "Oh no—the kids are going to be so disappointed!

❀ They'll be climbing the walls!

❀ What am I going to do with them all day?

❀ This will be a nightmare!"

The feelings arising from these thoughts will most likely be some variation of frustration, disappointment, irritation, panic, aggravation, anger and, perhaps, depression. Your actions in the expression of these feelings may include snapping at the kids, slamming things around the house, giving up and slumping down in a chair or venting on the phone to a friend. And, watching you, any observer would detect the negative emotions and know you are anything *but* happy, excited and relieved.

It is when you become aware that you are experiencing negative emotions, such as anger, frustration, hurt, fear, jealousy and the like, that you must learn to remember that you are creating this situation for yourself. Your thoughts are your captors, your prison and the creator of your misery. I don't mean to imply that bad things don't happen to people sometimes. Or, that you should or can be expected to enjoy them. But, when you are feeling negative emotions, know that your thoughts are creating your emotional reaction to the event you,'ve experienced. That fact alone empowers you to change it.

How do you do that? Take the example of our parent and the disappointed children. Rather than going with the negative set of thoughts that first popped into your head, imagine the difference if you entertained these thoughts: "Well, I need to come up with plan B. Let's see, we'll put a video in the VCR and have a picnic on the living room floor. We'll save the beach for next weekend and, after lunch, we,'ll all go out and splash around in the puddles!"

This change in your thinking process and the addition of those "Replacement Thoughts" leading to "More Positive Feelings" can be diagrammed as follows:

Granted, it probably won't make you happy, excited and relieved like our farmer, but you will most likely be a whole lot calmer, more relaxed and more neutral about the event than with the former set of thoughts. That's the effect the thinking process can have: enabling you to *choose* your reaction to events over which you, in most cases, have no control. For most of us, in this society, there are only too many such situations in our lives. What do you have to lose by managing your emotions more successfully?

While utilizing this process typically takes some work, it does get easier with practice. You are likely, at first, to notice that you remember to pay attention to your thoughts only after you have *again* reacted to a situation. But, in many cases, there is emotional baggage remaining that you can work on at that point with this process. The more you work with this, the earlier you will notice the effect you have. Pretty soon, you will stop yourself in mid-sentence as you react to an event and, before long, you will be thinking through the entire reaction before even opening your mouth.

As you get more accustomed to thinking this way, you will notice, also, that your mind takes over and completes the process for you. After a while, you might start down the path of a negative reaction, and your thoughts will stop suddenly, seemingly of their own accord. You may think, "Wait a minute, I don't have to go there. I can think about it this way instead!" It will seem as involuntary as the negative thinking does to you now—only you won't be nearly as miserable! But, as with any change worth making, it does take practice to make it work.

Two more points about the Event, Thought, Feeling Process bear mention here: repetition and outcome. First, if an event has happened to you a number of times in a similar manner, you are likely, in that instance, to move so quickly from Event to Feelings and Actions that you are not consciously aware of the Thoughts at all. They are, indeed, there. You will just have to work harder, and slow things down even more, to get to them.

Because this is a repeated experience for you, your thoughts have taken the same route many times in the past. Thoughts that we have create a neural pathway in our brain. Each time we have a similar experience and the thoughts repeat themselves, they follow the same pathway. Once an experience has repeated itself a number of times, your thoughts have dug a deep trench in your brain, as it were. Each time the same experience and thoughts happen, it takes less time to get through them and on to the feelings and actions. And each time the trench gets a little deeper and a little wider. Let me give you another example.

Let's say you've had a previous relationship in which your partner took to going out with friends and, when this would happen, frequently he would hook up with another woman and become involved in an affair. Whether this happened to you once or a thousand times (hopefully you did not choose to stay in the same relationship that long), you have a pattern of thoughts that will tend to happen pretty much automatically when your new partner announces he will be going out with friends Friday night. It goes something like this:

Event

Your partner announces he's going out with friends.

Actions

Thoughts

You ask him 20 questions:
- Where are you going?
- Who will you be with?

He'll meet someone else

He'll find someone
he likes more than me

You forbid him to go

He doesn't really care about me

You get upset and start
an argument

There's something wrong
with me

You give him the silent
treatment

I'm unlovable

You lie in wait to attack him
when he gets home

Feelings

Hurt
Afraid
Jealous
Insecure
Lonely
Angry

Because of your life experiences, you are uniquely set up to react to this situation. How you react is often largely dictated by what has happened in your past as well. But, just knowing this, you have the power and ability to change it!

It is also important, in the context of relationships, to think about outcome. You want to get in the habit of asking yourself, "What's my outcome here?" and "Are my actions getting me the result I want?"

In the example presented above, if you act on the first set of thoughts, your actions are likely to be snapping at your partner, giving him the silent treatment, or starting an argument. We are upset because we are afraid our partner will leave or not be faithful to us and we are feeling emotionally distant from him. Choosing those actions, however, we end up with exactly the opposite of what we want; we get greater emotional distance, rather than the closeness we prefer. Further, remembering that anger is a secondary emotion, we don't have far to look to find the feelings leading up to it in this case.

The bottom line in this exercise is, we want to feel closer to our partner, but all our actions are achieving is greater distance. In reacting to an event in the context of a relationship, always ask yourself, "Is this getting me greater emotional closeness? Or greater emotional distance?" Then act according to what you would prefer.

What might replacement thoughts be in a case such as this? How about these:

❀ This is a new relationship

❀ This is a different partner

❀ He and I have a good relationship

❀ I know I can trust him

❀ I know he cares about me

Again, this is how the replacement thought process might be diagrammed:

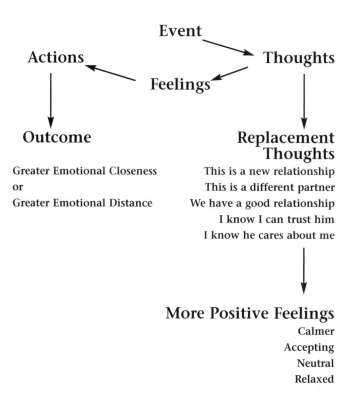

You may not find yourself happy and excited about your partner going out with his friends, but you will most likely be much calmer and more neutral about the experience than if you went with your first set of thoughts. You will be less likely to push your partner away with distancing behaviors and more likely to act in ways that increase emotional closeness with him.

In creating replacement thoughts, is it important to be genuine. Don't attempt to create positive thoughts that you can't believe, such as telling yourself you have no reason not to trust your partner if she has cheated repeatedly in the past. In that case, you may first want to ask yourself why you stay in the relationship in the first place. What are you getting out of the deal that keeps you there? Are you with her only because you feel you cannot find another partner? Do you have a need to "save" her from herself? Or, is it that you truly enjoy each other,s company when you are together and her affairs take little away from the relationship? If that is the case, your positive thoughts may need to be about this conscious choice on your part: "I know she sometimes sees other men, but our relationship is a good one and I can live with that."

Know, too, that the first time you travel this new path with your thinking, you will have to work at it to come up with the replacement thoughts. Remember, all of those old familiar destructive thoughts have dug a pretty deep trench by now. Creating a new path can take some work. But the more you force yourself to go through the exercise of creating positive thoughts, the easier and more automatic it becomes.

The point of discussing this thinking process now is that you can help your children do this as well. If you notice them getting into a pattern of negative or destructive thinking, you can help them out of it by suggesting replacement thoughts for them. Again, remember that all feelings are OK, even anger. It's how they are expressed that may not be.

You can also model for them how you do this yourself. When you are frustrated by a problem at work or irritated by a slow driver, you can verbalize your thinking process as you create replacement thoughts to improve your own mood. You can do this with some thoughts and feelings about the divorce as well, but be careful to focus only on the fears and frustrations that do not involve your children's other parent while you are talking to them.

Encourage Them to Talk

There are some other techniques useful in opening up a discussion with your child. Use what communications experts like to call "door-openers" such as "Tell me about it" in response to a subject he brings up, or "I'd be interested in your point of view." Essentially open-ended questions, these statements open the door for conversation and discussion because they cannot be answered with a one word response, such as "Yes" or "No."

Instead of asking your child, "Do you like this house?" put your query in the following form, "I'd be interested in your opinion of the house we looked at today." Your daughter cannot respond with a simple "yes" or "no" and is more likely to say something like, "Well, I like the living room, but the bedrooms are kind of small." From here you can open up a dialogue about the kind of home you would both prefer. It's much harder to get there from a one word response.

Engage Your Child in an Activity

If you find that your child is very guarded about her feelings, get involved in an activity together, such as putting together a puzzle or baking cookies and gently ask a probing question. This is similar to questions that come when you are driving children in a car to and from an activity. It is a safe time because you are not staring at each other, but sitting or working side by side. Again, don't forget to look for potentially divorce-related questions, even if they don't seem so on the surface.

Stay Available

Parents need to be aware that children may not be ready to share their feelings with them. If you are met with anger or avoidance, don't pry or push, but do stay available. Again, what you have done is opened the door to talking about these topics. Now you must wait for your child to be ready. If anger is the response you get, you may also help them to refocus it as discussed above and get to a more positive place.

Share Some of Your Own Feelings

Parents might also want to share some of their own feelings with children, being careful not to overwhelm them with the depth of your emotion or to badmouth the other parent. Be aware that they may have a number of mixed feelings, most children do, and may not understand what they feel or why they are acting the way they are.

Use a Children's Book to Give Them Information About the Divorce

A number of parents have found great success reading to their children about divorce. Hearing about feelings and events other children have experienced can help to normalize the experiences and feelings your own children are having and help them to deal more positively with them. As we discussed previously, books can also help to promote discussion of topics that may not come up naturally in the course of conversation and reinforce the message that the divorce is an acceptable topic of conversation.

A Few Final Thoughts on Communication with Your Children

As you talk with your children, about the divorce or any other topic, work to avoid lecturing, interrogating (especially about time with their other parent) or criticizing your children. At a time when most likely everyone in your family has taken a beating to their self-esteem, kids need to feel good about themselves in order to develop the resilience to survive and overcome this stress.

Create a Stable Home Environment

According to all researchers on this subject, by far, the most important thing you can do to enhance your children's long term adjustment to your divorce is to create a stable home environment. A stable home represents safety and security to the very young, reassurance and love to the school age child, and the safe haven necessary for a successful adolescence.

This one factor helps kids adjust to virtually any change they encounter in their lives, whether it is losing a parent or grandparent through death, experiencing familial divorce or the experience of adjusting to step-family life. As an aside, current research is showing that becoming part of a step-family is even more stressful for children than parental divorce.

This makes sense if you think about it. In a divorce, children see their parents one at a time, but, in most cases, still have a relationship with both parents. In a step-family situation, there is another adult moving into the children's lives and home. It often doesn't matter if they like or get along with this person, or how they feel about him. He will be living in their home or, possibly, they will live in his. And he has, depending on the particular family situation, some degree of authority over the child.

Even when parents successfully avoid making the new step-parent the "bad cop," so to speak, which, in itself, is a situation which often spells disaster, this stranger, at the very least, has the ability to provide input into expectations of children and family members. Talk about a stressful situation! But a stable home environment can help even this!

But what does this mean? What is stability? What follows are some ideas on how to achieve this in your home.

Set Up Regular, Organized Routines

There are many ways to achieve stability in your home. The most effective and successful is to set up regular and organized routines and schedules, making every effort to stick to them. These routines should include meal times, bedtimes, after-school schedules, chore lists and the like.

Does this mean that you all have to sit down to dinner every night at 5:00 p.m.? *No!* Not unless that works for your family.

My husband and I are both therapists and take turns working weeknights. That's not what happens at our house. But our children know what to expect and what is expected of them. That is the key.

Why is this important? As human beings, we take comfort and security from our rituals and routines. It's much like putting a toddler to bed. You have to put his pajamas on, brush his teeth, read him a story, say his prayers, wind up his lamb and only *then* can you turn out the light. If you do it in any other order it doesn't count and you must start all over again from the beginning!

Children, like adults, take great comfort from these rituals. The ritual enables them to perform the otherwise frightening task of separating emotionally from their parents for the night. Again, we need to apply this wisdom to children of all ages, not just the little ones.

So, what is it that makes up this stability? It's how your

home is run; what happens there. Stability is children knowing the answers to the following questions:

- ❀ Who makes dinner?

- ❀ Who does the dishes?

- ❀ What's expected of children after school?

- ❀ What's expected of children as far as chores are concerned?

- ❀ When is homework done?

- ❀ What is curfew on the weekend? On weeknights?

- ❀ Can friends come over on school nights?

- ❀ What time is bedtime?

- ❀ How are conflicts handled?

- ❀ How do we spend time together as family?

- ❀ When will children see each of their parents and under what conditions?

- ❀ How are rules and expectations enforced?

When your children can answer all of these questions, and their answers are consistent with yours, you have stability in your home. It may be easier, at least starting out, to keep most of the rules and expectations the same as before the separation. But, does this mean that if you had a rule in your family that the other parent believed in but with which you had always disagreed, you must keep it for the sake of stability? Absolutely not!

Now is the time to change it. But your children will have an easier time adjusting if at least *some* of the expectations are familiar to them.

How to get started? Family meetings are a great way to

begin. Sit down when all children are present and just have a conversation about "what the rules are in our family." Once you have that figured out, you can move on to "what do we want them to be?"

Be sure to give kids the opportunity for input in these decisions. They may have some valid reasons for objecting to specific expectations and often do a better job "thinking outside the box" to come up with creative and unique solutions to dilemmas their families are facing.

Many times I've been amazed at the wisdom of my own children in solving problems when they haven't been hampered by some of the same restrictions I may have unwittingly placed on a situation myself. Including children in solutions also gives them greater investment in the expectations and outcomes, so they are more likely to make the contributions to the family that you are asking of them.

This concept of stability and consistent expectations is so important in children's adjustment to parental divorce that I often tell my classes, "If you take nothing else away from this group, I want you to remember the concept of stability and what that looks like in a family." The most important thing I can teach you in this book is how to provide that stable home for your children so that they can, again, benefit from that security.

Judith Wallerstein refers to this concept in her book, *The Unexpected Legacy of Divorce*, as one factor that makes a difference between children who successfully accomplish the adjustment to their parents, divorce and those who continue to struggle in school, socially and in the community with difficulties that, in many cases, haunt them for the remainder of their lives.

Establish Rules and Limits

While answering the questions posed on the previous pages gets you a long way toward you goal of that stable home environment, there are other factors that play a part. It is important to establish rules and limits for your children and to use consistent discipline. This means that when you and the children make a rule or set an expectation, it should be clear to everyone. If you need to, write it up and post it on the refrigerator where all can see it or remind themselves if they forget.

We have found this technique very useful in our home, especially when chores change or are rotated among family members. It eliminates the excuse, "I didn't know whose turn it was" and gets the parent (i.e. you) out of the role of having to keep all of these details in your mind at all times. This is important because the first time you respond to "Whose turn is it to do the dishes?" with an "I don't know" you have provided an excuse that can be used every time by the child looking to escape responsibility.

Don't give them that out. Teach them to be responsible and accountable for their actions. I see many people each week that have reached adulthood and are still having difficulty with this concept. Whether it is a violent husband blaming his wife's latest beating on her "making" him angry, or a wife who had an affair because her husband didn't pay enough attention to her, many adults are causing enormous problems for themselves by not taking responsibility for their own behavior. Don't let your children get started down this path.

Rules, limits and discipline often fall by the wayside in divorcing homes, but their absence only compounds the chaos and confusion children feel. When their entire world seems to be falling apart, rules and limits provide children with the reassurance that some order remains after all. Remember, while children may complain about the rules or guidelines, they mean stability to your child.

Equally important to developing these expectations, however, is their enforcement. Expect that these guidelines will be followed, but also discuss when you are creating them, what will happen if they are not. Children are often better and more creative than adults at coming up with appropriate consequences for not following the rules.

Also, the punishment should fit the crime, so to speak. In other words, if your son cannot load dinner dishes into the dishwasher when it is his night because your daughter has neglected to unload it before dinner, it then becomes her job to do *both* chores. She then has an incentive to get her job done before dinner or it, in effect, doubles. This solution was suggested by one of our daughters, rather ingeniously, we thought.

Our ineffective solution prior to that point had been to deduct $1.00 from her allowance each time her task was not done. But that left her dad and me to do the task, as she had no incentive to do it once she was late in getting to it.

Now we have finally reached a point where Katie reminds herself to unload the dishwasher when she gets home after school. This is no longer my task either. Amen! The job, and her getting it done, has finally become more important to her than it is to me. This is your goal and it will make your life immeasurably easier and more pleasant.

Many parents are reluctant to impose rules and limits on children when they are going through a divorce, thinking they are "giving [the child] a break, because he's having such a tough time right now." Parents are especially lenient with young children and research is showing the biggest offenders to be mothers with sons. But fathers do this as well and both parents also with daughters, so I want to hear no gloating or "I told you so's." Again, the message that this behavior, by either parent, gives to children is that there are no rules and chaos reigns.

To give an example of this phenomenon in action, suppose Mom feels sorry for Johnny and tells him he doesn't have to worry about cleaning his room as she knows he's having a hard time because of the divorce. The next week, when the Health Department is threatening to visit Johnny's room, Mom is fed up! She comes home after a particularly difficult day at work and screams at Johnny to "Get this room cleaned up NOW!!!" The following week, Mom is in a better frame of mind and gently reprimands Johnny about the condition of his room, adding that he cannot visit a friend's house until his room is cleaned.

What has Johnny learned? Probably that he is never quite sure what the rule or expectation on him is or what will happen if it is not met. Essentially, he has learned that there is no rule about the state of his room in his family. Thus, chaos reigns! This is but one small example of the kind of thing that leads to children having continued problems adjusting to their parents, divorce—or to any major change in their lives. The bottom line is, parents should establish their rules and enforce them consistently so that children will have a clear sense of what is expected of them and what will happen if the expectation is not met. They can then take comfort in the security of these rules and the surety of their enforcement.

Seek Out Other Support People for Your Children

I want to address boys for a moment. Boys tend to have a greater difficulty adjusting to divorce than do girls. However, research done with sons of divorced families, in particular, has found that boys who have clear rules and firm limits, which are enforced, function better on a day to day basis and adjust better to divorce than boys with lax discipline. Although both boys and girls need rules and limits, boys seem to be in greater need of them.

Younger children tend to need very clear rules and limits even more than older ones do. In times of stress, very young children have a difficult time with self-control. They truly need external controls by parents, teachers and caregivers to guide them in their behavior.

I want to make another point about boys. We know from research that boys, in general, tend to mature more slowly, both socially and emotionally, than girls do. But this fact, alone, doesn't explain why boys have a harder time adjusting to divorce than girls, because that tends to happen across the board. However, even in this day and age, when boys and girls are raised more similarly within most families than at many other times in our history, these adjustment differences are still apparent. It has more to do with gender-based differences, than with environment.

If you drive past any elementary school playground, even today, you will typically see groups of little girls standing around talking or engaged in types of quiet play during which conversation is still not only possible, but most often taking place. You will also see groups of boys out running, kicking balls, jumping, dribbling, shooting baskets, etc. They are typically not talking, other than an occasional shout, and are most often engaged in behaviors that make conversation difficult, if not impossible. Of course, there are always the exceptions that prove the rule, but in most cases, these types of separate activities occur.

When your daughter, Susie, comes to school worried or upset about something happening at home, she very often will go to this group of friends and say something like, "This is happening at my house [in my family] and I'm worried [scared, frustrated, angry] about..." Her friends will listen empathically, ask questions, offer opinions and suggestions and typically relate similar difficulties that they may have dealt with.

When your son, Johnny, comes to school worried or scared about what is happening at home, he isn't going to stop the game, pull one of the other boys off to the side and discuss these feelings with his friend. He will go and join the game, enthusiastically running, kicking, dribbling, expressing his feelings just the same in vigorous physical activity, fueled by the adrenaline coursing through his body.

Johnny's behavior, in itself, is not a problem. As we will discuss in greater detail in Chapter Four, any time our bodies or minds perceive a stressor or threat in our midst, adrenaline will circulate throughout our bodies.

Physical exercise or exertion is one of the best ways to expel this excess hormone and get ourselves back on a more even keel. However, while Johnny expressing his negative feelings physically is not a problem, and is, in fact, a very healthy approach to dealing with stress, it still deprives him of a support system that your daughters have automatically.

Soon after they arrive at the playground, the school bell rings and Susie, Johnny and their classmates file into the classroom. Even with the awareness and attention to family problems in school these days, everyone coming in contact with our children, including the teachers, counselors, social workers, coaches, scout leaders and administrative staff, is more likely to say to our daughters, "I know you're going through a tough time at home; if you ever need to talk, just come to my office [stay after class, practice, etc.]." They are much less likely to say anything to your son.

It's not that they do this consciously, or are ill-intentioned or bad people. Your daughters often seem more approachable or, possibly, in greater need of reassurance than your sons, who, as boys and men still often tend to do, hide their emotions under a mask of nonchalance. Boys are still getting the message that It's not OK to show emotion, unless it's anger, which as we've discussed previously, is always preceded by other troubling feelings. In the business of everyday life, our sons are being lost or misinterpreted and, again, because of these messages, are not taking it upon themselves to reach out to these adults in their lives and acknowledging that they need to talk. Therefore, our daughters have two naturally occurring support systems that our sons do not have.

What is a concerned parent to do? Plenty! You can pull these people in to be a support system for your children—sons and daughters. You will want to contact the school and explain to everyone who comes into contact with your child and will listen, what is happening in your child's home and family. Ask them to invite Johnny or Susie into their offices once a week to play a game of Checkers. Again, it is when the child is engaged in or focused on some activity and feeling safe, that some of the best, truest discussion of problems happens.

Also, your child may feel awkward or as if he is being disloyal to his other parent by talking to you about the divorce or what goes on at his other house. Give him a caring adult to talk to by pulling in school personnel that will have contact with him anyway. I am not aware of any instances when these good people were invited to support a child in which they failed to step up to the plate and provide the extra services being requested. In the long run, it only makes their jobs easier and most are very appreciative of the added information and willing to do whatever they can to help our children. Build this support system for your child. It truly can make a difference.

Another good resource, in addition to people at his school, is anyone else that you trust who has contact with your child: the dance teacher, the karate teacher, the parent of your child's best friend that he sees whenever he is over at their house, etc. All of these people can be pulled in as part of your child's support system. Seek out the people who can provide your children with support, sensitivity and caring. They can help you out at the same time by giving you a break from being your children's sole emotional support!

Aside from these crucial components of establishing rules and limits, following through and enforcing them and helping to build a support system for your child, there are a number of other tips to enhance the security and stability that your child feels. Many of these are nothing more than common sense ideas, but bear mention based on what I have observed in divorcing families. What may seem obvious when you are not in the middle of a contemptuous divorce may not seem so when you are. If these ideas have already occurred to you, bear with me. This is not the case for everyone in your situation.

Resolve the Issues of Custody and Placement as Quickly as Possible

It is best for the children if parents resolve the issues of custody and placement as quickly and amicably as you can. While you may have the legal right to pursue primary placement of your children or to push for placement exactly 50 percent of the time, down to the last minute, get in the habit of asking yourself, "Is this what is best for my children?" In most cases, seeking to enforce every parental right to the last detail is not about the children, but about revenge and bitterness parents often harbor toward each other.

If you find that you and the other parent just cannot agree, please quickly review Chapter Five on custody and placement, Chapter Seven on "sharing with the enemy" and Chapter Nine on how to improve your relationship with that other parent. You would also be well advised to enlist the assistance of a family mediator as discussed in Chapter Five.

To the extent you can, develop a firm parenting schedule quickly that provides frequent, regular and reliable contact with the nonresident parent. It is important for children to know who them will be with and when. Great insecurity can develop when children have no idea when they will next see their absent parent.

CAJUN PUBLIC LIBRARY

Take Children's Developmental Needs into Account

You will also want to be sure to take children's developmental needs into account when determining a parenting schedule. This will also be covered in depth in Chapter Seven. No matter what age or developmental level your child may be, you should avoid very frequent transitions between parents. This tends to make children feel they are living out of a suitcase. Every day or every other day is too often to be moving between homes.

End Parental Conflict

It is also important to end parental conflict, at least within the child's earshot. Even if she can only hear your end of a telephone conversation, your child will probably be able to easily guess who you are talking to and can easily fill in enough of the rest of the conversation to feel concerned and insecure. Prolonged parental conflict is unsettling and destructive to the child's emotional health.

In fact, recent research points out how destructive this can be. Children were studied from conflict-ridden intact two parent families and from conflict-free single parent homes. The children from the conflict-free homes performed better socially, emotionally and in the community than those from the conflict-ridden homes, in spite of the fact that they had weathered a divorce in the process.[4] It is truly that important to end conflict and keep your children out of the middle.

Support Children's Relationships with Their Other Parent

You must also support the children's relationships with their other parent and that parent's extended family. Do not badmouth either in your child's presence, no matter how tempting or even if you have good reason to do so. Again, this is emotionally harmful to you child who must be your primary concern. See Chapter Seven for additional thoughts on this subject.

Encourage Your Child to Assume Age-Appropriate Responsibilities

It is also normal and acceptable in a single parent family to ask more of your children that may have been expected of them when you all lived together. After all, there is one less pair of adult hands to do the same number of never-ending chores. Be careful, however, not to burden children with adult responsibilities.

Do encourage and expect them to assume some additional age-appropriate responsibilities to relieve your burden. Children who contribute to the family grow in self-reliance and self-esteem, which most likely needs a little work right now, anyway. But they should be parent helpers, not parent stand-ins.

This can be a fine line, but if your 14 year old daughter is making meals every night and spending every spare moment caring for younger siblings, you are probably expecting too much. The same is true if your 16 year old son is spending every night and weekend working to make money to support the household.

If you are feeling too overwhelmed to reduce your extensive reliance on your children, take a look at Chapter Four on managing your own stress. Don't continue on your current path or it will be to the detriment of your children. Seek your emotional support from your adult support system. Do not rely on your children to fulfill your needs for support or adult companionship, no matter how mature they appear to be. Remember, they are interested parties and are in dire need of your nurturing and care at this time.

If the only way children feel they can get the attention they need is by supporting you, they may be only too willing to take on that role. Focus on meeting your children's needs when you are with them, and seek your support from other adults.

Resolve the Reconciliation Question Quickly

As we discussed in Chapter Two, the possibility of reconciliation between his parents is the most fervent wish of virtually 99 percent of children of divorced and divorcing parents. Resolve the questions of reconciliation and any associated indecision as quickly as possible.

Long or repeated separations are hard on children, placing them in a state of chronic stress. They are hopeful about the reconciliation and heartbroken if it doesn't work out. The only thing worse than losing your family once is losing your family twice, or even three times!

Get Counseling for your Child if Necessary

If you have created a stable and loving environment and your child continues to have problems, consider seeking counseling for him. Most children benefit from having a neutral adult to open up to in times of change. Sometimes that is best available in the form of a professional therapist.

Make sure, however, that you are working with someone who is experienced in working with children from divorcing families because some of the behaviors and reactions your child may experience may seem unfamiliar to one not well versed in normal post divorce

Limit the Amount of Change in Your Children's Lives

Many parents assume that their children experience only one loss or change in the days and weeks following a separation: that of living with both parents together. In actuality, children typically experience many losses as a result of separation and divorce.

The first and most obvious is that previously mentioned— the child no longer lives with both parents together in one house. Along with this, however, is the loss of time spent with the less-seen parent. And this loss can be significant.

Even assuming a very positive 50-50 split of placement to maximize the amount of time the nonresident parent is with the child, there can be many hours and times the child would, in the past, have had contact with that parent that would be in excess of the time she may see the parent now. For instance, assume parents alternate weekends and each has children for two weekday evenings. There are still all of those weekends the child is with only one parent during which they would otherwise have spent at least some portion of time with the other parent, be it at mealtimes, engaged in parent-child activities or even just being around the house together, where the opportunity for casual contact is lost. The same occurs with the weekday evenings the child must now spend with one parent or the other. This is a very real and tangible loss to the child of divorce. Time with parents now becomes more formal and calculated, even in the best of circumstances.

Further, seeing parents in separate homes, there is another living environment that is introduced into the picture. Gone is the opportunity for the child to spend nights and weekends in one bed or home. Now he must switch between two homes and accept this new reality as his way of spending time with his parents.

Additionally, often in a divorce, the family must move. Perhaps the primary home must be sold or the apartment is too large or expensive for one parent to afford. No matter whether it is from a larger to a smaller home or from a house to an apartment, the move is often not a positive one.

Also, the child then loses his friends in the old neighborhood, as well as adult neighbors he has had a relationship with, perhaps from birth, and other familiar resources associated with the location of the home. These resources can include a park, a corner store, the library, the school playground and the like. This adds innumerable potential losses for the child.

Sometimes when there is a divorce, a child must change schools. Perhaps this occurs because there is now a lack of money for tuition or because of the neighborhood change. When this occurs, the losses the child endures multiply exponentially. We must consider not just the school building, but also friends at school, teachers, counselors, janitors, cooks, coaches, scout leaders and the like that the child must leave. Some of these persons may now be part of the child's crucial support system as well. This number can include anyone your child has a relationship with that is affected by the move or family change.

Yet other losses may include the primary or previously

more available parent needing to take a job that makes them unavailable to the child for larger portions of time, changes in care givers or day care arrangements or contact with grandparents or other extended family. These often occur due to cost, location or relationships.

As you can see, we very quickly get into double digits in terms of the number of losses our children experience as a result of the divorce. The number of losses they experience has a significant effect on how well and how quickly they will adjust to the divorce.

Give Your Child Six Months Before Making Additional Changes

Understanding that there are any number of changes that children experience as a result of divorce gives you the awareness to make more sensitive choices in the months and years after your divorce. To the extent you can, strive for continuity and keep the details of your children's lives the same after divorce as they were before. These details can include the house, school, neighborhood, caregivers, activities, friends, household routine, your expectations, limits on their behavior and many others.

Also strive for continuity in your children's relationships with their other parents. Contact with that other parent should be frequent, regular and reliable, and should begin immediately after that parent moves out of the home. The children should also have clear information about when and where they will be seeing this parent.

If at all possible, temporarily delay any major changes, such as moving to a new house or apartment, changing schools or taking a new job that demands more of your time. Ideally, you will be able to give your children six months before adding any of these changes on top of the separation and divorce. Then you will add only one at a time. Even a delay of a few months will be helpful to your child.

Make Changes Gradually

When major changes must be made, make them as gradually as your situation allows. Again, it is not uncommon for children to face a number of these major adjustments in a divorce situation. But patience is the key.

Remember the greater number of children who were still struggling five years after their parents separated discussed in Chapter One? These were children whose home lives had not stabilized and who had been faced with one change or adjustment after another. They were hit with the separation, a move, a change of schools, a parent's new partner, another move, and so on.

Allow Six Months Between Major Changes

Try to build in at least six months between any major changes in your children's lives. If you can, wait six months after separation to move them out of their home. Then, if you must move, try to keep them in their old school, at least for the year, or until they are out of elementary (or middle) school, so it is a natural transition time anyway. Build in that magic six months between each of these major changes to allow your child time to adjust.

Continue Familiar Routines

Also, strive to continue with familiar routines in your home. Incorporate as many things as you can from the family home into your new home. This will bring comfort and stability to the new home and help your child settle in.

Give Children Time to Prepare for Changes

When changes must be made, inform your children in advance of what will happen so they will be able to prepare themselves for change. They should know they will be attending a new school by the end of their last school year or semester at the old school. They should have several weeks notice before moving out of their home and should be told before the "For Sale" sign appears on the front lawn. All of these things can help them to adjust to the changes that are often an inevitable part of the divorce process.

Provide a Positive Focus

Finally, if many negative changes in your children's lives are unavoidable, work to offset them by providing extra love, time, support and sensitivity. Introduce new positive events and experiences into their lives. Help them to look for the silver lining. For example, after moving from your large family home to a smaller, less desirable apartment, you may be able to incorporate an after dinner walk to the park in your new neighborhood as part of your new routine. Your own positive attitude can assist your children in being positive and forward-looking as well.

Guilt

Guilt is common in the divorcing parent. It may be comforting to know that children often emerge from their parents, divorce with greater psychological strength. Research is showing that the most effective way to foster that resilience in your children that we were discussing earlier is not to shelter them from stress, but to allow them to encounter stress in doses that are moderate enough for them to handle and overcome successfully. The key is for the stress to be moderate enough so it does not become overwhelming to the child. This resilience will serve them throughout their lives.

I have personally noticed that my daughter, Katie, is stronger psychologically and emotionally than many of her peers, and stronger than I was at her age. There is a sureness about her, a confidence, that is not typical in the average 16 year old girl. Her transitions to middle and high school were easy for her; I am more concerned about my two younger children making these adjustments. They are not children of divorce and do not seem to have developed that same adaptability.

While I certainly do not recommend divorce as a positive parenting technique as I stated previously, and it takes effort on the part of the parent to ensure this stability, I have seen many wonderful examples of how possible this is to do. And I have seen first hand the positive effect it can have.

In talking with Katie about how she feels the divorce affected her, her reaction is not uncommon. She says, "I'm more independent and a stronger person because of the divorce. I think I've learned a lot." This is apparent just from meeting her. And the good news is this is very possible for your children as well!

Just as we have done in previous chapters, take some time to go over the outline on the following two pages and think about how your children have been affected by your separation and divorce. At that point you can make some decisions about changes you need to make to enhance their long term stability and security.

"Ninety percent of the friction of daily life is caused by the wrong tone of voice."

~Anonymous

Fostering Children's Long-Term Adjustment to Divorce

1. Build Good Relationships with Your Children

❀ Spend time alone with your children

❀ Show children empathy and respect

❀ Reassure your children about your feelings

❀ Be interested in their activities

❀ Support their relationship with their other parent

❀ Build your own support system

2. Create an Atmosphere of Open Communication with Your Child

❀ Listen to your child

❀ Put yourself in your child's place

❀ Tune into divorce related questions

❀ Accept their feelings

❀ Use emotional regulation to help yourself and your child deal with difficult emotions

❀ Encourage them to talk

❀ Engage your child in an activity

❀ Stay available to your children

❀ Share a few of your thoughts and feelings

❀ Use reading materials to help your child

❀ Avoid lecturing or interrogating children

3. Create a Stable Home Environment

❀ Set up regular, organized routines regarding meals, chores, homework, curfew, friends, bedtime and enforcement of rules

❀ Establish rules and limits and enforce them

❀ Seek out other support people for your children

❀ Resolve custody and placement issues quickly

❀ Take children's developmental needs into account

❀ End parental conflict in their presence

❀ Support the children's relationship with their other parent

❀ Encourage children to assume age appropriate responsibilities

❀ Resolve the reconciliation question quickly

❀ Get counseling if necessary or desirable

4. Limit the Amount of Change in Your Children's Lives

❀ Give your child six months before making additional changes

❀ Make necessary changes gradually

❀ Allow six months between all major changes

❀ Continue familiar routines

❀ Give children time to prepare for changes

❀ Provide a positive focus

"Have patience with all things, but chiefly have patience with yourself."

–Saint Francis de Sales

CHAPTER 4

NURTURING FROM A FULL CUP
Caring for Yourself So You Can Care for Your Kids

Kasey looks up from the cartoon she is mindlessly staring at, as her mother staggers in the door after another ten hour day at work. She and her younger brother go running into the kitchen to greet her, clinging to her legs, expressing their need to have more time with her than they have of late. They see their exhausted mother slump down on the kitchen floor, with them still attached to her legs, sobbing uncontrollably. They don't understand her tears and feel frightened.

There is no question that divorce is an extremely stressful experience, whether this is something you are choosing to do, or whether the experience is foist upon you by your partner. In either case, you will be experiencing emotional stress in reaction to this change. Remember, stress is nothing more than our physical and emotional response to change. And divorce surely brings a large measure of change to all who experience it.

The other difficulty with divorce is that it endures. In my home state of Wisconsin, there is a mandatory 120 waiting period between the time the divorce papers are filed and when a divorce may be granted. Nonetheless, it is most often in excess of six months from the filing of papers until the final hearing in a divorce action. During that period of time, participants are typically in a state of chronic stress, never being quite sure what each day will bring; will it be a letter from their attorney, conflictual contact with the other parent, a child-related problem and on and on. It sometimes seems that *every* day brings a new problem or stress.

The effect of this stress can be overwhelming. When you are in a chronic state of stress, your body is aroused for a long period of time. This means that you have adrenaline and other stress hormones coursing through your body on a daily basis, elevating your heart rate, blood pressure, pulse and all of those other crucial systems that keep us attuned to our surroundings. What your body is doing is keeping you in constant preparation for battle.

Our physical responses to stress are much the same today as in the day of the cave man. When the stress hormones start to affect us, our hearing becomes sharper and our vision more acute. Our breathing becomes shallower, from the chest, rather than the deep, relaxing breathing that comes from the diaphragm. Blood is directed away from our hands and feet, and into the larger muscles of our arms and legs, preparing us to either fight our enemy or to run away. Our hands and feet can become cold or clammy in this situation.[1]

In the same way, blood is directed away from all other bodily functions deemed non-essential for survival, such as digestion. Therefore, if we have just eaten a full meal, it may feel like a rock in the pit of your stomach as the digestive process is halted. The immune system is also shut down. This is why we can be exposed to millions of germs every day and only succumb to that cold or flu when we are in a state or time of stress, or soon thereafter. Normally our immune system suppresses the illness; when this system is inhibited by stress hormones, we become ill.

While the effects of stress are designed to assist us in times of danger, they are unnecessary and unhealthy for most of the incidents which cause stress in our lives today. For instance, when the boss criticizes our work, we have no need to fight for our survival. Indeed, if we come off as if we are defensive and fighting for our lives, we may just end up losing our job, something few of us can afford. The same is true if the stress is caused by heavy traffic. What we now call "road rage" can be the result of the survival mechanism triggered by stress caused by traffic frustration.

As our bodies were designed, this stress mechanism was also not meant to be active on a constant or long term basis. It was designed for short spurts of use, such as when chasing prey or fleeing *as* prey. However, the process of getting through a divorce can lead to a chronic state of stress that lasts from before papers are filed until after the final hearing, often a period in excess of six months! In these instances, the chronic operation of the stress response can lead to long term health and emotional problems. For example, an individual whose immune system is suppressed for six months may catch every viral and bacterial infection he comes in contact with that entire period of time. That could make for a long and miserable six months, even aside from the divorce!

In addition, stress does not lead to a reaction in every system of your body at the same time. People are usually stress-reactive in only one or two systems each. That is where you will notice trouble during your times of stress. If you give it a little thought, you can probably point to other times of stress in your life and what illness or trouble you experienced to identify your own most reactive systems.

For instance, a woman with a family tendency toward adult onset diabetes may be, herself, diagnosed with this malady during or directly following a stressful time in her life. Or, a man with a reactive respiratory system may have his first asthma attack during a time of stress. Researchers are also now investigating the connections between depression, cancer, aging and stress.

There is another complicating factor here: the very reason you are reading this book in the first place. You have one or more little people depending on you to help them through this difficult time. How can you take care of them if you can't even take care of yourself? Simple. The answer is, you can't. It is difficult, if not completely impossible, to nurture others when your own cup is empty. It is important for anyone to take care of themselves during times of stress; it is especially important for parents to do so. Your children are depending on you.

To that end, one of the most important things you can do for your children is to take care of your own needs so that you can care for them. You must fill up your own cup so that it "runneth over," and then you can give to others, your children, from your overflow. If you cannot, you will probably end up feeling depleted, overwhelmed, bitter and resentful. And none of us is much of a parent at a time like that!

So, you're going through a divorce for the next six months and we have just learned that it's a major time of stress in your life. Accept that. What can you do about it? Many things!

Build and Use Your Support System

We have already discussed the how and why of developing your support system in Chapter Two. Know that it is important for you to spend time with other adults, away from the company of children or anyone who is likely to be making any demands on you. The purpose of this time should be purely social. So that work meeting you were going to use doesn't count!

As I stated previously, single parents are some of the most notoriously guilt-ridden people I work with! Accept that you need this time for yourself and talk back to that guilt. Remind yourself you are doing this for your children!

To accomplish this talking with your support system task you *must* have some time away from your children. This is not optional; it is essential. You can do this when your kids are with their other parent, but if they are with you most of the time, you may have to find someone to care for them for a few hours so that you can accomplish this task. You would have thought nothing of hiring a sitter on a Saturday night when you were married. You need the time to yourself even more now! As the Nike commercial says, "Just do it!"

You need to be able to talk about the divorce, your experiences, your feelings and whatever comes to mind with your support persons. Ideal support persons are warm, empathic, accepting, non-judgmental, positively focused and good listeners. This may seem like a tall order, but there are many of them out there. You may just have to dig a little to find them.

It may be that co-worker with the warm smile that you've thus far only said "hello" to. It may be that best friend from high school that you haven't called in fifteen years. It may be your child's friend's parent or, perhaps, that friend of yours whom you nursed through her own divorce just last year. Or, it may be a connection you make in a divorce adjustment group or a therapist you find it helpful to talk with. They are out there—you just have to find the right people. Compare the ones you find to that list of qualities at the beginning of the above paragraph.

Once you have found some supportive people in your life make a list of their phone numbers and keep it handy. You won't want to be digging for a phone book when you are upset or have news you are dying to share. Force yourself to open up to these people—for your own good and that of your children.

"My friends have made the story of my life. In a thousand ways they have turned my limitations into beautiful privileges, and enabled me to walk serene and happy in the shadow cast by my deprivation."

~Helen Keller

Get Information to Reduce Anxiety About the Divorce Process

Most persons experiencing divorce have not experienced it first-hand before. And, of those who have, most have not gone through it with this partner or, perhaps, with this attorney. These facts lead to a certain unpredictability that can be terrifying and debilitating if we allow it to get the best of us.

Fear and anxiety are normal reactions to situations in which we feel we don't know what is going to happen and that we have no control over what does happen in any case.

Participants in a divorce action do actually have a great deal of control if they know and understand the process. Knowledge also helps us to feel less afraid and puts us in a better position to start exercising some of our power over the process.

First of all, get some information about how the process works in your state *and* in your county. I say this because neighboring counties often have very different ways of handling an issue. Your friend in the next county may mean well, but may be giving you incorrect information in telling you how things happened in his divorce. Ask your attorney to explain the process to you—in layman's terms. Ask her to define any terms you don't understand. You are not stupid—you just don't spend as much time in the court system as she does. And that's a good thing!

If you still don't feel that you have a sense of how things operate or what comes next, look for a book on the subject to lay it out for you. Again, be sure it is specific to your jurisdiction. Your county courthouse may have some literature written for laypersons explaining the process of divorce in your county. I would start at the Clerk of Court's office or with the Family Court Commissioner. They can direct you if you need to be checking elsewhere.

If you still feel in the dark, ask a few other people. If you are seeing a therapist, ask her. You would be surprised how many people in the middle of a divorce have no idea what the process is or what comes next. A therapist should not give legal advice, but can give you some general information that you may not have. Often in sessions when I make reference to a typical event or part of the process, I get a blank look from a client. Investigating further, I ask, "Did your attorney tell you about that?" "No," is often the response, at which point I backtrack and give them what I hope is a clear explanation of the issue or process at hand, along with some questions to discuss with their attorney.

The relief on their faces is immediately evident. "Oh I had no idea that would happen," or "My attorney never explained that to me." Even in my Parenting Through Divorce classes, there are a number of procedural issues that I end up explaining to participants. Often attorneys are so familiar with the process they can forget all that you don't know. And, if you don't know what you don't know, how can you be expected to ask about it?

For this reason, I've introduced a number of topics about how divorce operates in Manitowoc County into my class. Most of the class is likely to be hearing it for the first time. A few of these issues will be discussed in Chapter 5 on Legal Custody and Physical Placement. Others are simply too specific to our locale to be of great importance to anyone not located in our County so will not be included in this book.

While my background as a former divorce attorney is extremely valuable at times like that, any therapist working regularly with persons experiencing divorce should have a thorough understanding of the divorce process. This is the kind of therapist you want to work with, even if you have no questions about the divorce process. In order to best help you cope and get through it, she must understand it herself.

I cannot stress this strongly enough. Ask, ask and, if you still don't understand, ask again! There is no such thing as a stupid question, especially when your children's well-being may be affected!

Secondly, remember your attorney is working for you and on your behalf. She can give you her best legal advice or recommendations regarding a particular issue and you are free to disregard it if you don't feel comfortable following it. In some instances, you may be asked to sign a paper indicating that you are making a decision against the attorney's advice, but that is just because the attorney feels her advice is the best way to handle the issue in most situations and does not want to be the subject of a lawsuit by you down the road if things don't turn out as you plan. But remember, you are the consumer and it is you who must live with the results of your decisions. If you have strong feelings about how you want to handle a particular issue, get all the information you need, but go with your gut reaction.

Third, taking action of some kind is a wonderful technique to reduce anxiety in any situation. Therefore, if you ask about the process and learn that you will need to place a value on all items of marital property, you have a task to accomplish. It can help you to feel like you have some control over what is happening in your life to pick up a notebook, walk around your house, list the items of property and set about researching reasonable values for them.

This may entail locating and hiring an appraiser (make sure there is not someone court appointed before you do this; you would also want to explore whether you and the other parent can agree on values before taking on the cost of hiring the appraiser yourself), checking values of like items selling on E-bay or elsewhere on the internet, obtaining the Blue Book value of a vehicle or getting a statement from the bank regarding the outstanding balance of a loan. Taking action of any kind, designed to further of affect the process, should reduce your anxiety about what is happening in your life and cal also be empowering to anyone feeling at the mercy of the court or legal system, or the other parent.

"To feel brave, act as if you were brave, use all your will to that end and courage will very likely replace fear."

~Anonymous

Take Care of Your Physical Body

When we are under stress, our body is stressed as well. However, it becomes even more stressed, and more likely to give out on us, if at the same time, we are not eating or sleeping and have no regular schedule on which it can rely.

I have worked with hundreds of persons experiencing divorce and I can tell you even from personal experience that many people completely lose their appetites and desire for food when enduring this process. Food becomes tasteless or, worse yet, leads to nausea, which most people decide feels worse than any hunger being experienced. Even people who have struggled with their weight all of their lives commonly find that they have mysteriously misplaced 10, 15 or 20 pounds while experiencing a divorce, without noticing how it happened.

The problem with this is not that losing excess weight is bad, but that, just like a car, your body needs adequate fuel to function. If you do not feed it, it starts feeding on itself. Not just on fat, but also on vital organs and tissues needed to keep you healthy. Then, this body that is already under stress becomes ill and unable to function. If only for the sake of being able to care for your children, you need to give your body the fuel it needs to maintain itself.

This unexplained weight loss and lack of any desire for food was something I experienced during my divorce. Believe me, that is the *only* time in my life that I have accidentally lost weight! My saving grace was my daughter. She was with me most of the time and, being only 18 months old, needed me to prepare regular meals and snacks for her. And, of course, she wouldn't eat unless I did!

While in those first few months I found I was never hungry enough for a full meal, I forced myself to nibble a few mouthfuls of whatever she was having as I knew if I was going to be able to care for her, I would need to care for myself. That was enough to sustain me and my appetite did gradually return, especially as I began to look forward to my new life. But at first, it was only the few bites I was able to consume with her that fed my stressed physical being.

Sleep is another issue with the newly separated parent. Many of us find sleep becomes quite elusive as we start down the road toward divorce. Either we put off going to bed, or when we get there, we lie awake worrying about all that we have to do. Or, we may wake regularly in the middle of the night and struggle to get back to sleep, or perhaps we wake for the day several hours too early. Perhaps we have some combination of all of these symptoms!

While sleep can be evasive, there are some things you can do to make it more likely to happen for you. Pay attention to your caffeine consumption and eliminate all caffeine after 5:00 p.m. or perhaps after noon, if the 5:00 p.m. limit doesn't do the trick. To that end, it helps to get yourself on a regular sleep schedule, going to bed at the same time each night. When it gets in the rhythm of a regular bedtime, you body will start to feel tired and more relaxed as your bedtime draws near.

You can also help to prepare yourself for bed by engaging in some night time rituals that help your body start to wind down. These might include a hot bath, listening to relaxing music, enjoying a cup of chamomile or valerian tea, reading a good (but relaxing) book, writing in a journal and the like. Avoid watching television from your bed. Make the bedroom just a room for sleep so that your body will start to relax just walking in the door to the room.

Alcohol is another substance that can interfere with getting a good night's sleep. As it is a depressant, alcohol may make us feel sleepy. However, it can actually prevent us from getting good, sound sleep and help us to wake up a few hours after we've gone to bed. Therefore, if you are having a problem with waking in the middle of the night, or it you wake in the morning feeling tired or not as rested as you usually do after a night's sleep, try eliminating the alcohol from your pre-bedtime rituals and see if that helps.

A final note about the bedroom. Most people find that if they are staying in the home they shared with the other parent they need to make some changes in the bedroom to make it different from the space that they may have shared a significant amount of intimacy and closeness, physical, sexual and emotional, with that person. Perhaps you would like to rearrange the furniture so that you awaken to a different view, or paint the walls a different color, or hang new pictures or window treatments. Some people switch rooms with one of their children to achieve even greater distance in terms of sleeping arrangements.

I remember that the day after Bill left, which happened to be a Saturday, I had a number of errands to run with my daughter. Interestingly enough, the most important thing on my own personal agenda was going to Shopko to buy a gallon of blue paint so that I could paint my bedroom walls! The way I felt, nothing short of being struck by lightening could have prevented me from making that trip!

The funny thing was, the room never got painted. My anxiety was appeased just by buying the paint. And, while I did intend to paint the room at the time, I got so busy putting my new life together that a month and a half later when I moved back to Manitowoc, the room was still the same off-white it had originally been. But the paint moved north with me. We ended up using it some years later to spruce up the master bedroom in Terry's home before we sold it. It served that purpose well and did end up in a bedroom—just not mine!

So, put yourself on a schedule, engage in activities that relax you and eliminate those that don't, especially later in the day. Plan to take the steps you feel necessary to make yourself comfortable living in your home. Whether or not you actually accomplish them may be immaterial.

Exercise is another wonderful technique to deal with stress. While it is obvious that exercise is good for the physical body, many people are unaware that it has as many benefits for emotional well-being. When we engage in physical exercise, our brain releases chemicals called endorphins, which help us to feel good. We may start out exercising feeling weighed down by the recent dilemmas life has thrown our way and end up feeling that life is good and any difficulties we are facing are resolvable.

Research is showing that the endorphins released while exercising are as effective as antidepressant medications in some depressed individuals at improving mood and functional behavior. Obviously, if you are taking medication, do not stop taking it without talking with your doctor. But whether or not there is medication in your life, exercise can have an incredibly positive effect on it.

One of the best things you can do for yourself, both physically and emotionally, may be to go for a run, ride a bike, cross country ski, go out walking, chop wood, etc. It matters little what you do for exercise; the important thing is that you move. Current research is also finding that, independent of its effects during divorce or on depression, exercise is something that holds back the clock and reduces effects of aging. Don't you owe it to yourself, and your family, to do everything you can to take care of yourself?

Exercise has long been a personal stress management technique of mine. I started running (slowly) in college, though I did speed up when I quit smoking in law school! Throughout my life, I've always had a habit of regular exercise—just because

I figured out that I simply felt better when I was working out in some way. I have solved many of the world's most troubling issues and problems, not to mention my own, while out running, biking or cross country skiing, and have become happier, healthier and more relaxed in the process. When Katie joined the track team at 15, I took great pleasure in having her company while running, and enjoyed being fit enough to help her improve her endurance. Long runs are also a great time to talk about life!

After a break of several years, I took up the running again while going through my divorce and a year later, ran my first marathon in four hours and 35 minutes! This was something I have never even dared to hope for as a personal goal; yet I actually accomplished this coming out of one of the worst years of my life! You can do it too! And get to be happier and more relaxed in the process.

"Life can be one satisfaction after another if we let it."

~John Schindler

Take Care of Your Inner Self ~the Spiritual Connection

A basic need all human beings share is the need to feel connected to something greater than ourselves. We need to feel that we have some purpose, a path; that we have a reason for being here. Many of us meet this spiritual need through practicing, to some degree, an organized religion. Perhaps you attend mass on Sunday morning or Synagogue on Saturday evening and feel a spiritual connection there. Or perhaps through volunteering at some type of helping agency you feel a connection with your spiritual calling.

Some people just don't feel connected to an organized religion. Perhaps you have tried to attend church regularly and left feeling cold and untouched. So you spend your Sunday mornings walking in the woods or along the lakeshore because it gives you peace. This is another important way to connect with our spiritual selves. You are actually meeting the same need as your neighbor who is rushing off to 8:30 mass. You are connecting with something greater than yourself through your contact with nature—in appreciating the beauty of the woods on a spring morning, or the majesty of the waves crashing down on the shore, or the miracle of millions of snowflakes falling to earth, all unique and different from each other.

That sense of awe is your spiritual connection. Do something regularly to inspire it. Put yourself in connection with nature on a regular basis. It doesn't have to be the same thing every time. Variety is the spice of life. It can keep you spiritually connected as well. Some Sunday mornings it may be church; others may call you to the woods.

My family and I are members of the Catholic Church. My husband and I volunteer to greet church members attending mass one Sunday morning per month and our two youngest children sing in the children's choir. All three children attend Catholic schools. Katie is now attending Roncalli, the Catholic high school in our area.

However, we try to get up to our cabin in the woods near Eagle River, Wisconsin, one to two weekends a month. While I know there is at least one Catholic Church in Eagle River, we have never attended there. We make a point of connecting with nature while we're up in the woods and this typically goes on throughout the weekend! So, our Friday, Saturday and Sunday benedictions may include taking a moonlit walk in the woods, cross country skiing on our own or other nearby trails, snowshoeing into the national forest next to our property, canoeing on the small lake across the road while a bald eagle soars overhead, teaching her babies to fly, running through the woods on a trail or just sitting on the screen porch to watch deer, bear and raccoons meander by. Each is more awe-inspiring than the last, and as much a part of my own, and my children's, spiritual enrichment as the Sundays we spend at mass.

Even if you have not done so throughout your marriage, give some thought to how you can connect with your spiritual self, to give it the spiritual nourishment it needs, especially during this very stressful time. You will probably find that you are making changes that last a lifetime!

Think Positively!

Often when we are feeling down, we become our own worst enemies. We see every situation in its most negative light, thereby perpetuating our negative experiences. We really do get more of what we pay attention to!

Did you ever have a day when everybody on the road seemed to be out to get you? Cars cut you off, pull out in front of you or nearly hit you? These days usually start out with one such experience, perhaps an inattentive driver cut in front of us, completely non-maliciously. We react to this event, and then tell ourselves we really need to be more cautious. So we become vigilant, paying attention to everyone who is likely to infringe on our space. Sure enough, we notice, many people are weaving into our lane, following too closely, cutting us off and seemingly out to cause us harm. We are seeing what we are looking for. What we are not noticing, however, because it is not what we are paying attention to, is the vast majority of vehicles following at a safe distance and obeying all appropriate traffic laws. This is the old "Is the glass half empty or half full?" question.

Your reality, like we described in Chapter Three, depends on your perception of it. If you are determined that your world is ending, it will. If you are aware that our greatest opportunities for growth and accomplishment come from our greatest challenges, then that will be your experience and your focus. I can tell you that how you feel about this divorce will depend on what you tell yourself about it. You will feel better if you tell yourself positive things.

You all know that my divorce was not my decision, nor was it my choice. However, it was one of the best things that have ever happened to me. The closing of that door has opened many windows of opportunity for me that I cherish and appreciate. The work that I do now would not have been possible in the same manner or time frame if Bill and I had stayed married.

Bill was not looking to have any more children. He was thrilled to be Katie's father, but one child was enough for him. I wanted more children and I was able to have my two youngest children because of my divorce. I have also built a thriving private practice, opened a business, designed and wrote the Parenting Through Divorce class and now this book, all because of this experience. I also now have a partner in my work as well as in my life and play. I would certainly say it has been a positive experience in my life.

That's not to say it has been easy. It started out as the most difficult and painful emotional experience I have ever endured. Erma Bombeck said, "When life gives you lemons, make lemonade." I would rephrase that to say, "When life gives you lemons, *it is your duty to yourself* to make lemonade!" Think about it.

> *"If you keep on saying things are going to be bad, you have a good chance of being a prophet."*
>
> ~Isaac Bashevis Singer

Boost Self-Esteem by Learning New Things

When we are in a marriage or long term relationship, it is easy to get and to feel stuck—doing the same old things with the same old people in the same old way. Many of those options may no longer be available to you as you proceed through a divorce.

Further, as any relationship breaks up, whether it is our choice or not, things are said and things are done that are harmful to us emotionally. Perhaps we exchange insults with our former partner and take a few hits. Perhaps we are struggling with guilt or rejection and are wounded that way. We all experience these moments of emotional damage as we travel throughout our lives. For this reason, virtually anyone in a relationship, or, as we discussed earlier, a family, that is breaking up can use some work on their self-esteem.

One of the best ways to improve your self esteem and to cope with the loss of some friends and activities is to find new ones. Now you have the time to learn new things. Take that class in watercolor painting you've always dreamed of. Learn to play the piano like you've always planned—you can always start with an inexpensive keyboard or rent a piano for a few months to see how you like it. Many are also available at reasonable costs. We found one at a rummage sale for $25.00!

Explore cooking a new type of cuisine, perhaps one your former partner didn't enjoy. You only have to please yourself! Learn a foreign language. You will feel better about yourself if you are moving forward, rather than looking back. Learning new things is one of the best ways to do this.

If funds are limited, there are often agreements you can make with the educational institution running the adult education classes to register other learners or perform some other administrative task in exchange for minimal or no tuition. It never hurts to ask. The worst they can do is say "No." But where there's a will, there's a way. If you want it badly enough, you'll figure out a way to do it. You are limited only by your imagination!

Venture Out!

Some people experiencing divorce have the impulse to hibernate; to hide at home, not talk to anyone, not go out or do anything. Most of us feel worse, more alone and isolated, when we give in to these impulses. Even if this is your desire, force yourself to get out, to do things, to be involved with other people. You will probably find that you feel better if you do. I know I did and most of my clients do.

You may be afraid that you no longer fit as well with some old friends, especially couple friends, as you did before the divorce. That may be true, but with the prevalence of divorce in our society today, many friendships are able to weather divorce fairly easily.

On the other hand, you may find that your interests and feelings of connection with some of your old friends have changed. This is a wonderful time to seek out new friendships. Strike up a conversation with that woman next to you in the Aerobics class that, up to now, you've only said "hello" to. Reach out to the person in your new art class who has the interesting style. Invite her to have a cup of coffee after class. Ask that co-worker over for dinner. He will most likely reciprocate and a new friendship is born.

Further, do not take any rejection of these attempts personally. Tell yourself it may just be the wrong time, a busy night or the wrong person. You are in a vulnerable state right now; don't take more rejection on than you need to. Keep trying. Most rejections have nothing to do with you, but with circumstances beyond others' control. Reminding yourself of this can give you the courage to reach out again.

Use Humor to Cope

We've all heard someone use the expression, "If I don't laugh, I'll cry," to describe a situation they are valiantly attempting to make the best of. As we go through a divorce, some of the situations we become involved in are so ridiculous that they would be humorous to anyone hearing about them. While it is typically difficult to laugh as we are emotionally involved in a trying situation, attempt to take a step back and view any situation with an outsider's perspective. This may put you in a better position to enjoy the humor in some of the situations in which you find yourself.

I think of the client who engaged in a bitter legal battle, involving many letters between attorneys, over "her spatula," or the client who endured many "mediation" sessions with his former spouse and attorneys over a visitation plan with the family cat, who reportedly couldn't have cared less! Both of these people were able to take that step back and laugh at themselves once the dust had settled. If you can achieve this ability while in the throes of battle, it can be a wonderful coping technique.

Humor is also useful when visualizing events the other party is dealing with. Bruce Fisher in his book *ReBuilding After Your Relationship Ends* shares an example of a woman, wounded by her husband's desertion, who sneaked over to his home in the middle of the night to write four letter words on his lawn with fertilizer, so that all summer long, whenever his grass grew, he could be reminded of her thoughts about him. I thought this was hilarious, but it is also criminal. So, remember, using humor to imagine an amusing event occurring for the other person is very different from acting on it. Don't make the mistake of confusing the two!

"Blessed is he who has learned to laugh at himself for he shall never cease to be entertained."

~John Boswell

Meet With a Therapist to Discuss These Issues

Many people get through their divorces just fine with support from friends and family and by caring for themselves. Others, many of whom I work with, find it helpful to speak with a therapist on their adjustment to divorce and single parenthood. Sometimes family and friends are very negative about divorce and, perhaps, toward the other parent. Baring your soul to a negative person can put you in the position of defending of that person, which is typically not very helpful to you.

Talking with a therapist can give you a neutral, and perhaps healthier, perspective and help you progress more quickly in dealing with some of the more typical issues that are necessary for most people to deal with during and after a divorce. Also, many therapists offer groups for divorcing persons that offer not only some structured activities to process the typical emotions experienced, but also function as a support system, connecting you with others experiencing divorce with whom you may have contact outside of or even after the (typically) time-limited group ends.

I offer such a group in my practice and have always had a favorable response. The groups benefit as much from their contact with each other as they do from any information I provide them. In fact, I currently have at least four groups still meeting sporadically in my community. Some choose to meet in a restaurant or the home of one of the participants. Others vary the location depending on the current preference of group members.

My divorce adjustment groups typically run six weeks and a different topic is presented each night the group meets. Topics include: Loneliness, Depression, Anger, Letting Go, Forgiveness, Self-Esteem and others depending on the needs of the group members. I typically assign homework, as this is helpful in either individual or group counseling to help persons take what is presented and start using it in their lives. Otherwise we could have a pleasant conversation and nothing about their lives ever needs to change.

Each week we start with a check-in, then homework, and moving on to our topic of the evening. I will usually present some information which may be followed by a discussion, then the assignment for the week. We finish each week by learning a new coping skill which can help participants deal with the stresses they are experiencing. Some of our coping skills have included: meditation, visualization, relaxing music, activities to boost self-esteem and the like. Groups such as this are typically available in most larger communities and may make it easier for you to get through the divorce process.

Be Creative in Your Response to Stress!

In this chapter, I have given you a number of ways to cope with any stressful experience in your life. These are general techniques that will work for most people. However, sometimes people come to me and share that they have discovered something, unique only to them, which helps them relax, calm down and deal with any stressor they may face. If you are aware of something that works for you, use it—even if it's not listed here. These are general ideas to supplement what you are already doing and will apply to most people.

To give you an example of how unique these techniques can be, I want to tell you about a woman I work with who gets stressed regularly for many reasons. She finds listening to *Metallica* CDs and watching *Rambo* movies on video to be the things that most relax her. For many of us, that would increase the intensity of our emotions and we respond more favorably to music designed to be relaxing and movies with a less intense, less violent theme. But for a variety of reasons particular to her make-up and her life experience, for Pamela, these work for her.

Many other people find listening to classical music on the radio to be relaxing. For me, however, it is too intense. I love some classical music, but on the radio the vast variation between pieces and the intensity of the music is too much for me, especially if I am driving. If I do listen to classical music in the car, I soon find I am exceeding the speed limit or am feeling quite edgy. I find I need to be able to choose the songs and this is more possible if I am listening to a classical CD or tape. Don't be afraid to use what works for you as well, even if it doesn't work for anyone else or it isn't listed here. Relaxation is a very personal thing.

Encourage Your Children to Use These Guidelines Themselves

We've already established that your children are stressed by this divorce. Many of the techniques that work to relax you will work with them also. Don't be afraid to suggest that they try some of them, or, if it doesn't interfere with your own stress management, invite them to do them with you. My children and I have had some wonderful walks in the woods together that have had a terrific effect on our relationship and I regularly have one of them biking along with me when I am running. Again, your opportunities to help your children are limited only by your imagination!

To finish up this chapter, take a look at the summary on the following page and take stock of all the good things you are doing to help yourself "fill your cup." Then give yourself a hearty pat on the back! You deserve it.

"Happiness is a butterfly, which when pursued, is just out of grasp. But if you sit down quietly, may alight upon you."

~Nathaniel Hawthorne

I am managing my stress by:

❀ Developing, enhancing and using my support system (and talking back to my guilt about this!)

❀ Getting information about the divorce process to reduce anxiety about the unknown

❀ Caring for my physical body by:

  · Eating healthy foods regularly

  · Getting adequate rest and going to bed at the same time each night

  · Exercising regularly to prevent/eliminate depression, etc.

❀ Caring for my inner self by incorporating spiritual nourishment in my life

❀ Keeping a positive outlook by reframing negative thoughts to achieve more positive feelings

❀ Increasing skills and boosting self-esteem by learning new things such as cooking, a foreign language, art and craft projects, etc.

❀ Venturing out and getting involved in new groups and activities of interest

❀ Using humor to cope with difficult times

❀ Meeting regularly or occasionally with a therapist to discuss these issues.

❀ Coping with stress in another creative way

❀ Encouraging my children to use these guidelines themselves.

"A ship in harbour is safe, but that is not what ships are built for."

~William Shedd

CHAPTER 5

DECIDING WHERE
THE KIDS WILL LIVE

*Unraveling the Mysteries of Legal Custody
and Physical Placement*

*"Jason, what is your home address?" asks his teacher on the
first day of school. "Well," begins ten year old Jason, "I have two
houses."*

*"No," corrects his teacher, "You have one home and the other
is a place that you go to visit your Mom or Dad."*

*"Uhhh, I don't know then," responds Jason, confused now
about which of his two homes is the "real" one and embarrassed that
his classmates have heard this conversation.*

Two of the most upsetting and emotionally wrenching
issues to be established in any divorce involving children are the
issues of legal custody and physical placement. I have witnessed
previously amiable, cooperative, positively focused couples who
had calmly negotiated the disbursement of all of their worldly
possessions, resort to ranting and raving over the issues of
custody and placement.

These tend to be decisions that bring strong emotions to
the surface so that, at times, it seems impossible to discuss them
rationally. It is possible to do so, however, with the ideas and
methods set forth in this book, especially with the awareness of

how the negotiations are affecting you and the potential for volatile conflict on this issue.

In all of my years as a mediator, I have never had a couple come to blows over these (or any) issues, but I must confess that I have had to call a time out on more than one occasion when the negotiations were disintegrating and emotions were rising.

In the Past

In years past, in Wisconsin as well as in a number of other jurisdictions nationwide, parents experiencing divorce would talk about legal and physical custody. While both were attempts to delineate a parent's rights, responsibility and time with a child, they differed slightly in application.

In most cases, legal custody conferred the right to make certain and fairly specific decisions about a child's life, such as whether or not they could get their driver's license at 16, whether they could receive non-emergency medical treatment, what religion they would practice and participate in, and the like. These are issues that typically do not come up often in the life of a child, but are important decisions nonetheless.

Physical custody most often referred to actual living arrangements. Typically, the parent with physical custody was the parent with whom the child lived. The other parent was said to have "visitation rights" to and with the child, and was usually relegated to some type of scheduled contact, often at the whim of the parent with physical custody.

Usually, the parent with physical custody would have the child most of the time. The other parent might visit on alternate weekends, with perhaps some after school or evening time thrown in one night per week. This was a typical visitation schedule back in the 1960's and 1970's.

Why Language Matters

These schedules and the language used to describe how parents would spend time with their children, led to a rather interesting development for the families involved, however. The parent with "visitation" in many cases began to feel unimportant and unnecessary in the lives of their children. Often this was the father, back in those days, and, as a society, we started to see more and more children whose fathers began to drift away. Limited to occasional contacts with their children and, not feeling true parental rights or responsibilities, these men began to feel more and more like mere visitors in the lives of their children. As a result, they became even less involved leaving the children truly without a father, creating a generation of children from divorced families without a male role model in their lives.

In the 1980's, the Wisconsin legislature noticed this phenomenon and decided to take on the task of attempting to achieve social change through legislation. They began discussing how they could encourage both divorced parents to continue to be involved in the lives of their children. In this quest, they began to look at the language we used to talk about these parenting roles. They sought to find words to talk about the time parents spend with their children that would more appropriately do justice to the actual roles these people played with respect to the children.

As a result of these changes, Wisconsin law now refers to all of the time parents spend with their children as "placement time." This language seems to do a greater justice to the true and actual role the parent with less contact actually plays in the life of the child. Even more importantly, however, it encourages the parent to actually play that role, which is so important for the child's successful adjustment to divorce and development in life.

The legislature observed the effect the language was having on children and families and took appropriate and successful steps to correct the problem. This is a positive example of your tax dollars at work!

Physical Placement~the Question of Time

The "physical placement" language quite simply refers to the time parents spend with their children. Parents are said to have primary physical placement, secondary physical placement or shared physical placement. *Primary placement* is somewhat akin to what physical custody used to mean. It is typically the parent with whom the child lives most of the time. The child most often spends more time with the parent with primary physical placement than with the other parent, although these days primary placement time typically involves somewhat less time than physical custody did in the past as both our country and society acknowledge the necessary role of both parents in children's lives.

Secondary placement is somewhat akin to the former visitation status, although it, like the flip side primary placement, typically involves more time and contact than visitation formerly did. Most couples these days are working toward more of a *shared parenting* arrangement, as long as children are old enough to tolerate longer periods of time away from the primary caregiver. Courts in Wisconsin, as in many other states, have a preference for more of a shared parenting arrangement, due to the assumption as established by researchers and experts in the field, that it is important for a child to have enough time with both parents to achieve a significant and meaningful relationship with that person.

There is also a less common variation or alternative in the placement field, *split placement*. In a split placement situation, some of the children live with each parent and have periods of physical placement with the other parent. In the days of the physical custody language, this was referred to as split custody. A common split was that all the girls would live with mom and all the boys would live with dad. Unfortunately, this adds yet another loss to those the children are already experiencing due to the divorce and associated changes, as we discussed in Chapter Three. They tend to miss the siblings they are accustomed to living with, even if they spent a significant amount of time in conflict.

I did have a man in my Parenting Through Divorce class share with the group that he and his wife had two children, a son and a daughter, who had been in conflict with each other ever since the second child was born. When divorcing, they decided to split placement. In their case, the daughter lived with dad and the son with mom and on alternate weekends, they would switch children for two days, so the kids would not have to spend time together. He insisted that all family members loved the arrangement and that it was working extremely well for his family. Perhaps this was true, but as a family therapist, I am inclined to wonder what was happening in this family that these two children were feeling the need to be in conflict so much of the time? Were they merely acting out the, perhaps unspoken, conflict between their parents, so that things calmed down considerably when the couple separated? If they had come to me for counseling, I would have advised them to put more effort into improving the relationship between the siblings, rather than simply writing it off.

In exploring your options for placement arrangements, it can be quite helpful to actually read over the statutes governing these issues in your state. If you are unable to access a copy on your own or on the internet, a trip to your local courthouse can be helpful. Courthouse personnel can often assist you in locating the statutes governing the issues you are interested in researching.

Legal Custody

While the "legal custody" language has not changed in the state of Wisconsin in the recent past, there has been a progression of sorts in the assumptions courts will make in awarding the same. Sec. 767.24(2), Wis. Stats. In the days of physical custody, one parent or the other was also often awarded legal custody.

About the same time the discomfort was developing with regard to the physical custody language, we started seeing more and more couples emerging from their initial and final hearings sharing joint legal custody of their children. As if in reaction to the language issue, the legislature responded regarding legal custody as well. It appears to have determined, on some level, that joint legal custody was more likely than sole legal custody to keep both parents involved with the children, and that in most cases children would only benefit from this result. The resulting action was that the laws in regard to criteria for making a determination on legal custody were changed to create specific conditions under which courts could, and should, order joint legal custody. The focus was on providing for more significant and meaningful relationships between the children and these parents.

Interestingly enough, with that new language, as recently as a few years ago, a Wisconsin court literally had to "stick its neck out" to order joint legal custody in a contested case. At that time, there was a general preference in favor of joint legal custody as discussed above. Legal custody could be ordered by a court if either, a) both parents agreed and requested this, or b) only one party requested joint legal custody, the other demanding sole custody, but the court determined that, even though they were not able to agree on the type of legal custody they would have, these two parents were likely to be able to reach an agreement on these significant issues that would, reasonably rarely, arise with regard to their children.

You can see that the court had to take a risk to make such a determination, but we saw quite a number of these court orders as both the legal system and society realized that children needed both parents to stay involved in their lives. Again, any temporary discomfort to the court or to the parents was certainly seen to be worth it for the end result of a healthy, well-adjusted child.

Recently we saw further movement in the direction from the legislature. In recent years, the Wisconsin legislature changed the statute again to create a rebuttable presumption that joint custody is the preferred form of custody to be ordered, unless it can be established that this would somehow be detrimental to the child or dangerous for one or both parents. Sec. 767.24(2)(am), Wis. Stats. In fact, the vast majority of the couples I come in contact with do share joint legal custody of their children.

Which Form of Custody and Placement are the Best?

While there is no one form of legal custody or physical placement that can be recommended as "the best" for all families and children, there are some general guidelines and presumptions that are applied by states, courts and attorneys in many cases that can help parents decide these issues. Knowing how you are likely to come out in a court contest on these issues can make a big difference in what you may be willing to agree to.

Again, it can be worth a trip down to your courthouse, a telephone call to your attorney or a bit of research on the internet to become familiar with the statutes in your state. Once you know what you are dealing with, you are in a better bargaining position.

Recognizing that this is a gross generalization and that there are exceptions to every rule, I would add my own presumption that in most cases, children fare best when parents do share legal custody of their children. However, what the research is finding is most important in a child's adjustment to parents, divorce is not the particular form of custody or place-ment they are exposed to, but the fact that all children have a significant and meaningful relationship with both of their parents. Time is a factor in establishing this type of a relation-ship. Parent and child must spend enough time together for such a relationship to develop.

In terms of physical placement, there is also an official or unofficial presumption in many states that, in most cases, if the children are old enough, shared physical placement is best for them. In Wisconsin, the standard is for a child to have "regu-larly occurring, meaningful periods of physical placement with each parent" which "maximizes the amount of time the child may spend with each parent." Sec. 767.24(4) and (5), Wis. Stats. This is dictated by statute in a number of other states as well.

To that end, even though my court order, in its discus-sion of physical placement, orders physical custody to me and "reasonable visitation upon reasonable notice" to Bill, we have always interpreted that the same way—according to what was best for Katie. You can see this was written back in the days of the physical custody/visitation language.

Bill and I have lived in different cities ever since we sepa-rated. At first I was in Manitowoc and he was in Madison so we were three hours apart. Now, I am still in Manitowoc, but he is in Green Bay, about 45 minutes away. Accordingly, we found that weekends would constitute the primary time Katie would spend with her dad. But we have always interpreted this language very loosely.

Since she became old enough to be away from me for that length of time, as I was her primary caregiver, Bill has spent every other weekend with Katie religiously, regardless of distance or business or how many other plans he had. We will talk more about how a child's age affects this scheduling in Chapter Six.

However, our loose interpretation of this statement has led to other arrangements as well. Because we both had as a goal maximizing the amount of time Katie and her dad spent together, as that is what is best for Katie, we have looked for as many other opportunities to get the two of them together as possible. For example, Bill will sometimes have business meetings in Manitowoc and will call to ask if he can pick up Katie after school and take her for ice cream. "Absolutely!" is the response he always hears.

Further, if we are shopping in Green Bay or just passing through, we will most often stop at Bill's store (he manages an automotive parts store) so that Katie can pop in and say "Hi!" because four days a month is too little time to spend with your child. And because that's what's best for Katie.

During the summer, Katie spends several planned weeks with Bill. Further, when we take our annual ten day camping trip to the mountains of New Mexico, Katie, who refuses to camp, spends her ten days in the air-conditioned comfort of her father's home. Everybody wins.

Initially, when we first started talking about shared placement in Wisconsin, we would see the *week on/week off* type of schedule. In this arrangement, children would spend seven days with mom, then seven days with dad. Parties most commonly switched placement on either Fridays, before the weekend, or on Sunday evenings, after the weekend was essentially over.

There were two difficulties that many parents had with this type of arrangement, however. For many parents, seven days was too long a period of time to be away from their children in a shared parenting arrangement. Second, it was difficult to have any degree of predictability with regard to children's activities.

For instance, if there was a religion class you wanted your child to attend every Monday evening, and you had placement every other Monday, you had to rely heavily on the other parent to be as vigilant as you were about getting your child to the religion class (or swimming class or scout meetings, etc.) as you were. This often was used to punish or retaliate against a parent you were unhappy with if negotiations during the divorce were not going your way.

A common example of this that I have heard from conflicted couples runs along these lines: "If you ask for maintenance, our son isn't going to get to swimming class when he's with me." It can put you at the mercy of a former partner, now co-parent, with an axe to grind. It also puts you in the position of trying to impose some control over the other parent's life, which can be a questionable move in even the most amicable divorces.

Several years later, some very clever attorneys came up with an alternative shared placement schedule that alleviated both of these problems. In this new schedule, the *three day/four day split*, Wednesday was alternated by parents each week. For example, during week one, the kids would be with Mom Sunday through Wednesday. They would then go to Dad's Thursday through Sunday. For week two, they would be with Mom Sunday through Tuesday and head over to Dad's on Wednesday, staying through Sunday.

The advantages of this schedule were that each parent had either three or four days with the kids each week, so they were never away from them for more than four days. In addition, they could plan activities for certain nights of the week when they were guaranteed placement. In the example, Mom could plan an activity for every Monday or Tuesday evening and Dad for every Thursday or Friday night, as they always had the children on those nights.

The chief drawback to this schedule is a big one, however. Without special arrangements, it messes up every weekend. You can never take the children for a whole weekend, or get away for a whole weekend, without making special arrangements with the other parent. That can be quite difficult, especially while the divorce is going on.

Again, some clever attorneys came to the rescue. A few years ago I began to see what seems like the perfect schedule for many families. This schedule involves a *two/two split* and alternating weekends. For example, in week one, children spend Monday and Tuesday with Mom, Wednesday and Thursday with Dad, then return to Mom's for Friday, Saturday and Sunday. They stay with her for her usual Monday and Tuesday, then go to Dad's for Wednesday through Sunday. Every week involves a five day/two day split, so parents are never away from kids more than five days and each parent sees the children at least two days every week. In addition they are guaranteed the same two weekdays, so planning classes and activities is easier. Entire weekends are alternated so it is also easier to plan activities for Friday through Sunday.

But, again, there is no one schedule that works for all families all the time. The two/two schedule works well for parents who work the same shift and have school age children, but there are probably better alternatives for parents who work alternate shifts. In those cases, it may be easier to split times of the day than days of the week. In other words, have the kids by the second shift parent during the first part of each day and with the first shift parent after school and in the evening.

The entire matter of scheduling will be discussed in greater detail in Chapter Six, but the best rule of thumb is to pay attention to what works best for your family, not what seems to work for everyone else! And remember, the most important factor is for your children to have enough time with each of you to develop that significant and meaningful relationship.

How Questions of Custody and Placement are Resolved

When couples are unable to reach an agreement regarding the issue of legal custody or physical placement, they have at least two options in the state of Wisconsin: a mediated agreement or a court decision. Further, Wisconsin law provides that before a couple can get into court for a hearing on those issues, they are required to sit down with an approved divorce mediator for at least one hour to determine if they can reach an agreement without court intervention. After that session, if they are unable to agree, either they, or their attorneys if they are represented, can schedule a hearing at which the court may decide the issue.

There are situations and circumstances that are inappropriate for mediation. Some of more typically excluded situations include relationships in which domestic abuse has been an issue, creating an imbalance of power in the relationship, and cases in which one or both parties has a significant alcohol or drug problem which may affect their ability to reason and to reach an agreement. Other exclusions involve allegations of child abuse and neglect and situations in which the safety of one of the parties may be negatively affected by a mediation session. Sec. 767.11(8)(b), Wis. Stats.

In Manitowoc County, qualified mediators are assigned by the Family Court Commissioner, after application by a party or an attorney. It is then up to the mediator to investigate the abuse issues with the couple, though these questions are asked on the application form. It is the responsibility of the mediator to ascertain that each party has approximately equal bargaining power.

The Advantages of a Mediated Agreement

I am a firm believer in the mediation process. I could not do this work if I did not believe strongly in it—it is simply too difficult. The idea of locking myself in an office with a couple who has been unable to work out their relationship conflicts, to help them work out conflict regarding another extremely emotional issue, is not very appealing. I am most certainly not a glutton for that much punishment!

But for most couples, reaching a mediated agreement regarding the custody and placement of their children is one of the most positive and empowering events happening to them in the course of their divorce. It is also wonderful for their children to see them working together to meet children's needs. In most cases it is good for the entire family!

The majority of my couples are able to reach a mediated agreement, which saves the court system tax dollars in unnecessary court time and, often, the police force from using tax dollars in enforcement time. Couples are much less likely to violate a parenting plan they are in agreement with, or at some point, have agreed to.

I also like to use my mediation time with couples to educate them about the co-parenting process and to back them away from power struggles they may have engaged in for years. I give them information about how they can help their children through their divorce. This can also help set the tone for an improvement in their relationships with their children and each other. Again, everybody benefits!

When I do get a difficult parent or couple in a mediation session, I like to point out that reaching an agreement in my office is their last best chance to have control of deciding how they will each spend time with their children. I also like to point what my mediation training very cleverly called the BATMA— their Best Alternative To a Mediated Agreement.[1] They might like to believe that a court would order placement with the other parent for only one day a month, but I can typically predict a range of alternatives that a court, following Wisconsin law, is most likely to award the other parent. I then refer them back to consult with their attorneys regarding these matters as well. This is another factor that leads to many mediation agreements.

I am also careful to explain that, unlike a judge, I do not decide a mediation agreement. My only role is that of a facilitator, to assure that both parties get to share their thoughts, feelings, preferences and feel that these are heard by the other parent. I focus strongly on some basic communication skills, such as having only one person talking at a time, as I can only hear one person at a time, and requiring partners to listen when it is the other person's turn to talk. My role is often similar to that of a police agent or enforcer.

Often I am talking to two people who have not agreed on anything for many years, but both care very dearly for the little subjects of our conversation. Procedural difficulties should not stand in the way of them making decisions for their little charges. Because of my experience working with other couples, and my lack of emotional involvement in the situation, I can often clearly see a solution that may have evaded them for months, or simple techniques that may help them to reach a decision on a difficult matter, such as visiting several potential schools together with their child to help make the decision of where she should attend.

The bottom line in most cases it that it is typically best for all involved if parents can reach a mediated solution. They are the best persons to be making these decisions as they are most invested in the outcome. Their children see them working cooperatively for what is in their best interests. The court system is not bogged down by holding unnecessary hearings. The only person who does not benefit is the attorney, who is not earning the fees for these extra hearings. But most of the best family law attorneys that I work with regularly are so busy that they will not miss the extra work, but be relieved by the lack of it!

While Wisconsin requires residents of all counties in the state to spend an hour with a mediator before getting into court on the issue of custody or placement, how the different counties administer this requirement varies greatly. In my home county of Manitowoc, one of our greatest benefits is that the county pays for the first three hours of a mediator's services. After that time, if the parties choose to continue meeting with the mediator, the services are billed to the parties at an hourly rate. Therefore, I strongly encourage every resident who has need of it to take advantage of this benefit. If you reach an agreement, some of that time must be spent typing up the agreement or reducing it to writing, but, in most cases a mediating couple can have two to two and a half hours of face to face time with a mediator at no charge to themselves.

In our neighboring Calumet County, a court can and must order couples into mediation, but they are required to pay the entire fee out of their own pockets. Do some investigation and find out if your county offers payment for mediation services. If so, be certain to take advantage of it. Divorce is an expensive process. Make use of every benefit to which you are entitled. Even if your county is one in which you are responsible for paying for mediation services, it is much cheaper and, often more effective, than working these things out through attorneys, who have good advocacy skills but can be somewhat lacking in the finer points of personal relationship and mediation skills.

The Advantages of a Court Decision

In some cases, especially when I feel a couple will be unable to reach an agreement, but even sometimes when I feel they may be able to if I push them hard enough, I will encourage them to pursue a court decision on the question of custody or placement.

I will usually take this position when I sense an imbalance of power, even in the absence of allegations of spousal abuse. There are many times when one partner or the other is quite controlling of the other's actions or access to the children, even though there may never have been physical violence between them. These partners can be quite effective at pushing the other parent to agree to something they are clearly not happy or comfortable with, and which may not be in the best interests of the children, such as very limited or very expanded placement times. In these cases, when the pushed parents starts to hesitantly agree, I may suggest that if this seems to be something they would have a hard time living with if they went along with it, they may feel better if a court would order this. Then they would also be able to tell their children that "It wasn't that I agreed to only see you at those times, but the judge ordered it." It gets them out of the role of "bad guy" with their children, which is ultimately better for both the parent and child, even if it isn't better for my record as a mediator.

There are also cases when I believe an agreement is fair, but one parent clearly isn't on board with it and will give the other parent (as well as attorneys and police agencies) no end of grief in trying to enforce it. I can often see these cases coming and will often, in those circumstances, stop encouraging agreement and encourage them to see what the court decides. These tend to be situations in which, in spite of the fact that parents are agreeing on the placement plan now, one of them will likely violate the agreement every chance they get. At those times, having them violate an order of the court, rather than a mediated agreement, will typically result in faster and stricter enforcement for the other parent. After 13 years of professional mediation, I can usually, not always but in most cases, predict which couples will fall into these circumstances. These are couples that will be much better off with a court decision than with a mediated agreement.

When a court goes to make a decision about physical placement, there are a number of factors it considers which are typically laid out by statute. In the state of Wisconsin, as outlined by Sec. 767.24(5), Wisc. Stats., some of these factors are as follows:

* the wishes of the parents,

* the wishes of the child,

* the relationship between the child and parents, siblings or other significant persons,

* the amount of quality time the parents have each spent with the child,

* the child's adjustment to home, school, religion and community,

* the child's age and developmental and educational needs,

* the mental and physical health of the parties, children and others in the household,

* the need for regularly occurring and meaningful placement to provide predictability and stability for the child,

* the availability of child care services,

* the communication and cooperation between the parties (including a refusal to cooperate),

❀ whether parties can support the child's
relationship with the other parent,

❀ whether there is evidence of spousal battery
or abuse,

❀ whether either party has a significant problem with
alcohol or drugs,

❀ reports of appropriate professionals regarding the
parties, and

❀ any other information the court considers
relevant to the best interests of the child.

You can see that this is quite a broad list. The bottom line seems to be that the court may consider any information it deems helpful in making a physical placement determination and arriving at the best interests of the child. Parents facing such a decision would be well advised to check out the statutes in their state that outline these factors as well.

The Parenting Plan~Do It or Suffer the Consequences!

Another change the Wisconsin legislature made several years ago was to require each parent to file a form entitled a "Parenting Plan" with the court prior to the pre-trial conference in the divorce action. Sec. 767.24(1) Wis. Stats. The consequence for not having a plan on file was to give up your right to object to the other parent's version of the Parenting Plan. So you can see, especially in a case where custody or placement was contested, it would be crucial not to miss this deadline. It is an issue important enough to most parents that even if there were not a contest, they would want to have input into these important issues regarding their children.

To that end, in each of my Parenting Through Divorce classes, I give participants a copy of this form and warn them about the deadline. This way, they can have some time to think about the questions asked, how they would like to respond and touch base with their attorney so that this deadline is not missed.

What we have discovered together, the parents and I, is that most of the attorneys in our county are not handing a blank copy of this Parenting Plan to the parents I come in contact with, but are presumably completing one on their client's behalf and submitting it to the court.

This is another argument in favor of my giving them a copy of the plan in class. There are questions on this form that many parents would have strong and, perhaps, unique feelings about and would, in many cases, want to provide some input to their attorneys on these issues. I am certain that if s/he did not know how to respond to a question, most attorneys would call the client in and discuss it with them. However, I also know that there are times when attorneys use standard responses or answers and have personally talked to more than one client who was disgruntled with the standard response, even when the average person might not be.

To that end, I have also included a copy of Manitowoc County's version of the Parenting Plan form in Appendix D at the end of this book. Keep in mind that this is one county's version of what they are looking for and your state and county might expect something quite different if there is a requirement to this effect.

This form has a rather interesting history that I want to briefly share with you as well. I have it on good authority, which shall remain nameless, that interested parties in Manitowoc County had devised this form shortly after the Legislature passed this requirement for the state. A few months later, the State Bar developed a standard state-wide form to meet this requirement which Manitowoc County then adopted. Apparently, the powers that be in Manitowoc County were somewhat disgruntled as they preferred their own form to the Bar Association's version, so they made the decision to use their original form rather than the uniform state form. Manitowoc is probably the only county in the state not using the standard form, but I tend to agree with them; it is a much better form. For that reason, I share it with you. But be warned: your state or county may require something quite different.

The other reason I have included this form in the Appendix is that you can use it for "unofficial" purposes as well. If you and your children's other parent want to sit down and try to work out custody and placement arrangements on your own, and believe me, there are many advantages to doing so, ranging from achieving from an agreement that fits your lifestyle to reducing your attorney fees, the form can act as a trigger to identify some of the key issues you will want to discuss. Some of these things may not occur to either of you independently if you have never experienced divorce before. Then, when you do reach an agreement, you can record it on the form, if you like, both sign and date it and make sure each of you has a copy. This can eliminate misunderstandings later on.

Variations on a Theme~How Other States Determine These Issues

While Wisconsin's laws and preferences are the only ones with which I am familiar, I do not believe they are especially unique. A little progressive, perhaps, at times representing the direction other states are moving toward, but not alone in their attempts to encourage both parents to stay involved with their children.

I would even imagine that, if you had access to old and recent statutes from your state, you would see a progression, similar to that which I explained that Wisconsin experienced. The values we are trying to encourage here are pretty universal across the country and the world. Courts and legislatures have much more information in recent years about how important contact and relationships with both parents are to children's development and well-being. Therefore, much of this information should be reasonably accurate with respect to how any court might be predisposed to decide an issue, or the factors which they will be considering. To be sure, however, please consult with your attorney to get a clear picture of how courts in your state and your county are likely to decide your custody and placement issues.

Another development of which I have become aware is the tendency of courts and counties to establish policies requiring divorcing parents to attend classes, similar to my Parenting Through Divorce Program, and upon which this book is based. While I probably would not have been thrilled to be court ordered to attend this type of class when I was going through my divorce, the information presented is valuable and helpful at a time in our lives when we are not always thinking clearly or able to focus, unless reminded, on the best interests of our children.

Ask your attorney early in the process whether your county requires attendance at such a program so you have time to schedule it at your convenience. In our county, parties may not schedule a final hearing until both parties have attended the class. I, personally, have entertained many frantic telephone calls from parties whose attorneys "forgot" to tell them this or were not aware of the requirement at the time the papers were filed.

Also look into the "Parenting Plan" requirement. You do not want to be surprised at the pre-trial conference or the final hearing by discovering that the court is going to order exactly what the other parent wanted because you failed to file your version of this required form. Discuss this with your attorney early on so that you can give her some direction with regard to how you would respond to some of the questions and to insure that preparation of this form is in process.

You can see that there are a number of issues for parents to consider in the areas of legal custody and physical placement. Your attorney is there to advocate for you. Use her expertise to help make your decisions in this area.

At the end of this chapter, I have again included a worksheet to help identify and record the information you receive and your preferences with regard to these issues. If you are using a library copy of this book, please make a copy of this worksheet rather than writing in the book. This way you will also be able to keep your responses and refer to them later on.

Use this worksheet to help yourself to wade through the legal morass and achieve some clarity about your rights and preferences. Use it also to record your reactions to the information you are receiving and your reasoning for the choices you are making. This will help you discuss these emotional issues with the other parent, your attorney and, if necessary, the court, more effectively. Add any additional questions that arise as you are driving away from your attorney's office (don't they always?).

And remember, if at first you don't understand the information your attorney is giving you, ask and ask again! There is no such thing as a dumb question—only someone who hasn't experienced divorce before!

"I long to accomplish a great and noble task, but it is my chief duty to accomplish small tasks as if they were great and noble."

~Helen Keller

Checklist on Legal Custody and Physical Placement Issues

❀   *I have discussed the issues of Legal Custody and Physical Placement with my attorney.*

My reactions were:

_____

_____

_____

New Information I received about these issues:

_____

_____

_____

New or remaining questions I have about these issues:

_____

_____

_____

❀   *I would like Legal Custody of our children to be:*

_____ Joint _____Sole with Mother _____ Sole with Father

because:_____

_____

_____

The other parent:

_____ Agrees _____ Disagrees _____ Unsure

❀   *I would like Physical Placement to be as follows:*

Primary Placement with _____ with Periods of Physical Placement with _____ as follows:

_____

Shared as follows: _____

_____

_____

Some other arrangement: _____

_____

_____

_____

I believe this is the best arrangement because:

_____

_____

_____

The other parent:

____ Agrees ____ Disagrees ____ Unsure

❀ *Mediation will take place* with _____

_____

_____

❀ *A Parenting Plan was filed with the court on* _____

by _____

❀ *I attended the Parenting Through Divorce class*
on:_____ with_____

❀ *My Certificate was filed with the court on* _____

"There is no security in life. There is only opportunity."

~Douglas MacArthur

CHAPTER 6

A MATTER OF TIME

How to Structure Co-Parenting Schedules to Meet
Your Children's Needs

T*he first night at Mom's new apartment, six month old*
Melanie threw up her dinner, experienced diarrhea and then
cried for over an hour before falling into an exhausted sleep.
Later, she woke in the middle of the night screaming. Her parents
were baffled. When they separated and happily agreed to a shared
placement arrangement, they thought that working things out
amicably, with each spending 50 percent of the time with Melanie
would "make it easy for her." What went wrong?

If we accept, as we discussed in Chapter One, that parental
divorce is a trauma for children and that different age groups
typically exhibit diverse symptoms identifying their difficulty
in adjusting to it, we can also accept or assume that there are a
variety of recommendations for schedules that best take these
developmental needs into account.

Children of all ages need stable and frequent contact
with both of their parents. However, just as children of different
ages respond or react in dissimilar ways to parental divorce,
they also have diverse needs regarding a placement schedule,

also related to their developmental level. For this reason, a parenting schedule that is appropriate for a six year old is not appropriate for a six month old, nor is it appropriate for a sixteen year old.

Further, because of this fact, the schedule that you develop now will need to change several times over the course of your child's life. This may seem like no earth-shattering revelation to you, but it may be to your attorney. When I was a young divorce attorney at 25, I had never been a parent. I had my first child at 28. I assumed that once we got the placement, or physical custody schedule as it was called at the time, ironed out in the divorce proceedings, it would remain as it was, as if carved in stone, until the child turned 18. It sounds ridiculous now, but back then, I never gave it much thought.

Now that I am a mother of three children, I realize how ridiculous this assumption is. But don't assume your attorney understands this. In addition to being a naive attorney, myself, I have worked with a number of Guardians ad Litem who have recommended simply appalling placement schedules for children of all ages. Don't assume that yours is the best judge of what's best for your child. Guardians ad Litem can be young, naive and inexperienced when it comes to children. They can learn from you. Take the time to educate them.

No one knows your child like you do. Therefore, the court will agree you are in the best position to determine a schedule for your family, especially if you and the other parent can agree. But even if you cannot, you have a special expertise with regard to your child. Educate your attorney about this and have her advocate for what you have determined is the schedule that will be easiest on your child.

If your focus is the best interests of your child or children, you cannot go wrong. However, as you will soon become aware, what is best for your child may sometimes be difficult or uncomfortable for you. Depending on the age and developmental level of your child, this may involve seeing your child less than you would like or having the nonresident parent spend time with your child in your home.

Remember, also, that these are guidelines, not hard and

fast rules. If you have children in a variety of age groups, it will be impossible to follow all the guidelines for every age group and end up with one schedule. Do the best you can at meeting the greatest, or most important, needs of the greatest number of your children, without driving yourself crazy in the process. At the end of this chapter, we will discuss other variables that may moderate the recommendations for a particular schedule.

Schedules for the Littlest Ones-Infants (0-12 months)

The reaction of Melanie, in the example at the beginning of this chapter, is typical of this age group. She is upset and traumatized by the disruption in her routine. What parents are likely to see in the event of an inappropriate schedule are any of the stress-reaction behaviors we discussed in Chapter One. This is about the only way Melanie can show she is upset by the separation or by the schedule. Her reactions are about the same with any stress in her life because she has such a limited repertoire of behaviors from which to choose. A more appropriate schedule for Melanie would be to live with whichever parent was her primary care giver before the separation, while spending several hours with her other parent three to four times a week.

Infants' schedules are the most difficult to arrange. This is because infants need an extremely stable environment, including stable caregiver(s) and a regular schedule. In addition, overnight visits with the nonresident parents are typically not recommended because, due to their developmental level, infants have no way of knowing that their primary caregiver will return when they are separated from her.

Ideally, infants will have frequent contact with both parents, but only sleep at home with their primary caregiver present. Due to the task of establishing a secure bond with one primary caregiver, infants must be afforded one primary home, with frequent short contacts with the nonresident parent. Overnight visits are not recommended. In addition, they need stable caregivers and a regular schedule.

Experts agree that infants should have one primary home and not be separated from a primary caregiver for long periods of time, or overnight.[1] Babies see themselves as an extension of their primary caregiver and the caregiver as an extension of themselves. Therefore, just as a baby in a high chair does not realize that a rattle still exists after it falls off the edge of the chair and they can no longer see it, they also do not realize that their primary caregiver will return when he leaves for an extended period of time, or when the child is left in another location. An extended absence from either the home or the primary source of comfort is traumatic for an infant.

Researchers have also noted that infants, sleeping in their own homes in their own beds, but with the primary caregiver gone and the other parent at home, experienced some symptoms of distress: they smiled less often, became fussy and aggressive, had a harder time falling asleep, woke more frequently during the night and were more likely to wake up crying than infants with their primary caregivers at home. Therefore, if you cannot see your baby frequently, don't try to make up for lost time with very long visits. The baby is likely to find it distressing to be away from a familiar setting and primary caregiver.

We have dealt with this issue in the context of our own family. The summer between college and law school, Terry's son, Cavan, lived in Milwaukee with his mother and stepfather, working to earn money for school. He met a woman and became involved in a summer relationship. As fall approached, both agreed the relationship had run its course and parted friends. Cavan moved on to law school in Illinois and "Lisa" moved to Indianapolis, Indiana to be near family. Approximately one month into the school year, Cavan received a telephone call from her telling him she was pregnant.

Aside from the innate difficulties of becoming a single parent and becoming a parent while participating in a demanding educational program, such as law school, Cavan's situation was made even more complex because of the distance involved. His youth and inexperience as a parent didn't help, either! He had a hard time understanding why he just couldn't swoop down and pick up Taylor every other weekend. The first step for his father and I was educating Cavan about child development and how such behavior would likely affect his daughter.

Once he understood that such an arrangement would be traumatic for her, Cavan was able to regroup and attempt to fashion a schedule that would maximize his time and relationship with Taylor, yet not compromise her development in any way. What he did was travel to Indianapolis one weekend per month for about the first 18 months of her life. He would check into a motel, and then visit her, typically at mom's home on Friday afternoon or evening. He would come back Saturday and, perhaps, take her to the zoo or a park, then come back to see her Sunday before he left to return to Illinois.

This continued for about the first year and a half of Taylor's life. Gradually, he established that significant and meaningful relationship with her, in spite of the obstacle in their path. Everybody in the family breathed a collective sigh of relief as Taylor became old enough to spend weekends at Cavan's home and, eventually, became able to come for a week or two per month in the summer.

The scheduling is so much easier now that she's older, but, in looking back, the inconvenient schedule lasted for such a short time in her life as to seem almost insignificant. This is what it is important to remember. The true inconveniences last for such a short period of time and the damage done by not adhering to these simple guidelines can last a lifetime and affect every significant relationship a child will have.

The topic of my master's thesis was "Bonding and Attachment: A Story of Love and Relationship."[2] Through a close and comprehensive look at the most cutting edge research at the time, I explored the myriad of problems and difficulties people can develop if their attachment to their primary caregiver is insecure in the first 18 months of life. It appears that everything from depression to alcohol abuse to personality disorders can result from an insecure attachment in childhood. There is also a screening tool that has been developed to assess the security of this attachment. With all of this information available to us, there is no excuse for playing with fire by not adhering to as many of these guidelines as are practicable when experiencing divorce. I would be happy to share more detailed information on this with anyone desiring it. Feel free to contact me at the number in the back of this book. It's truly fascinating stuff!

As I have said before, our mission as parents is not to prevent children from experiencing stress in their lives, but to help make the stress they do experience moderate enough to be manageable for them. We can do this by paying attention to guidelines such as these, and not forcing our children to endure uncomfortable overnights in unfamiliar surroundings to enhance our own comfort and convenience.

Toddlers (1-2 1/2 years)

An appropriate schedule for two year old Kristine would be to live with her primary caregiver, but see her other parent several times a week, for example Tuesday and Thursday and all day on Saturday.

As babies grow, they continue to need a great deal of security, such as the stability of one primary home and caregiver, but they can gradually handle longer times away from their primary source of comfort and nurturance. They still need frequent contact with both parents, but can also tolerate gradually longer times between seeing their non-resident parent. In addition, any placement times should involve physical, hands-on contact, such as holding, rocking, feeding, bathing, changing, playing and the like, so that the child can begin to transfer the secure bond they are developing with their primary caregiver to their other parent.

But there is more flexibility in the scheduling now. By the time a child is a year old, she may be ready to spend a long day with the non-resident parent each week, but should have at least one shorter contact in between. By the time the child reaches 18 months of age, the more liberal guidelines suggest that she may benefit from a two day, one night stay with the nonresident parent, providing she is quite familiar with the parent and they have a good relationship. Longer stays can still be very upsetting for these children, in part because their concept of time is so poor.

When Bill and I first separated, and I moved northward, he would drive from Madison to Manitowoc every other Saturday to take Katie for the afternoon. They would visit his parents, go to McDonald's, play at a park, etc. At the end of the afternoon he would bring her home, exhausted, but happy and content.

Within three months, we had graduated, first to all day visits, then one night overnights in Madison. By the time Katie was two, approximately six months from the separation, she was spending every other weekend in Madison from Friday evening to Sunday evening.

You can see from this schedule that we moved more quickly than the guidelines recommend. But we were watching Katie for signs of distress. What you will look for from your child as you make any change in the placement schedule, is any of the signs and symptoms of distress discussed in Chapter One. For a toddler, that would have been becoming irritable and aggressive, having more temper tantrums and regressing to earlier behaviors. Not new behaviors, necessarily, but in greater frequency than prior to the schedule change.

As I stated previously, immediately upon our move, Katie regressed in her use of the pacifier and bottle. This was an immediate reaction to the separation. As we increased her time with her father and away from her primary home, Katie showed no new symptoms and no increased unpleasant behaviors. This was our key that she was tolerating the change in a positive manner.

It is often difficult for parents to understand why a child who seems so familiar and close to them would have difficulty spending a weekend at their new home, even at 18 months of age. Children do not process information like adults do. In fact, our brains are not fully developed until we are 18-25 years of age![3] For this reason, something we see as non-threatening and "no big deal" may, in fact, be a very big deal for our child.

I want to share with you an experience from my life that has nothing to do with divorce that will illustrate this point quite clearly. My son, Ryan, is a very intelligent, active and curious fellow, who likes to investigate how things work, taking them apart and occasionally getting them back together in one piece. To spend time with him, one would notice he is full of questions and that sitting still is not his best thing.

When Ryan was about four years old, his father and I took him canoeing for the first time. It was not without some fear and trepidation, due both to Ryan's personality and the fact that we were using a whitewater canoe, which tended to be a bit tippy, but we would be on a small, quiet lake in northern Wisconsin and he would be wearing his life jacket.

As soon as we set off, I noticed a change in Ryan. As we paddled away from the dock, he was sitting stock-still and not saying a word. The entire time we paddled out, he did not move, which, also, was very unlike him. After about thirty minutes we figured we were pressing our luck, so we turned the canoe around and headed back to shore. As soon as he spotted the dock we had pushed off from, Ryan's behavior changed again. He became very animated and very much his usual self. But what he was saying shocked his dad and me. He began shouting excitedly that, "Now we can see our cabin again and our blue house in Manitowoc and Nanny and Bumpa and our swingset...!"

For some reason, Ryan assumed we would forever be floating on this lake, I guess, or at the very least, that we would never see anything or anyone near and dear to us again. I am sure neither his dad nor I said anything to give him that idea. That sure wasn't *our* intent. His four year old brain just processed the information it received and came out with a new start in life—for all of us!

Even older children can struggle with this kind of thing as their brains are not fully developed so the information and event processing mechanisms work differently than for adults. We recently returned from a raft trip on the Rio Grande. While on the trip, Meghan, our youngest daughter, did something rather peculiar. An avid swimmer, Meghan refused to swim when given the opportunity to do so in midafternoon, on the river when the temperature was approximately 90 degrees Fahrenheit. We made the offer and encouraged her several times, but she was adamant.

After we returned to our home from our trip out West,

she started talking about the hike we had taken the year before, down to the Rio Grande on the Big Arsenic Trail. As she talked, I recalled that she had asked what arsenic was and had been told it was a poison. I asked her if that was why she hadn't wanted to swim in the Rio Grande and she told me that she had been afraid of being poisoned. She added, "Whenever I took a drink from my water bottle, I was careful to wipe off the top in case some of the water got on it." Here this child had been terrified of poisoning the entire day and thought her parents were encouraging her to swim in a poisoned river. And she is 10 years old. Another example of the fear that can arise in children in even the most innocent of circumstances!

You can imagine what something like this can do to a child being separated from a primary caregiver for an extended period of time. Therefore, even if the changes don't seem to be upsetting your child or you can't understand why they would be, it could very well be occurring. Watch your child's reaction closely whenever there is a schedule change. If he suddenly becomes irritable, aggressive or wakes up crying during the night, you may want to back off for a couple of months to give the child time to mature a bit so he can more easily handle the schedule. He may be better able to handle any changes a few months down the road. It is also a good idea to start any new schedule gradually, for instance on alternate weeks or once a month, to give him time to adjust. In addition, it is helpful if the child has telephone contact between actual visits and shorter in-person contact between longer visits, if possible.

Preschoolers (3-5 1/2 years)

Four year old Ricky would benefit from living with his primary caregiver and seeing his other parent two days or evenings a week and every other weekend. This is getting closer to a shared placement as he is more able to tolerate longer separations from his primary source of comfort and nurturance.

Preschoolers still need familiar routines and consistent schedules, which provide a great deal of stability for them, but they can now typically handle longer visits with the non-resident parent. By age three, the more liberal guidelines suggest that they may be able to handle two night stays away from the primary caregiver. As I stated previously, we did this with Katie before she was three with positive results. Your key and guideline has to be your own child's reaction. If you are making the changes gradually and your child is not reacting negatively to them, it is likely she is tolerating them well.

Ideally, your child should have contact in between longer or weekend-long visits, both in person and by phone, and should not go more than seven to ten days without seeing a parent. That said, however, I want to acknowledge that distance and scheduling often makes this guideline difficult to follow to the letter.

We did not follow this rule with Katie, largely because of the distance we were dealing with. It was a three hour one-way drive from Madison to Manitowoc. As single parents, both working full time, neither of us had the luxury of time to make that six hour drive on a weekday. Still, we watched Katie for her reactions and she tolerated it well. We did have extensive telephone contact between Katie and Bill, however, and since she has learned to read, they also keep in touch via email.

Bill has always called Katie at least once a week. He did so more often before she had the social schedule she has now and was more available to him. In our home, we have always had an "open phone" policy: Katie is able to call Bill at any time, except to get out of a consequence for misbehavior. The only request I make is that she let me know when she is calling him so I can maintain some kind of a running total of our long distance telephone bill. We have recently obtained a cell phone for her with free long distance at certain times of the day and week. A significant portion of her calls go to contacting her dad.

The bottom line is that preschoolers need predictable, frequent and regular time with the non-resident parent. They still have a poor concept of time, so it is often difficult for them to grasp the meaning of next week or three days from now. Help them to visualize on a calendar, as we discussed in Chapter Two, when they will be seeing their other parent. The markings can help you keep track of these dates and times as well! One parent in my class color-coded her calendar with a different color for time with mom, dad and caregiver, so a non-reading child could quickly understand where they were going to be. What a wonderful idea!

Bill happened on a rather inspired solution to this problem as well. For Christmas one year, he bought Katie a book on tape entitled, "When Is Saturday?"[4] It involved one of the Sesame Street characters, perhaps it was Grover, who was going to spend a night at his favorite uncle's house the following Saturday night. The book starts out on Sunday, with text that explains everything Grover did that day. The last thing before he want to bed that night was to cross out Sunday on his calendar. The book walks the child through an entire week, giving him a concrete picture of how long a week actually is.

I know Katie loved the book. In addition to helping her understand how long before she would see him again, it also seemed to help her feel closer to her dad at times when he wasn't physically available to her. She listened to it over and over and over! By summer I could recite the darn thing without the book in front of me! But the important thing was, it made a big difference in Katie's life.

These days, with the frequency of divorce holding steady, there are likely to be even more options for teaching tools such as this, so you wouldn't have to listen to the same story every day! Take a walk through the children's section of your library or local book store. See if you can't find something to help your child understand this elusive concept as well.

School Age Children (6-8 years)

Eight year old Stephanie can be quite comfortable spending half of her time with each parent, without one parent having "primary" placement or responsibility for her.

School age children need longer periods of time with each parent. Once kids are about six years old, they are usually ready and eager to spend extensive time with the parent they see less often. This is also a good time to begin shared parenting, if that is a goal.

The difficulty with this age is that once they enter the

school system, children also develop a social calendar. They get involved with more outside activities with peers, sports and other interests, which are essential to their appropriate development, and end up spending more time with peers and less with both parents.

School age children may also need to spend more time with the same sex parent at this time in their lives, depending on you family structure and their relationship with both of you. But the bottom line is that they need permission to love both parents and all family members. Verbally give them permission to enjoy spending time with their other parent and to look forward to their times together by making comments such as, "I'm glad you had fun with dad this weekend," and "It's great that you look forward to going to Mom's."

Remembering our discussion of brain development, kids often see parents as competitive and assume the worst, i.e. that you will be hurt if you know they enjoy seeing their other parent and look forward to going there. They may assume that you want them to hate or dread going over to the other parent's home and many children need for you give them the verbal permission and acknowledgement expressed above. In this way, they will be better able to accept the arrangement in a positive manner and make a healthy adjustment to it.

Kids also tend to benefit the most when both parents are interested and involved in their lives. This includes participating in parent-teacher conferences, sports and other extracurricular activities and interests. Go to the conferences, contact the school, attend the soccer games, and show up at the dance recital! Even if you feel momentarily uncomfortable, or are somewhat inconvenienced, it will mean the world to your child. You are showing them that you care.

One of the things Bill has done, ever since Katie has been in school, is to make the drive from his residence in Green Bay to Manitowoc, about a 45 minute one-way drive, for the 15 minute parent-teacher conference. This puts him on the road many times longer than the actual meeting, but if you could see the look on Katie's face when he walks in the door, you would understand why he does it! They he usually makes a point of taking her out for ice cream or a Mountain Dew to maximize his time with her as well. She even gets a treat out of the deal. What kid wouldn't love that?

Pre-Adolescent Children (9-12 years)

Ten year old Kyle can split his time equally with both parents, but what they will most likely discover is that they spend many of their evenings and weekends chauffeuring him to and from the various extracurricular activities which have become his priorities: basketball, soccer, boy scouts and sandwiching "quality time" in between his planned activities. This is necessary and appropriate for him.

Pre-adolescent children are old enough to successfully adapt to a schedule that best suits the family as a whole, but at this age, they are often extensively involved in school and extracurricular activities. Any parenting schedule must accommodate these activities, as well as time with peers.

As a parent interested in your child's well-being and wanting to support their positive adjustment to your divorce, you must accept these extracurricular interests. Do not penalize your child or make him suffer by preventing him from going out for basketball, because practices are on Tuesday evenings and that happens to be "your night" with your son. There are few ways to achieve disaster as quickly as punishing your child for being a product of divorce.

Look at this as a unique opportunity to participate in your child's life. Accompany him to practice, where he can show you what he can do on the basketball court, then on the way home, stop and grab a burger or ice cream cone.

Therefore, while the good news may be that you get your kids more often, the bad news is that you may be spending that extra time ferrying them from one activity to another. However, do remember that this is an ideal time for all of those big questions about the divorce and changes in the family that he was not comfortable asking you when you were staring at him eyeball to eyeball. As you are driving him to basketball practice or dance class, he may finally summon the courage to ask the questions that he has been pondering and just waiting for the perfect opportunity to discuss with you. At these times, as we discussed in Chapter Two, you will want to tune into any questions that are, or could be, divorce related, so be sure to be on the lookout for those!

Teens (13-17 years)

Fifteen year old Sarah is able to move quite freely between her parents' homes, as they live within two blocks of each other. But she advises friends, "Try me at Dad's first. If I'm not there, I'll leave that info on his answering machine message so you'll know to call me at my Mom's." Her parents content themselves with catching a movie or burger with her when she has "nothing better to do" and to keeping tabs on her for her own safekeeping.

With regard to a parenting schedule, teens need privacy, activities with other adolescents, flexibility to reschedule plans with parents when something more important comes up, freedom from responsibility for major family decisions, continued guidance from parents about rules and standards for behavior and ongoing contact with both parents. Developmentally, teens can accommodate to any schedule that works for the parents or the family as a whole, but typically prefer one home base so that they have one phone number for friends to call to make plans. However, teens are also very adaptable and can quickly take over your life and your answering machine, changing the message to something such as, "Hi, this is John. I'm at Dad's this week, so call me at 555-1234."

The flexibility comes in when the social event or party of the year comes up. It is normal and appropriate for teens to want to cancel plans with parents to attend. You will do them a great favor if you can allow this to happen and not take it personally. Actually, you can take this as a good sign—your kids are normal.

Teens also thrive on flexible, impromptu meetings with parents, such as a movie date when both parent and child find themselves hanging around the house on Friday night or a quick game of basketball when both are available on a Saturday afternoon or after school. If you can accommodate this type of flexibility, it will go a long way toward improving your relationship with your teen.

Teens need to be free from major decisions, such as whether or not to sell the family home and choosing which parent they want to live with. They will have definite opinions about these issues, but you can get the information about how they feel without backing them into a corner. Don't make them choose between you and their other parent. Even at this age, it is emotionally damaging for them.

If parents live close to each other, some teens are comfortable moving back and forth between homes quite informally, leaving messages on each parent's answering machine indicating where they are at any given time so friends can reach them. This can be an extremely positive situation. However, you want to make sure that both parents understand where the teen will be so they will be provided with regular supervision, and are not just spending time at each parent's home when the parent is not available to supervise them.

Again, remember teens need that "safe harbor" from which they can come and go. Make sure the stability is there for them. Any schedule at this age must accommodate school, peers and employment. These are the areas on which teens *must* be focusing at this point in their lives.

Young Adults (18+ years)

While 21 year old Jake initially rejected his father's attempts to have contact and talk about his decision to seek a divorce, he eventually relented as Dad lovingly but firmly and persistently conveyed the message, "You are important to me. I want to spend time with you to talk about these changes." Eventually they did have dinner and the "heart to heart talk" that helped Jake understand and forgive his father.

No specific time-related recommendations exist for this age group as each parent's relationship with their adult child is different. Playing it by ear is the word of the day. Further, as most young adults no longer live in the family home, there is no built-in pattern of contact. Parents are advised to invest some time in assisting adult children to accept the changes in the family. This will vary for each family, and will often be related to patterns of contact prior to the divorce.

Adult children can be the most angry and hostile of all children regarding the divorce. Much of the anger is often directed at the parent who chose to leave. This is because adult children have often made choices and decisions in their own lives based, at least in part, on the parents' choices and values. If they are now married, working full-time and supporting a family, and the parent who modeled this behavior for them now wants to "chuck it all and move to Utah at age 55" this child is typically going to feel betrayed and angry. This may take some time to work through. But one thing we see from adult children is strong emotion, typically involving anger directed toward the parent choosing to leave.

If you are that person, hang in there and keep trying to talk to your adult child. Eventually the emotion will subside and they will be able to listen to what you have to say. It will be your continued attempts at reaching out to that child that will make the difference and heal the relationship, even if they seem not to want that contact at first. Remember, you are still the parent in the relationship. Take responsibility for attempting to have contact with your child.

This concludes the summary of scheduling recommendations for the various age groups. One of the keys is to remember to be flexible. This schedule will need to be changed a number of times throughout the life of the child. Also, if you are the first to extend an olive branch when the favor of temporarily altering the schedule is requested, you are more likely to receive that treatment in return when you are doing the asking.

A family mediator can help you work out some of these placement and custody issues if you and the other parent are not immediately able to resolve them. In our county, as I have described, the first three hours of the mediator's time cost you nothing so you really have nothing to lose. After that, it is still less expensive than paying an attorney. Inquire how your county handles mediation and save your attorney for the issues you really need her to resolve.

Other things to consider, these are guidelines, not hard

and fast rules. If you have children of a variety of ages, do the best you can to meet the greatest needs of the greatest number without driving yourself crazy in the process.

In addition, if a nonresident parent has been very involved, a child is likely to benefit from more time with that parent than the guidelines suggest. Additionally, a young child who is close to older siblings is often likely to be able to handle longer visits than suggested for her age because she will have the comfort and security of living and being with her siblings at placement times.

Distance is also an important consideration. Your placement arrangement will be different if you live across the street from each other than if you live on opposite sides of the state. Midweek visits that would be easier for your child and seem to make good sense if you live nearby, become an onerous and unreasonable task if such visits involve a five hour one way drive. Use common sense. Your child will survive. You are reading this book to try to make things easier on your child— not to make life impossible for you! If you have children in a variety of age groups, do the best you can to meet the greatest needs of the greatest number without driving yourself crazy in the process.

On the following pages, I have compiled a checklist to help you look at the parenting schedule you have arranged and assess how this meets the various needs of your children. Look it over and, perhaps, make some changes after you have a chance to take a look at how your children's lives might be affected and enhanced by your spending time with them. Enjoy!

"The art of acceptance is the art of making someone who has just done you a small favor wish he might have done you a greater one."

~Russell Lyons

Co-Parenting Schedules to Meet Children's Developmental Needs

Infants (0-12 months)

❀ Need a very stable environment and a regular schedule.

❀ One primary home and care-giver to develop primary attachment.

❀ Should not be separated from primary care-giver for long periods of time.

❀ Should not have overnight visits in most cases.

❀ Need frequent and regular contact with non-resident parent.

❀ Placement times should include lots of physical, hands-on interaction (holding, rocking, cuddling, bathing, feeding, playing) to help transfer this bond.

Toddlers (1-3 year olds)

❀ Need the stability of one primary home.

❀ Can handle longer stays away from primary care-giver and longer times between visits.

❀ Need frequent, regular contact with both parents.

❀ Still needs placement times to be very physical.

❀ May be ready to spend a long day with non-resident parent; should have one shorter contact in between.

❀ By 18 months, may handle a two day, one night stay.

❀ When schedule changes, start gradually and watch child for signs of stress: increased fussiness, aggressiveness, tantrums, separation fears, lack of smiling, waking through the night, masturbation.

❀ May work up gradually to overnights once per week if the child tolerates them well.

❀ Should have phone contact between visits.

Preschoolers (3-5 1/2 year olds)

❀ Still need familiar routines and consistent schedules.

❀ May be able to handle two night visits with non-resident parent.

❀ Should have contact in between visits and should not go more than 7-10 days without seeing parent.

❀ Predictable, frequent and regular time with non-resident parent is important.

❀ Still have poor concept of time so use teaching tools: calendar, books on tape, etc.

School Age Children (6-8 year olds)

❀ Need longer periods of time with each parent.

❀ Usually ready and eager to spend extensive time with the less-seen parent.

❀ Good age to begin shared parenting arrangements.

❀ More time with same sex parent may be important.

❀ Need permission to love both parents.

❀ Extracurricular involvement must be accommodated

❀ Need both parents involved in school and activities.

Pre-Adolescents (9-12 year olds)

❀ Involvement with peers of primary importance and must be accommodated.

❀ Have more outside activities involving sports, etc.

❀ Listen for divorce-related questions.

❀ Hormones affect mood and development.

❀ Can handle shared parenting schedules easily as long as time with peers is accommodated.

Teens (13-18 year olds)

❀ Need privacy, activities with other teens, flexibility to reschedule plans with parents and ongoing contact with both parents.

❀ Should not be responsible for major family decisions

❀ Need guidance about rules and standards for behavior.

❀ Often prefer one home base and one phone number.

❀ Need "safe harbor" from which they can come and go

Young Adults (19+)

❀ Most are not living at home so no specific recommendations exist.

❀ Regular contact with both parents is important.

REMEMBER: Be flexible; the parenting schedule may need to be changed a number of times throughout the years. Stay focused on the *Best Interests of Your Child(ren)*!

CHAPTER 7

SHARING WITH "THE ENEMY"

*Why You **Must** Support Your Children's Relationships With Their "Other Parent"*

auren and Luke are frightened and confused. It is apparent that their mother is furious! As soon as they arrived home from their father's house, she began questioning them about what they'd had to eat and what time they went to bed over the weekend. Thinking it was "pretty neat" to have Kool-Aid and candy for breakfast and to have no formal bedtime, the kids eagerly shared this information with their mother. Now, not understanding why she is so angry, they begin to think **they** did something wrong. They had fun spending time with Dad. Now, they're afraid they won't be able to see him anymore.

The information in this chapter is directed toward parents with either primary placement or operating under a shared placement arrangement. We will focus on how and why you must support your kids' relationship with their other parent. Information for parents with secondary, or non-primary, placement will be provided in Chapter Eight.

However, I would encourage all parents to read both chapters because it can be very helpful getting a glimpse of the other parent's perspective and reality.

Often parents with primary physical placement of children seek to discourage children's contact with their other parent and think they have good reasons for doing so. Perhaps the kids are upset both before and after visits. Maybe they come home wired from eating nothing but sugar or junk food for two days. Perhaps the other parent continually disappoints the kids, showing up two hours late or not at all, while they stand in the hallway with their jackets on asking when he will arrive. Maybe the kids are out of control for several days after visits because they've had no rules, limits or bedtimes all weekend, so it takes you three days to get them back to their typical schedules.

However, when parents discourage contact between their children and the other parent, the biggest losers are the children. Further, this loss is usually profound and long lasting, typically their relationships for the remainder of their lives, and certainly affecting their long-term adjustment to the divorce.

This is an area being actively researched by social scientists. All of the research is showing that any harm caused to children by loss of sleep, eating a weekend of junk food, being exposed to lax discipline and different values or even when children are repeatedly disappointed by the other parent, pales in comparison to the loss children experience by not having that relationship with their other parent. It matters not how much sleep they've lost or how many times they've had Kool-Aid for breakfast. None of these losses are as significant in the development of the child as being deprived of continued contact with their other parent.

Child development experts agree that this relationship between a child and non-resident parent should *always* be encouraged and nurtured unless there is clear evidence that the parent is abusive or neglectful. Even in situations such as those, most experts feel that the relationship is significant enough that it should continue as long as the safety of the child can be provided for, such as with supervised visitation.

Access to this other parent should also be very liberal or free, providing that the conflict between the parents is under control. In the event it is not, I would strongly encourage both parents, or at least the one reading this book, to take responsibility for doing whatever they can to remedy that situation. If you are convinced that you have done everything you can to alleviate the conflict, I urge you now to skip ahead to Chapter Nine to read bout how to single handedly make some changes in that relationship. It's crucial for your children that you do so.

Support Contact Between Your Children and Their Other Parent

One of the best things you can do to help your children adjust to your divorce is to support a great deal of contact, in any appropriate manner, between your children and their other parent. I have already made the argument that this contact is essential for your children's life-long well being. It is no stretch to imagine that this, also, is crucial to their adjustment to your divorce. If you can't bring yourself to support this contact for the sake of your former partner, see it solely in the guise of what you must do for your children. Then get back to work on your own adjustment to the end of this relationship. You obviously still have some work to do.

Your children's time with their other parent should not only be regular and frequent, but of sufficient duration to allow them to build and maintain a meaningful relationship. They must have enough time together to actually have a relationship. As the parent with more contact with the children, you have a significant amount of power to either support or inhibit this process.

Come out loudly and verbally in support of your children's contact with this parent. They will often take their cues from you. If you say nothing, many children assume the worst: that you don't care whether they have contact with their other parent or, worse yet, that you are mad at them for wanting this contact. Tell them out loud that you understand how important their relationship with that parent is and encourage them to have that contact. Most children need to hear this from you. Say it often.

Support this with your actions as well. Encourage them to call when they have good news to share, such as making the basketball team or getting good grades. Have reasonable rules regarding telephone and internet usage and long distance charges; rules that will encourage that contact. As the parent with much control over your child's life and time, you can find very subtle ways to either encourage or inhibit this contact. For example, developing a family policy that each person has to pay for their own long distance calls will inhibit your 16 year old from regularly contacting a non-local parent, whereas reasonable rules could encourage such contact, such as paying for all calls to adults.

In my family, as I have shared with you previously, we have always had a very open policy regarding Katie's telephone calls to her father. She may call him any time, except to avoid a consequence for inappropriate behavior. There has only been one instance when I have had to enforce this expectation. Kids understand these rules, if they are reasonable and make sense. The only other request I make is that Katie let me know when she calls, so that I have some idea of what our long distance telephone bill will be.

Another way to encourage and support this contact is to honor placement schedules, but not be rigid about them. Unexpected things happen in everybody's life. Do not penalize your children when this happens. Remember, if you are the first to extend an olive branch when a favor or change is requested, you are more likely to receive that type of response when it is you who is making the request.

Re-evaluate the schedule occasionally to make sure it is still working for everyone involved. As we discussed in the previous chapter, the schedule will most likely need to change a number of times over the life of your child. If you are on the phone every week or two negotiating a change, perhaps the time has come to overhaul the entire schedule. Maybe it's just not working anymore because your needs, or those of your child, have changed.

Keep in mind that sometimes changes will be necessary because of conflicting demands or due to variables over which you have no control. Keep your attitude positive and try to work out another time for your children to see their other parent. If you convince yourself that you should not have to make adjustments and dig in your heels, you will only be harming your child. All divorced parents experience these things; it is your attitude that will enable your child to succeed in spite of the challenges.

Let me give you an example of what I mean by change over which you have no control so you can get a clear picture of what this may look like in your own life. When we were first separated, Bill and I had a very easy and amicable relationship as far as switching our weekend times with Katie. If either of us needed to switch weekends due to a conflict, we would simply call the other and the upcoming weekend most often would be exchanged for that immediately following.

This convenience lasted approximately three years, until Bill became involved in a new relationship, with Anne who had a son, Christopher, from her previous marriage. I have never met Chris' father, but he has been described to me as a pretty unreasonable man, rarely agreeable to switching placement times with Chris.

Bill and Anne had a very healthy and positive goal of having their children with them on the same weekends each month so they could all spend family time together, then having them with their other parents (i.e. me and Christopher's father) at the same times so that they could enjoy some "couple time." There is nothing wrong with the goal and it is, indeed, one way to carve special time out of a very busy schedule to build and maintain a relationship.

However, this change made my life very difficult. All of a sudden, switching weekends took on all the difficulty and complication of negotiating a peace treaty. More often than not, Bill was agreeable to my having Katie on an extra weekend for one event or another (the dance recital for example, when she would need to be available Friday, Saturday and Sunday as I was expected to do her hair and makeup), but was unable to take her for the exchanged weekend for months down the road.

Well, I was incensed by this! This was not right; it was not fair! I wanted our easy scheduling back. I screamed and hollered and stamped my feet, but nothing changed, except that I got myself all upset. I finally realized that I was hurting no one but myself and, probably, my daughter, even though she was not at home when most of these arrangements were made. I eventually decided to let this issue go but this process took me several painful, angry months. Bill continued to be involved in Katie's life throughout our difficulties and I can recall several very upsetting telephone calls where one or the other of us ended up saying, "I guess we can't talk about this right now. I'll call again in a few days." Once my attitude changed, however, it all got much easier.

As a divorced parent, you, too, will experience events in your life and that of your child over which you have no control. You can be unhappy and not like it and want the old ways back, but none of that will matter. Learn from my experience. Don't take three months to work through this like I did. Let it go now. Accept it like death and taxes and both you and your child will be happier.

> *"If you don't like something, change it. If you can't change it, change your attitude."*
>
> ~Maya Angelou

Problematic Behavior Before and After Placement is Normal

Your child may not be able to articulate this in a way that you are able to understand, but making the transition from one home and family to another is difficult for children. Each transition requires them to shift gears to adjust to the differing rules and expectations of the parent or household. Further, each change triggers several understandable and predictable emotions that children may act out, rather than articulate verbally.

Children feel loyal to both parents; this becomes conflictual for them primarily when you are both together, such as at pick up and drop off times. Also, they are typically excited to see the parent that is picking them up, yet sad to leave the parent and home they will leave behind. Most children are confused by all of these feelings as well, and feel awkward and uncomfortable in the presence of both parents as they are not quite sure how to act. Transitions also force children to wrestle with guilt about leaving one parent for the other, or about wanting to be with a parent who may be causing the other parent much pain. This is especially acute while the divorce is happening. And remember, each transition requires them to say good-bye to one of the most important people in their lives!

I worked for a period of time while attending graduate school at an agency in Madison, Wisconsin called The Respite Center. We provided emergency and respite child care for children at risk for abuse and neglect. You can imagine the emotions running rampant in the children we saw.

I noticed early on that one of the things the childcare providers at the agency did was to take great pains to make each transition as calm and relaxing as possible for the children involved. The agency was housed, at the time, in an old Victorian style home. Our offices were upstairs and the downstairs area was where childcare was provided. It had a huge living/dining room combination that was a gigantic play area filled with noise, activity and more toys than you can imagine.

The home also had a front room that had probably been the parlor area, which could be closed off from the play area by pocket doors. This room was where all transitions took place. Whenever a child was arriving at or departing from the agency, childcare workers would take care to close the pocket doors to separate the room from the somewhat chaotic play area. Further, in this room the lights were kept dimly lit, curtains were drawn and often soft music was playing on the stereo. This enabled the child joining or leaving the group to focus solely on their emotions and not be affected by all of the noise, chaos and stimulus of the busy play area.

Similar to your children, leaving to be with their other parent, these children were experiencing a variety of emotions as they were coming or going: excitement, sadness, fear, confusion and more. The calmness of the parlor gave them a setting to sort out those emotions in a positive manner.

Do this for your child as well. Keep your home calm as you prepare for the transfer of placement. Do not have it filled with every child in the neighborhood and don't have every light in the house on. Draw the curtains and consider soft music. Calm yourself so your emotions and tension do not spill over to your children. Set them up for success. Help them to handle these transitions as calmly and easily as possible.

Tensions tend to be even more intense when parents are in conflict as this exacerbates the loyalty conflicts that children naturally experience. Don't use pick up or drop off times to attempt to negotiate a change in the placement schedule or child support. Have these discussions when your child is out of earshot and, preferably, out of the house or asleep. Even if they can only hear your end of the conversation, most kids are aware enough to know who you are talking to, even when you are speaking appropriately, and witnessing a negotiation process involving them can, in and of itself, increase the tension they are feeling. Spare them this agony. Have these discussions when they are not around.

The other thing parents need to understand about acting out behavior and transition times is that, from a child's perspective, it's much easier to leave a parent who's mad at you than it is to leave a parent who's being kind, warm, loving and nurturing. For many children, subconsciously, acting out and getting a parent upset, makes it easier for them to say goodbye. If the parent you are feeling guilty about leaving is angry with you, it is much easier to say, "See ya!" and leave with a clear conscience.

This can be a healthy mechanism for children to help themselves separate from their primary caregiver, for a short period of time. Eventually, the child should become able to separate without the inappropriate behavior and able to understand and accept their own feelings of discomfort. But, especially while the divorce is pending, and often for a time afterward, depending on the age of the child, acting out behavior at transition times is a coping skill that is frequently used. Bear with it—it won't last forever! Think of it as a positive sign that your child will miss you and cares a great deal about you.

Some children become withdrawn before they leave for a period of placement with their other parent. They may go spend time in their bedrooms or, if they do stay in the main area of the house, may don headphones or read a book, making interaction with them all but impossible. This is normal as well. They are emotionally preparing themselves in a positive way to separate from you and from your household and to be with their other parent. They are emotionally distancing themselves from you. This is something they need to do to make the transition in a positive and healthy manner.

In addition to making the home atmosphere calm, keep yourself calm and relaxed as well. Don't use this preparation time to nag children about homework or chores not done. Take care of any of those issues several hours before children leave so they can use the last two hours or so to prepare themselves for the transition. Give your kids some space. And, most importantly, remember to give them verbal permission to have a good time with their other parent. Do not lay a guilt trip on them for wanting or being excited to go. Remember, as difficult as this is for you, it is essential for their well-being.

When children return home, all of the same emotions are in play: excitement, sadness, loyalty, guilt, confusion, fear, etc. In addition, the atmosphere is often strained, so do not be surprised if you see some similar behaviors. You may notice acting out; you may also notice emotional distance. This is normal. Your child will let you know what she needs from you. Just give her permission to do this and take your cues from her. It will make a big difference in her adjustment to your divorce.

Even if you are aware of what your child is feeling, be aware of the subtle and not so subtle messages you are giving them. When Katie was three or four years old, I would always miss her terribly on the weekends she spent with her dad. My solution to my discomfort was to plan some spectacular family activity for Sunday night when she came home, followed by a big family dinner and so on. Invariably, these occasions ended with Katie in tears, stomping upstairs to her bedroom, where she might stay for 15-20 minutes, at which point she would come back downstairs and rejoin our confused family. Things would usually proceed uneventfully for the remainder of the evening.

In pondering these events, it became apparent to me that I was the one causing the problem in this situation. I was putting too much pressure on Katie to reconnect with me, and our family, too quickly upon her return; more quickly than her four year old mind was able. We were meeting my emotional needs, i.e. missing her, and not hers, i.e. needing to reconnect more slowly after a great weekend with dad. Her outburst was her four year old attempt to manage that pressure. She had just come from a wonderful weekend with her Dad; she wasn't the one feeling sad and lonely over the weekend. That was me. As soon as I identified and accepted responsibility for the problem, it became much easier to resolve.

Katie was also letting me know exactly what she needed from me when she returned home. Did you pick that up or did you miss it like I did at first? She needed time and space to reconnect on her own schedule.

So we decided to have the solution without the problem. The very next weekend when she came back from her Dad's, I made the following suggestion to her, "Katie, why don't you take your stuff upstairs and put it away and, when you're done, come on down and we'll have something to eat." We have since kept Sunday nights very low key; no special plans, just a simple meal, baths, any last minute homework and then bedtime.

Things have gone much more smoothly since that revelation. Katie takes her things up to her room when she gets home. They rarely actually get put away, but she putters around in her room for a few minutes, often jumps on the internet to reconnect with her friends, then rejoins the family as she is ready. But the tears and strong upset emotions are not part of her placement weekend experience anymore; now that I've wised up and realized the emotional pressure I was putting on her.

Take a look for yourselves at any messages you may unintentionally be giving your children about these times as well. Are you giving them the information that you want them to have a good time and that you will be okay when they are gone?

Or are you sending the message that you will pine for them and need them desperately? This may greatly affect how comfortable they are leaving you to spend time with their other parent. Give your children the gift of freedom from responsibility for your emotions. This is difficult enough for them without carrying you on their shoulders as well.

Even though we had solved the emotional connection problem, leaving her dad for two weeks was still difficult for Katie. Bill came up with a solution, a ritual as it were, that helped make it easier for Katie to leave him as well.

Even if they spend the entire weekend with the rest of the family, Bill usually attempts to make the drive home, from Green Bay to Manitowoc, strictly father-daughter time. Therefore, even if she has had to share his attention all weekend with family, work or hobbies, for that 45 minutes at the very least, she is the center of his universe. Of course, now that she's driving, both of them are a little distracted when on the road!

He also established a ritual with her that helps, in a very small way, to prepare her to separate from him. He developed the practice of buying her a "going home treat," which she has begun to view as an absolute entitlement. It's never anything expensive; often just an ice cream cone of a can of Mountain Dew. But it is a token of his affection that also helps her prepare emotionally to be separated from him for the next two weeks.

Explore for your own children and family whether there are any rituals that could help your children adjust to making this transition. They may be telling you unconsciously what would help them. You may only need to pay attention and listen. Good luck!

Make it Easy for the Other Parent to Continue Parenting Your Children

A part time schedule makes it difficult to truly feel like a parent to your children, as opposed to an occasional visitor in their lives. Research is showing that parents who begin to feel useless and peripheral to their children are more likely to drop out of their lives and to stop paying child and family support. We have already discussed how important just the relationship is for your children. In this day and age, with what it costs to raise a child, few of us can do without the financial support as well.

As the parent with more contact with the children, you have a significant amount of power to affect the ease or difficulty of that other parent in continuing to have a significant relationship with your children. Use that power wisely, for what is in their best interests, rather than to exact revenge or punishment even if you feel it is justified.

Studies also show that parents who are able to maintain a significant and meaningful relationship with their children often develop even closer relationships with them after divorce. Even if this feels unfair to you, because that other parent never spent time with the children before the separation, ask yourself which is better for your kids?

With this power, you have the ability to enhance the development of a closer relationship, and to make it easier for the other parent to "be there" for your child, at school functions, parent-teacher conferences, basketball games and dance recitals. The list is endless. These events are important for your children. Give their other parent every opportunity to be there for them.

As the parent the child lives with, you have access to all of the important information to make this possible. It is mailed to your home or brought home in their backpacks in the form of school schedules, basketball schedules, dance recital information and the like. When you receive it, share it immediately with the other parent. If Bill finds out on May 31st that Katie's Dance Recital is on June 2nd, how likely is it that he will be able to attend? What if, instead, he has that information on August 31st like I do? Doesn't that make it easier for him to be there for his daughter? Get in the habit of asking yourself, "What is best for my child?"

Give the school the other parent's home information. Katie has always attended the Manitowoc Area Catholic School system. Even with how we Catholics feel about divorce, the registration form I have completed for her every year has included the following questions:

❀ With which parent does the child live?

___ Mother ___Father ___Both

❀ If Mother or Father, do you want school information sent to the other parent? ___ Yes ___ No

❀ If Yes, please provide that parent's name, address and telephone number in the spaces provided.

Every year I have included Bill's information on the form and every year, without fail, the schools have been religious (no pun intended) about keeping him informed. He even receives Katie's report cards before I do because they are sent to him in the mail and I have to wait for her to bring them home in her backpack!

To his credit, most years Bill has also called and introduced himself to school personnel, even before the parent-teacher conference, and requested that the information be sent to him. But I see none of these behaviors as exceptional. We are only two parents attempting to do what is best for our daughter. You can easily do likewise. These actions are neither costly nor time-consuming, but can be significant in your child's adjustment to your divorce.

Respect Your Children's "Other Family"

Accept that your children's other parent has the absolute and inalienable right to develop his own relationship with them; to parent them. Go out of your way not to interfere when it is their time together. Do not call them when they are with their other parent or you insert yourself, front and center, right between them. You remind your child that you are alone and trigger all of those difficult emotions they struggle with at transition times. Give them the opportunity to have placement time together without you being on their minds.

I can count on one hand the number of times that I have called Katie at her Dad's house over the 14 years we have been divorced. Those times have been pretty spectacular, such as when her ballet teacher called her to tell her she was ready to go "en pointe," a goal she had been working toward for ten years! Make it a significant event or occasion before you will pick up that phone and interfere with their time together.

I am not talking about shared placement arrangements, here, but about situations where you have primary placement and your children are with their other parent on alternate weekends and, perhaps one night during the week. Four to six days a month is little enough time to spend with your children to try and develop a significant and meaningful relationship. Go out of your way not to interfere in that time.

For those of you who do share placement, use some discretion as well. If you are away from your children for four or five days at a time, it is alright to contact them briefly by phone once or twice, but make it at a time that you are less likely to interfere with the happenings at their other household. Call at bedtime or first thing in the morning, not in the middle of dinnertime. Do not call so often that you make a pest of yourself.

Help Your Children Adapt to Different Rules in Different Households

Think of your children's other parent as their "other family" with whom they live on a part time basis. Ideally, the two of you will agree on a set of basic rules and expectations which will make it easier for your children to know what to expect.

In the event that the two of you just can't agree on some basic rules, I can tell you that children do understand and can quickly adapt to different expectations in different households. By the time Katie was four, she understood which rules were different in each of her homes. If your children try to convince you they just can't remember, write up your expectations and post them on the refrigerator so it is the first thing that hits them in the face when they walk in the back door after a visit! I would bet you will hear less argument after that.

When your rules are different, be clear about what your expectations are and expect them to be challenged. Give some thought to the reasoning behind your rules so that you can explain them to your child and answer questions about them as they arise. When you have a difference of opinion about the rules, feel free to share your reasoning and your thinking with the other parent, but absent abuse and neglect situations, you have no right to impose your rules on their household-even if you think there is only one right answer and you have it!

As you know, my husband Terry is also a therapist. The two of us have always shared an interest in violence and its effect on children, stemming partly from our work together early in our relationship at the Manitowoc County Human Services Department.

When Katie was about three, we became aware of the studies being done about how children were affected by violence in television programming. We obtained a number of the studies, which were pretty damning in their recitation of the effects of such programming on children.[1] Children's cartoons were found to be some of the most offensive programs studied, often containing more acts of violence per second than some of the more obviously objectionable "slasher" movies. Many times the violence was gratuitous; not necessary to the story line, but added to increase children's excitement and lengthen attention span. Often no ill-effects were shown from the violent act, which is deceptive and can have deadly consequences for young viewers.

As an example, imagine any typical popular cartoon. Each week, the lead villain gets a large rock or other heavy object dropped on his head or incurs some other grievous bodily harm. He gets squashed to the pavement, and we laugh, yet shortly thereafter he pops up and is back to his old tricks. To a six year old child with magical thinking and childish reasoning that can send the message that a two year old brother clubbed on the head with a hammer or rock will, likewise, suffer no injury! See also the discussion of brain development in Chapter Eight.

The studies that we read also indicated that children exposed to violent programming were more aggressive and violent, themselves, especially in day care settings. They also tended to engage in more tantruming and other acting out behaviors.

After reading several of these studies, Terry and I decided that we would not allow violent cartoon programming in our home. This meant that at our house we did not watch most of the popular television shows on Saturday morning, as well as a number of other programs. Even though many of these programs were promoting values of right over wrong, they did so by proclaiming and using violence as a means to an end.

As soon as our decision was made, I shared it with Bill. I even provided him with copies of the studies and patiently explained our reasoning. He listened calmly and respectfully and, at the end of my explanation, stated something to the effect of, "Well, I grew up on cartoons and I turned out okay. So I'm going to let Katie watch them at my house."

That was my cue to back off. I had no right to make rules for Bill's household, even if I think I have the "right" approach or know more about a subject than he does. It is his home and his responsibility to run it and make rules as he sees fit.

My greatest challenge, however, came from Katie. When she was about four I started getting the questions, "Well, how come I get to watch that at Dad's house and not here?" This is where your reasoning comes in. I explained to her that through my work I knew that kids that watched these kind of shows hit other kids more, hurt people more and were more violent themselves than kids who didn't watch them. I further explained that Dad (Terry) and I decided we didn't want her to be that way, but that as she got older, she would be able to make more decisions about what she wanted to watch. I added that her Daddy was in charge of making the rules for his house and that sometimes these rules would be different, but that we would help her remember them.

Note that I said *nothing negative about her father or his rule*. This is crucial. I have no right to pass judgment on her father's rule, even if I disagree with it, or to encourage Katie to disrespect it or him.

We are now at the point that if I am in the kitchen on Saturday morning making breakfast, I trust her judgment in supervising programming for our two younger children. In fact, she is more familiar with many of the offensive shows than I am, so can usually pick them out more quickly than I can. As an added benefit, she has come to share my belief about children and violent television programming!

In an earlier chapter, I discussed the resilience that children can develop when faced with stressors that are manageable for them to overcome in life and that, while I would never recommend divorce as a parenting technique, it can provide an opportunity for children to grow and develop qualities that they may not have the chance to develop otherwise. I feel that this television violence issue had that effect on Katie.

As a result of our differing rules, I was forced to have many conversations with Katie about violent television programming. We would talk about whether a violent scene was necessary to tell the story or whether it was gratuitous, inserted to excite or to hold attention, and about whether it was shown in an unnecessarily graphic manner. Katie and I regularly discussed violence and television.

When the first Lion King movie was released, I remember discussing it with Katie, in deciding whether or not to allow Ryan and Meghan to see the movie. One of the issues we discussed was whether the scene in which Simba's father was killed in a stampede was necessary to the story line. She had seen the movie with her father and we both decided that it was not shown graphically and was, indeed, necessary to the adult lion Simba would become. We did all see the movie.

At age 16, Katie is making most of her own decisions about what television programs and movies to watch these days. She enjoys watching "Law and Order: Special Victims Unit" which often has graphically violent scenes, or at least the aftermath thereof, but I am confident that she can handle it. One significant reason for this is that, as an added benefit, Katie has become a very sophisticated consumer of television and movie programming. She is much more mature and competent in her assessment of this medium than I was at 16. I am also quite sure that she is more sophisticated and mature than she would have been if Bill and I had stayed together and developed some uneasy truce about what we would allow our child to see.

In this small way, being a child of divorce has enhanced her development.

This is my hope for all of you. See differences of rules and opinions not as a negative or divisive element in your child's life. Take them as an opportunity to educate your child and help them to grow in a way that, perhaps, you would not if these opportunities did not present themselves.

Placement Times are Essential-Do Not Use Them As Rewards or Punishments

Placement times with both of their parents are essential to your children. Do not use them as rewards or as punishments. They are necessary for your child's well-being. Honor and respect this fact.

Further, most states have gone to great lengths to separate the issue of placement from that of support, even to the extent of creating separate enforcement agencies and courts to handle them. They will not take kindly to a parent withholding support because of missed placement times or vice versa. You may get more than you bargained for in terms of legal consequences if you attempt to do this. If you are having some trouble with either of these issues, you would be well advised to make sure you are using the correct resource for the remedy you are seeking. If you are unsure, consult your attorney about these issues.

Keep Your Children Out of the Middle of Your Relationship With Their Other Parent

Do not ask your children to report back to you about their other parent. This puts them in the middle and floods them with feelings of disloyalty and confusion.

This does not mean you can't ask if they've had a nice weekend. It is also appropriate to ask, "What did you do over the weekend?"

It means you may not ask, "Did Mommy have any men at the house when you were there?" or "Did any ladies call at Daddy's house this weekend?" You know where you are going with these questions and it has nothing to do with your children or their well-being. They pick this up as well. Refuse to play this game.

Be Cautious With Suspicions of Child Abuse or Neglect

If you have good reason to believe that the other parent is being abusive to or neglectful of your children during placement times, the Child Services Department in your community is typically available 24 hours a day. But be aware that in the heat of divorce, many former spouses are willing to think the worst of each other with little provocation. Make sure you have a legitimate complaint before you make the call.

On the following page is a summary checklist of the main points in this chapter. Read it over and think about how you can best implement each of these points to aid your children in making their best adjustment to your divorce and help to simplify the placement times they experience with their other parent.

"It's not the load that breaks you down, it's the way you carry it."

~Anonymous

Supporting Your Children's Relationship With Their Other Parent

❀ Support a good deal of contact, both in person and by phone, between your children and their other parent—enough to build and maintain meaningful relationships.

❀ Understand that children's upset or problematic behavior before and after placement times is normal. Do not mistake this as a signal that their time together is harmful.

❀ Encourage and make it easy for your children's other parent to continue as a full-fledged parent in their children's lives.

❀ Respect the other parent's right to develop their own relationship with your children and to parent them. Do not interfere when it is their time together.

❀ Understand that placement times are necessary and not a luxury. Never use them as rewards or punishments and do not cancel visits because of missed child or family support.

❀ Do not ask your child to report back to you about the other parent—this puts them in the middle.

❀ If you have good reason to believe that their other parent is abusive or neglectful, the Child Services Department is available 24 hours a day. But be aware that in the heat of divorce, many former spouses are only too willing to think the worst of each other.

CHAPTER 8

STAYING INVOLVED

*How to be a Full-Time Parent
on a Part-Time Schedule*

Blake hangs back as his daughter's mother engages in an animated conversation with her eighth grade home room teacher about a homework assignment fourteen year old Katie had completed the previous week, and with which Mom had apparently assisted. Katie feels hurt and confused. She doesn't understand why her father, previously very active in her schooling, is not talking much with her or her teacher and seems like he's not interested in her schoolwork. Doesn't he care anymore? After all, he completely missed the Science Fair and didn't even see her project or her blue ribbon. Maybe she just isn't as important to him anymore...

Incidents and feelings like this are not uncommon. Often parents with secondary physical placement feel excluded, left out and wonder if everyone involved would be better off if they just drifted away, sparing their children the need to split their time and attention between two homes and parents. The answer to this query is, unequivocally, *NO!* See Chapter Five for a more complete discussion of Secondary Physical Placement.

It is crucial to children to have a significant and meaningful relationship with *both* of their parents. This one variable makes the difference between positive and troubled adjustment to parents, divorce. The research shows that it is not so much the *type* of custody or placement that helps children adapt, but the fact that they *do* have significant and meaningful contact with both parents.

Parents having secondary physical placement with their children come from a wide range of parenting experience. Some have been very active in parenting their children before the divorce; others seem to make children a priority only after the separation. Parents at both ends of this involvement spectrum will find helpful ideas in this chapter full of useful suggestions for how to involve yourself in your child's life when you only have a part-time schedule with them.

Remember, time is only one variable in your relationship. How you choose to use the time you have with your children can make the difference between the significant and meaningful relationship they need with you and a situation in which you are all just waiting for the time to pass, and feeling emotionally disconnected from each other.

Provide Stability in Placement~the Importance of "Just Being There"

The first and most important requirement of maintaining contact with your children after divorce is to show up. Make this continued contact an important and critical part of your post-divorce life. It must become a priority for you or it will be too easy to find other things you need to spend your precious time on other than being with your children. It will be easy to convince yourself that your child has another parent he is closer to and would rather be with. Just know that your time is critical to their adjustment to your divorce, if not for yours.

Be there when you say you will be. I have been told heartbreaking stories of children so excited that mom or dad is coming to pick them up at 6:00 p.m. that at quarter to six they put their jackets on and station themselves at the window watching for the beloved parent. As the minutes and hours pass, their little shoulders begin to droop and their eyes tear up, realizing they are once again forgotten or postponed. When the parent finally materializes at 8:15, they are not only physically tired, but now, also, emotionally exhausted from their two hour wait. The parent is usually then treated to explosive, withdrawn, whiny or other acting-out behavior brought on by his own actions.

The child is overwhelmed with feelings of abandonment (by the lateness of the arrival and long wait), excitement (at finally seeing the parent), guilt and sadness (for leaving the other parent), confusion (about their own emotions) and desperately wanting to please the less-seen parent. You can imagine the effect that this jumble of emotions can have on their late-night behavior as you pack them up to carry them off at 8:30 in the evening.

This is a typical scene when the parent finally *does* materialize. You can imagine the situation if the parent *never* arrives for the children. Many of these feelings become even more intense, along with a disappointment and loss that can overwhelm the child.

Do your children, and yourself, a favor. Get there, and arrive on time or when you say you'll be there. Make this time early enough in the evening to allow them to get settled in to their new, or less familiar, environment. Put their comfort and adjustment ahead of your own, even if you have to skip out of work or another social engagement a little early the night you are picking them up. Put yourself in their shoes. What would you want? Remember our discussion of stability in Chapter Three—this is crucial for their long-term adjustment to the divorce.

Be Flexible

There are times in your child's life when you will need to adjust your plans to accommodate theirs, or when the other parent asks you to change arrangements for their, or your child's, convenience. Whenever possible, attempt to accommodate these requests. Changes arise in everyone's life—even if you have a conflictual relationship with the other parent, if you are the first to extend an olive branch when a favor is requested, you are more likely to receive a positive response when you are the one requesting a change. Remember, you are setting the tone for your future co-parenting relationship. See Chapter 9 for a further discussion of this developing relationship.

You can also choose to look at flexibility as a personal challenge for yourself; an opportunity for personal growth, as it were. It is good for us to challenge ourselves this way and usually we feel good about doing something nice for someone, even when it is a person who has hurt us deeply in the past. We are not letting the other person's behavior or actions choose our response—we are choosing to "take the high road" even if they, in their previous contacts with us, did not.

You may need to read these words several times before you are ready to accept them. Our society often does not espouse the value of cooperation and gentleness, even if we like to think it does. My husband, who is one of the gentlest men I know, tells a story that quite wonderfully illustrates this principle.

A monk in Tibet was praying in his temple when a band of marauding intruders barged in and raised their swords to him. He calmly continued praying.

Stunned, one of the marauders shouted at him, "Don't you know who I am? I am the one who can kill you."

The monk looked up and answered, again calmly, "And I am the one who can let you."

These are values not commonly espoused in our society where we tend to value aggressiveness and individual rights above all else. We tend to focus on our own rights in parenting controversies and demand what we are entitled to as far as time with our children is concerned. Develop the habit, instead, of asking yourself in assessing your choice of actions, "What is in my child's best interest?"

Be Sensitive to Your Child's Needs

There are times in our children's lives when the placement

schedule that is best or most convenient for them is inconvenient or uncomfortable for us. Put their needs ahead of your own desires at these times and it will make a world of difference in your relationship with them. And, when they get older and can understand and appreciate the sacrifices you made for them, it will mean even more.

There are a number of typical times or developments in your child's life when this can be the case. Some of the most common situations in which this arises include:

❀ when your child is an infant and overnight visits are not recommended

❀ for toddlers, when less than a shared 50/50 placement is best

❀ for school age children who are, and need to be, involved in school and sporting activities, even on "your nights" with them

❀ when kids are teens, who should, and usually do, prefer to focus on activities with friends, school or jobs, rather than focusing their schedules around spending time with their parents.

❀ in situations when a parent has not been very active in a child's life and the child needs time to get to know you better, no matter what her age, before being comfortable with a more typical schedule for her age or developmental level.

See Chapter Six for a more complete discussion of placement recommendations and guidelines for these times in your child's life.

A number of years ago, I was assigned to mediate with a couple who had a son together, but had never been married. The relationship had ended just before the woman discovered she was pregnant. The boy was now two years old and had never had contact with his father. Dad, however, had had a change of heart and was now very interested in pursuing a meaningful relationship with his child, so had petitioned for mediation to set up periods of physical placement. At first, having never been a parent, dad demanded that he be able to have placement of his son every other weekend from Friday through Sunday. The mother, knowing how her child, or any two year old for that matter, would react to a perfect stranger picking him up and taking him away from the only source of comfort and nurturance he had ever known, went into a panic and became very defensive.

Understanding that I needed to educate dad about child development, I explained the effect this would have on his son. Then, cautiously, I suggested the alternative that I had been formulating in my mind since he had started to speak.

I suggested a period of "getting to know dad," explaining that this could be rather difficult and uncomfortable for them, given the current state of their relationship. What it would involve, is dad "visiting" with his son several times a week, for an hour or two, at mom's home. Mom would initially be present at the visits, but after a couple of times, she would only be present at the beginning and end of the visits, leaving the room in the middle to make phone calls, throw in a load of laundry, etc.

While they were understandably reluctant and cautious to agree to such an arrangement, we got a calendar and plotted out, over the next three months, a series of progressively longer and more independent visits between father and son, ending with him taking the boy away for the day. I then instructed the couple on what to look for as signs from their son that they were moving too fast, as outlined in Chapter One, and advised them that at the end of three months, it would be up to them to get together and figure out a plan for how to increase the visits gradually, with the ultimate goal of the child spending alternate weekends with his father. If they were unable to agree on a future plan, I suggested that they request to be re-referred to me for mediation and we could work it out together. I have never heard from them again, so I am assuming they were able to work things out. But this is a perfect example of a parent (actually both parents in this case, given my suggestion) putting his own preferences, needs and comfort aside in order to accommodate what his child needed.

At these times, it will be a challenge for you to put the other parent's suggestions ahead of what is easiest and most convenient for you. But focus on what is best for your child. It may be helpful to refer to Chapter Six for a more complete discussion of the reasons behind these suggestions.

Remember, the time you are likely to be inconvenienced is miniscule compared to the lifetime of difficulty or damage that can be done to your child by insisting on what is easiest for you. Look at the whole picture and train yourself not to react negatively to suggestions offered by your children's other parent.

Handling Demands for Toys and Treats

Children are very smart and can be extremely self-centered. They will know if you are feeling guilty about seeing them less often or getting a divorce and may try to use that information "against you" by demanding toys and treats during placement times.

A common way for this to occur is by taking the kids to McDonald's for lunch, then on to Wal-Mart for a new toy or a new pair of jeans during one of your first placement times with them. This can continue when you are feeling at a loss for how to spend time with them, so you repeat this behavior. They can begin to assume that you need to do this every time you see them, something which few parents can afford. Even if you can afford it, most parents begin to feel used and taken advantage of after a few such excursions.

I will give this to you in black and white so you can copy it and share it with your children. *They do not need treats, meals out, ice cream, new clothes, or anything you can buy them, at each placement time.* If they try to convince you they do, you now have it on good authority, from me, that this is a *lie!*

What children *do* need is your time, your affection, your attention and discipline. They need you to teach them responsibility and self-control. The need you to care about them and they need to know they are important to you.

So, spread out the trips to McDonald's and Wal-Mart. Focus on spending time with and enjoying your children. Stay at home with them. Rent movies or make a pizza together from scratch. Look at or create photo albums of all of those pictures we all have lying around. Shoot baskets together, play catch or baseball. Go for a bike ride. Go rollerblading. Cook out on the grill or take a picnic to the park. In colder weather, go ice skating or skiing. You will notice that most of these events are inexpensive, or free. These are just a few ideas, but should be enough to help you start your own list.

Look for Creative Ways to Stay in Touch

Often parents with secondary placement struggle to figure out how to stay in touch with children when they only see them a few days a month. If you had previously been very involved in your children's lives, you may feel that you simply don't have enough time to truly be a parent to them. If you had not been very involved in parenting activities, you may feel that it is difficult or impossible to try to establish a significant and meaningful relationship on such a limited basis. Even if you share placement with your children's other parent and see them approximately one half of the time, the ideas below can give you some clever ideas for how to do all of the above.

Use the Telephone

Reaching out to touch your children with one of the oldest and most obvious ways to connect, is often one of the best ways to establish a relationship or maintain a connection. Get into the habit of calling them on a certain day or night of the week, just to catch up. If you see them only on weekends, it is difficult to remember all of the day to day events that make up their lives. They want to tell you these things; make it easy for them to do so by calling during the week as things happen that they can share them with you. They will feel more connected to you this way and actual placement times will be easier and more pleasurable because they will have more to tell you, i.e. follow up to the events they will remember sharing with you during the week.

Bill has always called Katie during the week just to visit with her and hear what's going on in her life. She is at the point now when she will often call him about an important event or situation before telling me. And this is after spending 14 1/2 years seeing her essentially four days per month. I would say he's done a remarkable job maintaining that relationship and making it a significant one for Katie. It can be difficult, and take some creative thinking, but it is by no means impossible. And it is certainly worth it, especially to your children!

Use the Computer

All children today are computer literate and many homes today contain computers. If your child has a computer available to them at their other home, and it is within your budget, get yourself online. If you cannot afford a computer, most public libraries have computers with internet access and you can use them to open an email account with which to contact your children.

I would recommend you do this if your children are on line, even if you live in the same town. Most kids these days are doing homework on the computer while also maintaining conversations through Instant Messaging programs with several of their friends, for several hours every evening. What an opportunity to connect!

For those of you unfamiliar with Instant Messaging, unlike typical email programs where you send the message and at some later point in time, it is received by the other party, who then responds, this is instantaneous. It is like having a telephone conversation online. You type a greeting, your child responds instantly. You can have an actual conversation that might not be possible via telephone as the phone line may be busy for hours on end because they are online, or they may beg off to do their homework. They can have an Instant Messaging conversation at the same time they are writing that paper or doing that project as it takes less time and they are doing it anyway with their friends.

This can be a wonderful opportunity to have spontaneous, unscheduled contact with them. You can pop in when you notice they are on-line and send them a quick note, or an "I love you. Hope you had a good day. I'm thinking about you!" What a neat way to connect!

Even if the response is, "Can't talk now, I'm too busy; have a big project due tomorrow," you got your point across. And don't take that response personally; It's par for the course for your typical 14-17 year old. You've still made a connection and gotten your point across.

This leads to another point I want to make about reaching out to your children. Make sure you choose your actions without expectation of return. Decide what you want to do and how you want to do it, without being dependent on your children's response for validation and appreciation. While I am not absolving them of any responsibility in your relationship with them, remember you are the adult in the relationship.

As their brains are not fully developed and matured until they are 18-25 years of age, they cannot and do not process information and events the same way as adults do.[1] They, therefore, cannot be held to the same standards of responsibility and accountability as an adult.   Be the adult in the relationship. Take on the responsibility for maintaining contact, even if your child doesn't meet you halfway. Most children will not do their half of the work in a relationship with a parent.   Their priorities are, and should be, their friends, extracurricular activities and school work, often in that order. Know this and don't take their indifference personally. This is one of the most effective and positive techniques for parenting teenagers—even when there is no divorce in the family.

Even if your children are not into Instant Messaging, or you choose not to participate in it, you can email them regularly to maintain contact. This is a terrific option if you live in different areas or have very different schedules. If you work second shift and use email to help you wind down after a stressful night at work, you can go online at 1:00 a.m. (hopefully your child won't be on!) and send them a message that they will receive the next time they sign on. Again, you've connected.

Parents using this technique are more likely to maintain regular contact because even if you think about them when you get home from work, you cannot call. Even if you make a mental or written note to call them the next time you are both awake and available, much can intervene to prevent this from happening. And it is usually a better contact if you are thinking of them—you have more to say and it is more genuine if it comes from the heart, rather than a reminder note.

Put Their Pictures on your Refrigerator

Keep reminders of your children around in your home. Paper your refrigerator with their drawings or school papers. If you have none, ask them to do a special one for you. Kids love this!

Contact the school if you haven't already to ask that school papers, report cards, school schedules be sent to you as well as to the other parent. Post these in a prominent place as well. They will keep you thinking of your children as you go through your life and plan other activities. In this way, you will be more likely to be there for your children. And you are more likely to call them about the "awesome test" they took in math that week. You will be sending the message that they are important to you even when they are not with you.

Attend Games, Practices, Recitals, School Events

Get involved in your children's lives by attending events that are meaningful for them. Even something as simple as sitting through a basketball practice can cement that bond. Your child can run over to you afterwards and ask, "Did you see that awesome shot?" And you are the parent there to share the experience with them.

Make it a priority to attend these events in your child's life. When you see the basketball or soccer schedule or the date of the dance recital or parent teacher conference, write it in your calendar and re-schedule any conflicting engagements as soon as you can. If your focus is your child's best interest, you will know what you must attend and what you need to rearrange.

In the 12 years Katie has been involved in dance, Bill has never missed a recital. This is even more impressive because his home is located in a city 45 minutes away from where the recital is held, his job requires that he work many weekends and that we've always arranged that on dance recital weekends Katie stays with me because with hair, makeup, pictures, dress rehearsals and two recital performances, she really needs to be in town. He has always brought her flowers to the recital and most often arranged to spend a little time with her afterwards. He can truly say he is putting her interests ahead of what would be easiest for him.

Write Letters

Letter writing is fast becoming a lost art. When you have something you want to share with your child or something significant to explain to them, writing a letter to them can be a good way to make that connection. It is also a kinder, gentler way to communicate with your children and one which they can hold onto forever. Share loving sentiments with them in writing so that they may keep them to review in times of stress, loneliness or whenever they are troubled.

If you are conveying news or an announcement to your children, a letter may not be the best way to communicate as they typically need to talk with you and at least have you available for questions about anything that will affect their lives. But getting home from school to a general newsy letter can be a wonderful surprise at the end of a difficult day.

Most children love to get mail and typically receive little. Cut out pictures from magazines; send small items of interest to them. Again, you are letting them know you are thinking of them and that they are important to you.

Find a Special Interest or Hobby to Share

Look for a hobby or an activity for you and your child to share. This can be the subject of your letters, telephone calls or emails as well as providing a way to spend time together on actual visits. It should be something that is interesting to both you and your child and, ideally, is something they do not do with the other parent.

Fathers of daughters and mothers of sons often struggle with this. But be creative. Even though I am not divorced from his father, I was searching for an activity to share with my son. This was a bit difficult because I don't get into playing with trucks or skateboarding, and I am not much interested in Pokemon. Then we discovered the Harry Potter books and we were hooked. Together we read the first four and are now eagerly awaiting the fifth volume. We also enjoy bike riding, rollerblading and, occasionally, canoeing together.

Being a divorced father, Bill struggled for awhile trying to find something to do with Katie. They finally discovered they shared an interest in auto racing and, when he started building a car, Katie was thrilled to discover that she knew more than most of her male classmates about how to repair and maintain it. Racing is something I am not interested in and her self esteem has improved by virtue of the fact that her father introduced her to it and shared it with her. Again, everybody benefits!

You may have to search a bit. Try out new things and don't be afraid to give up an interest that you investigate but neither of you is impressed with. Just the project of finding a shared interest or hobby can *be* your shared interest or mission for now. See how many different things you can try together!

Maximize Your Contact

Look creatively for ways to include your children in your lives other than at your regular placement times. If you know the other parent is working through a spring or Christmas break or, you notice in looking over your child's school calendar that you have asked the school to send you, that your child is off school one day next week, contact the other parent to see if it is possible to spend that day with your child. Obviously, if the other parent has made special plans for that day, don't stir up trouble by interfering with them. But they may be thrilled that your child can spend the time with you, especially if they have to work.

If you have special activities that you can include your children in as well, think about how you can do so. Even if your placement schedule is every other weekend, you may be able to arrange to pick them up every, or an occasional, Wednesday night to take them to the races or go for a bike ride or check out a new restaurant. The more you incorporate your children into your life, the more significant and meaningful the relationship becomes to them as well.

Look for Other Ways to Include Your Children in Your Life

A parent with primary physical placement is always thinking about the children. They are faced every day with what arrangements are in place for the kids, special activities or needs the children have that day or week, and the like. When your children are not living with you, it is much easier to forget about them for longer periods of time and to not include them in activities that they can enjoy or learn something from.

If you were a very involved parent during your marriage, it is often difficult to think much about your children when you are first living without them. Know that this pain will lessen and pass and you may find that you actually have more quality time with your kids after the divorce as you are making it more of a priority in your life. Help yourself to think about your children by keeping their pictures and things around. Work through the initial discomfort with this so that you can move beyond it to involving them more completely in your life.

When you are planning your holidays and vacation times, try to find things your children would enjoy doing and on which they can accompany you. Don't forget to connect with the other parent about the scheduling issues, even if this is difficult. Explore divorce mediation, even after the fact, if the other parent is resistant or unwilling to discuss vacation or additional placement times with you.

Support Child Support

Many children experience a reduced standard of living after parents separate. Paying support is one way to show your support for your child.

Some people struggle with the amount of child support they are required to pay, feeling that it is excessive. Many states have come up with formulas that they use to determine the dollar amount of child support to be paid and most often, if parents understand how these formulas were developed, they would more readily accept the child support determination.

In Wisconsin, a ten year study was done which investigated what percentage of a parent's gross wages in an intact family was typically spent on providing and caring for their children. This included money spent on housing, food, clothing, utilities, transportation, medical expenses, in addition to all the extras children receive. Their goal was to arrive at a formula for child support that would not penalize the child for being a product of divorce; a formula that would require parents to spend the same amount on the child as they would if the family was still together. What they discovered was that the minimum amount of each parent's gross salary spent on the children was as follows: 17 percent for one child, 25 percent for two children, 29 percent for three children and so on. This became our formula for determining child support.[2]

You will notice that even though these amounts may seem high, there are families in which the child is penalized, because the figures used were the minimum amounts spent. There will, thus, be cases in which children do receive less because their parents are divorced. But it was a valiant and reasonably scientific attempt to maintain children's standard of living after divorce, certainly a worthwhile goal!

One of the best ways to maintain your child's standard of living is to be an advocate for child support. Make sure your employer's name and address are listed correctly in your court documents so that they will promptly begin sending on the amounts due for your children's care. If you change jobs, make sure the new information gets to the court as well. Notify the other parent so that they will expect and can plan for a delay or brief interruption in support payments. This will help both of you provide for your children's needs.

Use Rituals to Help Your Children with Transitions

We established in Chapter Three that rituals help to stabilize a family and provide comfort and security for children. They can be used to help with placement times as well.

See Chapter Seven for a further discussion of how rituals can be incorporated into placement times and several examples to illustrate their usage. Look for rituals to make transitions and placement times easier for your children.

Keep Your Children Out of the Middle

As recommended for parents with primary placement, do not ask your children to report back to you about the other parent. This puts them in the middle and floods them with feelings of disloyalty and confusion.

This does not mean you can't ask if they had a good week or what they did during their free time with the other parent. It means you may not ask, "Did Mommy have any men at the house when you were there?" or "Did any ladies call at Daddy's house last week?" You know where you are going with these questions and it has nothing to do with your children or their well-being. They pick this up as well. Don't play this game.

Be Cautious with Suspicions of Abuse or Neglect

If you have good reason to believe that the other parent is being abusive or neglectful of your children, the Child Services Department in your community is typically available 24 hours a day. But be aware that in the heat of divorce, many former spouses are willing to think the worst of each other. Make sure you have a legitimate complaint before you make the call.

On the following page is a summary checklist of the main points in this chapter. Take time to look it over and give some thought to how you can best implement each of these points to aid your children in making their best adjustment to your divorce and help to make placement times easier on them.

I am staying involved with my children by:

❀ Showing up and taking my children at placement times,

❀ Being flexible and cooperative in making arrangements with my children's other parent,

❀ Being sensitive to my child's specific placement needs,

❀ Not buying their affection with treats and toys, but truly spending quality time with them doing activities they enjoy,

❀ Looking for other ways to stay in touch:
  ~Calling them at appropriate times,
  ~Maintaining contact via the computer,
  ~Putting their pictures on the my refrigerator,
  ~Attending games, recitals and other events,
  ~Writing letters
  ~Looking for a special hobby or interest to share,
  ~Maximizing my contact at other times when ever I can,
  ~Keeping my eyes open for other creative ways to stay in touch,

❀ Supporting and advocating for my children's other parent to get the child support to which they are entitled,

❀ Using rituals to help my children with transitions

❀ Taking care to keep the children out of the middle of my relationship with their other parent,

❀ Giving the other parent the benefit of the doubt when appropriate.

"The best cure for anger is delay."

~Seneca, A.D.63

CHAPTER 9

BUT ALL WE DO IS YELL
AT EACH OTHER!

*How to Re-Structure Your Relationship
with Your Children's "Other Parent"*

Watching silently from the doorway, Sam and Meghan see
their mother grab the phone on the second ring. "Why
are you calling me again?" they hear her shout into the
receiver. "Listen to me—or I'm taking you back to court!" She utters a
few profane words, as well as several unflattering names, and then
slams the receiver down, only to have it promptly begin ringing again.
They watch as she lets the machine pick up the call, revealing another
string of profanity in an angry, yet familiar, male voice. Sam leans
over and puts his arm around a frightened Meghan, saying, "Come
on, sis—I'll read you a story." Meghan pushes him away and runs to
her room.

This is the part of the class that gets the greatest
amount of positive feedback! It is initially met with eye rolls
and groans, but participants quickly start listening and
thinking about how what I say applies to their own relationships. By the end of this section, and it is with this that I end
the class—I like them to leave with these ideas fresh in their
minds—I can see hope in their eyes that transformation is
possible in their relationships as well.

And indeed it is! These are some simple ideas that any partner can practice individually, even if the other person persists in their provocative or conflictual behavior. This is a section that was not included the first few times I taught the class, but my groups gave me the information I needed to understand that it was necessary.

As any good teacher should do, I ask every person attending my class to provide "feedback" about the class in the form of a short questionnaire, similar to the one provided at the end of this book in Appendix E. While I am unable to accommodate all suggestions provided (i.e. structure classes focused just on a certain age-group) this was one suggestion, arising from a number of different Feedback Sheets, that was easy enough, yet crucial, to accommodate.

The comments from those parents included comments, such as, "Your suggestions about negotiation and scheduling are all well and good, but what if my ex and I can't even be in the same room with each other without screaming at each other? How are we supposed to negotiate anything?"

I have worked with enough divorced and divorcing couples to know that there are some couples for which this is true, at least while the divorce is pending. There is so much hurt, frustration and tension between them, that the slightest untoward comment sets them against each other. This is a problem, but it is by no means insurmountable. This is what I tell them.

Essentially, we get out of a relationship what we put into it. And a marital, or other intimate relationship, is going to have to undergo some significant changes as it is coming apart. For example, the two of you may have been best friends in the not too distant past. Perhaps, as is typical of many couples, you have shared all of your hopes and dreams, along with many of your thoughts and feelings with your partner. Now, they typically are not interested in that information, but even if they are, they are not entitled to it anymore. Nor are you entitled to ask those things of your former partner. Those issues have become "off limits" in your new relationship.

It is changing this mindset that can cause difficulty

among even the most amicable couples. The game and all of the rules, on which you have relied for all the years of your relationship, have changed. Getting on board with the new rules takes some work and some time. It is this process of adjustment that causes difficulty, largely due to the feelings of hurt, rejection and guilt that are often triggered by these topics. It is normal to feel like you just don't know how to act around that other person. And to feel like you don't know them anymore.

Being unprepared for this change makes it more difficult and increases the chance of a struggle when it is happening. I like to make parents aware that this change is necessary and give them some ideas for behaviors they can try out to make this adjustment less painful.

Disengage In All Areas Except Parenting

Perhaps the most important issue divorcing parents need to deal with is how to relate to the other parent. Though they are divorcing, the mere fact that they have children together means that they will be forced to deal with each other, in one capacity or another, for, in most cases, the rest of their lives. While much of this contact will appropriately revolve around the children, the transition of moving their relationship from one of intimate partners to one of partners in the business of co-parenting their children does not come naturally to most people.

Given all the changes discussed in the past few pages, it is understandable that this is difficult and confusing for couples. And the tension of a divorce, dividing children and property and negotiating maintenance and support certainly don't help. But you *can* make it easier! What follows is how to do it!

Create Clear Boundaries for the New Relationship

It is important to create some emotional distance in your relationship with your children's other parent. To that end, you will want and need to break with the way you have interacted with each other for a number of years and to interact in a new way.

As couples live together, it is common for each to take on different roles and responsibilities in their day to day lives. She may mow the lawn; he might take on the laundry. He might cook or bake special meals; she might shovel snow in the winter. Because we all get so busy just handling our day to day responsibilities, especially now that most families have both parents in the workforce, it is just easier to take responsibility for the same things on a regular basis.

When the marriage ends, however, one of the most important adjustments the couple must make is NOT relying on each other in the same ways for the same things they have for many years. One of the best and most important changes you can make is not relying on the other parent for any of the tasks, except parenting, they previously assumed in the marriage. This includes making home cooked meals or special treats, car and home maintenance, laundry, bill paying, lawn care, snow shoveling and the like. In the long run, it is easier, healthier and cheaper to find a new plumber, mechanic or whatever than to count on your former partner to fulfill these responsibilities.

The one temporary exception to this is that while the divorce is pending, even though only one of you may be living in the family home, both of you may be responsible for the upkeep and maintenance of the home because you both technically still own the property. Your court order may have given these responsibilities to the person living there. At any rate, if you still share this role, you may be responsible for some of these tasks until your divorce is final. However, on the date of the final hearing, most often one of you is declared the owner of the home. At that moment, your joint responsibilities unrelated to parenting cease.

Be sure to look closely and carefully at your reliance on the other parent. It can be very subtle. When I initially typed these words in preparation for adding them to my class, I had been divorced approximately Eight years. I realized, in thinking about sharing this information with others, that I was still counting on Bill to perform one of the roles he had taken on in our marriage. I was surprised at myself! And not a little embarrassed!

While we were married, Bill worked in sales at a large television, stereo, furniture and appliance dealer in Wisconsin. His area, for the greater portion of his time there, was insurance replacement sales. He worked with large accounts, such as schools and hospitals that were looking to replace a large quantity of televisions, video cassette recorders and stereo equipment. As a result of this work, he knew just about everything there was to know about these items and, in fact, had always had a real aptitude for that kind of information. He could tell which were the best brands to buy, what features to expect, how much to pay and, in many cases, how to fix something that wasn't working properly.

Of course, given the vast amount knowledge he had in this area and his work in this field, electronics specialist was a role he played in our marriage. He decided what we bought and when, what we paid for it and how. This was fine with me as I have no aptitude and little interest in this equipment. As long as it plays when I turn it on, I'm good. In fact, one of my least favorite times of the year is when daylight savings time changes, because then I have to figure how to set whichever of my clocks I plan to actually use. I have given up on both of my VCRs and simply pull something over the front of them so they stop blinking at me! I just don't retain that kind of information easily and It's just not important enough to me to worry about.

But now, here I was, divorced from the man eight years and still counting on him to play that role for me. When Terry and I moved into our house in 1989, I was on the phone to Bill on moving day asking him how to hook up the television so the sound would come out of the stereo speakers. When we were looking for a little TV for the kitchen in 1991, I again called Bill to ask him what brands were most reliable and what I should expect to pay for it. When we were looking for a new stereo in 1994, I again called on Bill.

Bill never complained about this imposition on his time. He was always polite and courteous and answered my questions. My husband Terry didn't mind that I was counting on Bill for this information; he has even *less* interest in electronic equipment than I do! If *any* of our clocks are going to get changed during daylight savings time, I'm going to be the one doing it!

But the fact of the matter was it was me imposing these demands on Bill. It was not a mutual arrangement we had set up, such as my sharing counseling information with him in return for him providing the data I was seeking, for example. As fun as that could have been it didn't happen. No mutual arrangement existed at all; it was all imposed *on* him *by* me.

I vowed at that point that I would not put Bill in that role again. I would seek my information from another, more willing, source. And I have been true to my word. I will also tell you that since that time, I have taken some risks: we have purchased two televisions, two VCRs and, two Christmases ago, a DVD player! And we have done just fine.

As a humorous aside, last Christmas Terry and I were trying valiantly to figure out how to transfer some camcorder tapes onto VCR tapes. After an hour or so, Katie came home and within 15 minutes, she had used a mirror behind the VCR to hook up cables and was transferring the tapes for us! She was 15 at the time. I guess she inherited that aptitude from her father!

Formalize Parenting Roles and Responsibilities

Some couples do very well working out placement schedules and parenting roles and responsibilities on a day by day or week by week basis. For other couples, however, especially while they are in the throes of divorce, this is an impossible dream. For these couples, it is often preferable to put plans in writing and work out a regular schedule of responsibilities. Feel free to use the Parenting Plan discussed in Chapter Six, and included in Appendix D, as a format for your arrangements if you find it helpful.

Also, if you find yourself on the phone every other day making arrangements, or working something out with the other parent, you are not getting the emotional distance you need from the marital relationship. You are still having too much contact—even if you are just talking about the kids.

Build some distance into your relationship. Put a pad of paper and pen by the phone. Whenever you are tempted to call to discuss an issue, write it down and limit your calls to one or two per week. Or discuss the issues when the other parent calls you. Two calls per week is adequate to deal with most of the issues likely to arise with your children that the two of you need to discuss. It is better for both of you to limit your contact to this amount.

Further, if you are at all in conflict, the more clearly parental roles and responsibilities are spelled out, the better. Then everyone's expectations will be the same and there will be fewer occasions for future conflicts. Whenever you make some arrangement or agreement, reduce it to writing, perhaps on the Parenting Plan or some similar form, both sign and date it and make sure each of you has a copy. This, also, can eliminate future conflicts.

Communicate As Business Associates

Working out the details of your parenting arrangements will require talking and negotiating. This is when your attempts and resolve to form a different kind of relationship can be tested. However, there is much you can do to increase you chances of a successful transition of a co-parenting relationship.

Imagine yourselves as a "Parenting Coalition," something similar to a business partnership or team. You will want to work out basic rules for your children as best you can, just as you would in a business setting, and both of you will have input into the guidelines regarding new issues your children are facing, such as getting a driver's license or starting a dating relationship, especially if the two of you have never dealt with these issues before. The more the two of you can work together regarding these and other issues, the easier the transition will be for your children.

While working out the details of your parenting plan, it usually works best to establish a businesslike atmosphere for your discussions. Try to meet in a public place when discussing volatile issues. It is possible that having a cup of coffee in a local restaurant, where you can be observed by members of the public, will keep both of you on your best behavior.

Imagine, before you arrive at your destination or, if you are talking on the phone, before you pick up the telephone, that you are actually talking to a business associate. I don't mean your best friend at work, with whom you share all of your deep, dark secrets. I am referring to a co-worker with whom you have a business-like relationship, someone you know well enough to make polite conversation with, but would never dream of asking, "So, what time did you get home Saturday night?"

Remember, you no longer have the right to that information.

Discuss only practical, child-related matters. Steer clear of personal, controversial topics such as your marriage, spending habits, new relationships, and the like. You must change the idea that you have the right to comment on these issues with your former spouse. This time is all about gaining emotional distance from that person and those types of issues. Distance yourself during these discussions, as if you are in a business meeting, even if the other person says or does something provocative. Ask yourself how you would respond to such behavior if you were in an actual business meeting. This is an ideal gauge for your choice of actions.

Treat the other parent with respect and expect to be treated the same way. Take the "high road" in your responses. Refrain from sarcasm or digs, even if the other party uses them. Then reward yourself liberally with a special treat! You deserve it—this is not an easy thing. One thing we learn being married to someone is how to push their buttons. You are the two best experts on how to do this for each other. But *don't*! Your children will pay the price.

Another technique that has worked for many couples is to pretend that a third party is present with the two of you that you greatly respect and hold in high esteem, such as your priest, minister or a friend of the family. It should be someone that you want to convince that you are the epitome of rationality. Keeping this person in mind, don't say or do anything you would not want to do in front of this observer while you converse with your children's other parent.

"I often regret that I have spoken; never that I am silent."

~Publilius Syrus

Redefine the Relationship in Your Own Thinking

To establish true change in this relationship, you will need to take steps to think about it differently than you have been accustomed to doing. The techniques listed below should help you to do just that—modify how you think of your children's other parent and your relationship with her.

Quit Using Negative Labels

A key step in restructuring your relationship is to decide what to call your children's other parent from now on. An important consideration is how what you call that person affects your treatment of him. For instance, if you think to yourself, "I have to talk to that witch today," or "I have to see that jerk tonight", how do you think you will respond to him? Think for a moment just how willing and agreeable you would be to working things out with "the jerk" or "the witch." Will you value their opinions or their point of view? Will you treat them with respect? Probably not. You are setting yourself up for failure by approaching a discussion with that attitude.

Not sure? Imagine, if you will, your home telephone ringing. You look down at the caller ID and recognize the other parent's name and number. Your first thought is, "Great, now I have to talk to that jerk (witch) again!" You pick up the receiver and politely say, "Hello." When a request is made from the other side to switch placement times, just how willing and accommodating are you likely to be with that mind set? What is best for your children? If you do not accommodate, how likely are you to receive a favor next week when it is you doing the asking? What are the implications for your long-term relationship with this person? Profound questions to explore. And again, what is best for your children?

One of the most important and challenging opportunities many parents have in eliminating negative labels is when speaking with members of their support system: co-workers, family and friends. Even if you start out with the best of intentions, because of their support and empathy for you and, perhaps, because of past conversations you have had with them, you might, with the best of intentions mention the other parent's name. The response could be something like, "So, what's that jerk done now?" It could take everything in your power to change the tone of your conversation by calmly responding, "Well, Bill took a day of vacation to take the kids to the beach last week," even if you had been about to say something negative.

Most people will get the idea with only your subtle messages that you have changed how you are talking about the other parent. A few will not and you will need to be more direct, saying something like, "I've realized it isn't good for me to talk so negatively about Bill; and it certainly isn't good for the kids. So I've turned over a new leaf and am really working on changing my attitude about him (her)." If they still don't catch on, avoid them as much as possible until you are beyond being influenced by their attitudes.

Think of the Other Parent as Your Business Partner or Co-Parent

You will have noticed that throughout this book, and indeed throughout the four hour class that I teach, I refer to Bill as Katie's father or, simply, as Bill. There are other names or terms I could have used. But it keeps me more open, respectful and cooperative if I think of him as my daughter's father. That's what is best for Katie—and for me, too.

Give some thought to how you talk and think about that other parent. If you find yourself thinking and speaking negatively, experiment with these ideas by trying out your new, more positive way of thinking about that person and see if it doesn't make a difference in your attitude, as well as in your treatment of him. Don't be surprised if he notices this and comments about it to you.

This is the one section of this class that I get the greatest number of telephone calls about—well after the class is over. I make myself available for questions over the phone, in the event something arises down the road. The calls I get in response to this issue usually start out, "You won't believe how different my relationship with my kid's father (mother) is and how much nicer he is being." When I investigate a little further, it is usually after the caller has made some changes in their attitude toward that person. This is no surprise—and it can happen for you, too.

> *"Wisdom is divided into two parts: a) having a great deal to say, and b) not saying it."*
>
> ~Anonymous

Focus On the Present, Not the Past

You will notice that throughout this book, I haven't even referred to Bill as my ex-husband. While he is that, I believe that this term refers to the past, and in a negative way. I prefer to focus on the present and to talk about Bill as who he is now: my daughter's father, Bill and Katie's dad.

The more you focus on the present, the better you will feel and the more you will adapt to the changes that have happened in your life. People who stay focused on the past tend to immobilize themselves to act for the present and the future. They also tend to be negative and unhappy because they are stuck reliving events that they can't change and have no control over.

Empower yourself. Focus on the present. It is in your hands!

Build a New Life for Yourself!

For the same reasons, we want to focus on the new positive changes that are happening in our lives, because the better we feel about ourselves, the more positively we find ourselves dealing with the other parent and with our children as well. Usually, as people feel better about themselves and are successful at rebuilding a new life, they find themselves better able to establish more comfortable and less conflictual relationships with their children's other parent.

It will probably be helpful to work on rebuilding your self-esteem. Most people experiencing divorce have taken a hit in the esteem area, because as a marriage is breaking up, things are said and done that are harmful to us emotionally. Anything we can do to improve how we feel about ourselves will help us deal more positively with others with whom we come in contact. See Chapter 12 for some ideas about how to do this.

It also helps to work on creating an identity separate from your former spouse. This could take a bit of work, depending on the length of the marriage, but will most likely involve developing new interests and building a wide network of friendships. This will be discussed in greater length in a future book which will focus on personal adjustment after divorce. Contact the author for more information about this upcoming title.

Let Your Post-Divorce Relationship Develop

After the old ways of relating to each other have been eliminated and new patterns and behaviors established, you will have achieved the emotional distance you need from this relationship. You are then free to write your own ticket for it. Whatever your relationship with this other parent looks like down the road is completely up to the two of you.

If, a year from now, you and your co-parent realize that you are the only two people in your town who enjoy sky-diving at midnight on the first Thursday of each month, by all means, share that hobby. Or, if you decide to get re-involved romantically, that is up to you as well. Review Chapter Two about how to handle this with your children.

I am aware of many different arrangements that agreeable couples have stumbled on after they have become divorced. One couple I knew became platonic roommates. Their romantic relationship of 20 years didn't work out, but they realized they did very well living together.

Another couple purchased a duplex together so their children would only have one backyard to play in. Yet another couple became re-involved romantically but chose not to marry a second time.   Others do remarry.   As I stated previously, whatever your relationship looks like is completely up to the two of you.

So, get your distance now. Look at how you are relating. Make it more of a business relationship—you *are* in the business of co-parenting your children, after all. Work on making your attitude toward this other parent more positive and set your own course for your new life. Later on, reconnect as you wish. It may be just as co-parents; it may be as much more. The rest is up to you.

As you struggle to make these changes, however, be gentle with yourself. Your progress may not be steady but don't get discouraged. This is a difficult change to negotiate. Relapses are common. The feelings of attachment, attraction, love and anger often hang on. Find your own ways of dealing with these emotions, independent of this other parent. But don't be too hard on yourself. You're only human, after all. Just do the best you can and keep your focus positive. It will come in due time. In the meantime, use the checklist on the following page to check your progress.

"No act of kindness, no matter how small, is ever wasted."

~Aesop

I am taking responsibility for my role in changing this relationship by:

❀ Disengaging in all areas except parenting. *My most difficult expectations to change include:*

_____

_____

_____

~I am creating clear boundaries for this new relationship by _____

~We are formalizing parenting roles and responsibilities
by _____

~We will have contact with each other to discuss
parenting issues as follows:

_____

❀ Communicating as business associates. *These are the changes I have made to help accomplish this:*

_____

_____

❀ Redefining how I think about this relationship. *This is how I have decided to refer to my children's other parent in the future:*

_____

_____

❀ I think of this person as a business associate.

❀ I am focused on the present, not the past. *These are some of the changes I have made in my life that I am happy about:*

_____

_____

❀ I am working on building a new life for myself, independent of the other parent. *These are some of the exciting opportunities I am looking forward to:* _____

_____

_____

CHAPTER 10

GETTING OFF TO A GOOD START!

When and How to Introduce a New Partner To Your Children

Twelve year old Josh slammed the door of the room he shared with his ten year old brother at his mother's apartment. Having just arrived to spend the weekend with her, she had greeted him with the "wonderful news" that her new friend, whom he could call "Uncle Bob", would be spending the weekend with them, joining in all the activities the three of them had planned to do together. Josh remembers the last "Uncle Bob" he'd had to share his mother with. That one had been named "Dave" and his mother had spent the entire weekend mooning over him—barely even noticing he existed. She'd even forgotten to make his dinner on Saturday night because she and Dave went out together. Josh turned up the stereo, daring his mother to confront him about the noise.

As a therapist working with divorced and divorcing couples, I am often asked, "Is it OK to introduce my new partner to my children?" In most cases, if you are asking this questions, are recently separated and currently in the process of a divorce which has not yet occurred, the answer is a resounding *NO!* Most persons experiencing the throes of a divorce are in no position to even be thinking about a new long term relationship yet. They have too much baggage left over from the marriage to be able to create a healthy new relationship. And if you are not thinking the relationship will be a long term or significant one for you, you have no business even thinking of introducing your children to this person—you are just buying them another, yet guaranteed, loss. Review Chapter Three for more specific information on this.

As I tell my Parenting Through Divorce classes, there is an entire process to adjusting to the end of a long term relationship. If you short-circuit that process, you end up buying yourself more trouble and grief in the long run, and taking much longer to get through it. In addition, you will most likely end up with a bumpier road and more loss, yourself, than just putting off getting involved until you are through it.

I want to highlight some of the steps in adjusting to the ending of a marriage, but want to reinforce that this is just an overview. I plan to write an entire book on this topic in the near future, but until that time, I refer you to *Rebuilding*, written by Bruce Fisher (Impact, 1981). This book will give you a more comprehensive and detailed view of the steps that must be taken to be ready for a new relationship. This chapter will highlight some of the most common and difficult of these steps.

Adjusting to the End of Your Marriage

While this book does not have the room to discuss the entire adjustment process, nor even to thoroughly do justice to the stages being identified here, it will give readers an idea of some of the most important issues and complexities in making this adjustment in their lives. It is hoped that merely identifying some of the stumbling blocks and fleshing them out a little will provide enough information to peak the curiosity of the individual experiencing divorce so that she will seek this information in a more complete fashion elsewhere than this volume. I repeat, we cannot begin to do this justice here—just give you a flavor of the experience.

Denial

One of the first emotions people identify in response to their divorce is denial. Most aren't aware at the time that it is denial they are describing, but I label it for them because I believe it is helpful and healthy to identify what you are dealing with. Denial was first explained and described in our discussion of the Grief Process in Chapter One. Please review that discussion briefly now to refresh your memory as you will encounter a number of other stages of the grieving process in this adjustment period. This should be no surprise as you are experiencing a loss as you walk the path of your divorce. Even if the divorce was your choice, you are experiencing a loss, or a major change, in your life and should expect to grieve it.

Denial looks different, depending whether you are the person leaving the relationship, or the person being left. If you are leaving, denial often starts two, five or ten years before the separation, when you are thinking to yourself that the marriage is not what you had hoped. It is my professional experience that the decision to leave a marriage is seldom, if ever, a quick one.

In most cases, the person leaving has been convincing themselves for years that things will change, get better, etc. The leaving is what happens when the denial is gone. It is the denial that pulls the wool over the eyes of persons seeing insurmountable problems in relationships years earlier. It is the act of convincing oneself to hang in there because things will get better, when they know at gut level that nothing will ever change; they will never get what they need from the relationship.

Denial can also feel like shock, numbness or a complete lack of feeling. This is often the experience of the person on the receiving end of the divorce announcement. Many times that person is unaware of the depth of the unhappiness on the part of their partner. Or, if they are aware, they believe that the situation is workable or "Not that bad." Most feel the shock when the word is uttered and travel the path of the divorce experience with that feeling not far from the forefront of their minds.

The second way denial expresses itself to persons being left is convincing them that reconciliation is imminent. I have never had a first session with a client who was surprised by divorce papers that did not include some version of the statement, "I know we could work this out; if I could just get her to come and see you."

In many cases, the partner has been asking to go to counseling for years and, over time, with no change and no effort, her feelings have dwindled to nothing. By the time he is willing to go to a therapist, there is no point, unless it is to improve their post-divorce co-parenting relationship. But in most cases, it is my job to help him work through this early denial until he can see the reality of his situation.

Loneliness

Immediately after dealing with the denial, and in many cases, right along with it, is the intense loneliness experienced by one who is accustomed to living with a partner for years but who is now separated and living alone. This is experienced equally by persons leaving and persons being left. In my work to prepare people for the intensity of this feeling, I often hear, "I've spent my whole life living his lifestyle. I will welcome my time alone." While many people assume persons leaving are ready and prepared for it, I get as many calls on my crisis phone from persons leaving as those being left. "I feel so alone. I don't know what to do."

One mistake many couples make when this intense loneliness hits is to explore reconciliation. The person leaving thinks, "Maybe it wasn't so bad after all. I could learn to live with it." The person left is still in the throes of denial and thinks this is just great!

However, this is absolutely the worst time ever to consider reconciliation. And these are the wrong reasons to do so. Many couples who reconcile at this point do so because a "known evil", as it were, is less frightening and less threatening than all of the unknowns of what life may bring in the future. Most of these reconciliation attempts are short-lived and unsuccessful. Don't short-change yourself. Experience and revel in the excitement of infinite possibilities!

This is also another very dangerous time to enter inappropriate relationships with new partners. We are in pain and alone. We meet someone else who is lonely. We cling to each other for dear life, because it feels better than being alone. Six months later we wake up and wonder what we ever saw in that person. We have nothing in common and no shared interests. But now we have typically bought ourselves and, often, our children another loss to work through.

Fear

Many fears haunt the newly separated person. The most common is, "Will anyone ever want/love/care about/desire me again?" This anxiety is almost universal among persons experiencing divorce.

I know this from both personal and professional experience. I felt it myself and I have heard it from virtually every divorcing person I have ever spoken with.

Add to this the myriad of other fears that assault one who is experiencing major life changes at or near mid-life. Everything from "what will tomorrow bring?" to "will I be able to make it without him/her or financially? These fears are simply too numerous to mention in this book.

Working through this step involves facing and coming to terms with all of these fears. Those who don't do this, end up in a relationship to assuage their fears—and little else. Don't settle. In the long run it is easier and much less costly, financially and emotionally, to simply face and work through your fears. Use the thinking process described in Chapter Three to help you with this.

Guilt/Rejection

These emotions are funny because they are both felt by persons leaving and being left in a relationship. Of course, those who are leaving feel most guilty and those being left feel most rejected. This much is just common sense.

However, it surprises many people to learn that both parties experience both emotions. Those leaving also feel somewhat rejected because their partners were not able to be the kind of spouse they needed them to be. And those being left feel guilty for not being the kind of partner their spouse needed.

Working through these emotions before getting into

another relationship is essential or, again, you will most likely end up with a relationship that meets the need you are stuck on. Therefore, you may end up with a relationship where the only thing you have in common with the new person is occasional companionship, even though you spend little time together because you have no interests in common. The relationship eventually fizzles out, but, in the meantime, you have co-mingled assets and, often, children, so everybody now loses.

Depression

We have discussed the depression/withdrawal stage of the grieving process briefly in Chapter One. It is a common part of the adjustment process to experience symptoms of depression, including sleep and appetite disturbances, weight loss or gain, teariness, fatigue, hopelessness, tiredness, anhedonia (activities you used to find enjoyable do not please you anymore), suicidal thoughts, irritation, memory and concentration problems and anger and temper disturbances.

Most of the persons I see who are experiencing divorce qualify for one of the DSM IV diagnoses for Depression, even though the cause is situational.[1] Many find that they benefit from short term therapy and/or the use of an antidepressant medication. It is not essential, but is often helpful to take the edge off of the very painful emotional situations people are facing. It is obvious that anyone suffering from these symptoms has no business getting involved in a new relationship.

Anger

There is an element of anger in the divorce adjustment process that is quite different from normal, ordinary, everyday anger. It contains strong elements of bitterness, vengefulness and resentment even if these are not typically part of an individual's personality.   Often friends and supporters who have not experienced the end of a significant relationship cannot understand how you can feel this way about someone you once professed to deeply care about. It doesn't matter if they understand. Know that this is normal and that you must work through it.

There are a number of ways to work through this process.

Most involve feeling and expressing these emotions, whether in writing, verbally or both. Know that expressing them to the object of your affection will most likely not have positive results, so if you express them verbally, do it with someone who cares to listen, and can empathize and provide the support you need and deserve. But whatever you do, get it out. Do not hold onto this anger or it will poison all of your future relationships. Express it; regurgitate it so that it does not become toxic to you.

Letting Go

Withdrawal involves making peace with the ending of your relationship. You may initially find yourself looking for your spouse's car at the places you used to frequent or checking for their number on your caller ID. When you are no longer engaging in these behaviors, or you find yourself doing them less often or with less intensity, you are beginning to let go of this relationship.

When you are ready to let go, take out all of the mementos of your relationship together: your wedding pictures, special keepsakes, souvenirs from trips you have taken and the like. As you go through them one by one, you may cry, sob, scream, shout, mourn or rejoice. But you are expressing strong emotion; get it out and let it go. You will know when you have let go when you no longer feel any strong emotion connected with your former partner: not love or hate, not fondness or irritation.

Remember, the opposite of love is not hate, but indifference. Some couples, who have difficulty expressing intense emotion positively, express it negatively, by bickering, fighting or arguing. Choose not to do this; identify and settle these emotions in a positive manner. ⌐

Responsibility

Any relationship involves two or more people. Each has a role in determining what happens in the relationship.

Taking responsibility involves nothing more than identifying your role in what happened in your relationship. This does not mean finding someone to blame. But taking a good, hard look at what you did and didn't do and making some decisions about how it affected your relationship.

The second part of this stage involves looking forward. After you determine what you were responsible for, you make some decisions about what you want to be the same and different in future relationships. Then you take appropriate action.

For example, if you determine you were irresponsible in this relationship, you may decide to be more responsible in future relationships. Then you identify and practice more responsible behaviors.

Most people are not able to work through this issue until later in the divorce process. Normally, before we are able to take a good hard look at our role, we have to work through the anger, hurt and depression we are faced with first and usually make some headway at letting go of the emotional attachment to this partner and this relationship. Know that this stage is coming, but do not rush to it. Lay this important groundwork first.

Self-Esteem

The last emotion we spend time on in my divorce adjustment group is rebuilding our self-esteem. We all get more than enough negative messages about ourselves every day. When we are experiencing a divorce, this only multiplies, because as a marriage is breaking up, things are said and done that are harmful to us emotionally. We take a beating during this process and need to take steps to feel better about ourselves.

One of the last activities we do together in my group is to share one piece of positive feedback about each of the other group members. These are written on separate sheets of paper, read aloud to this person, then collected and given to him. That way, in his darkest moments, and we all have them, he can pull them out, read them over and acknowledge that someone who started out as a perfect stranger, and met him at one of the worst, most painful and difficult times of his life, had some very nice, positive things to say about him. It is a wonderfully soothing exercise. Even if you cannot locate a similar group, see if you can't find someone to give you positive feedback about yourself as well.

"No one can make you feel inferior without your consent."

~Eleanor Roosevelt

Why It Is Important to Work Through These Stages

As we have previously stated, if you do not work through these issues as you are experiencing your divorce, you will find yourself dealing with them later. One of the men attending my divorce adjustment group confessed that he had been divorced for ten years. When his wife left him for another man, he was so devastated that he threw himself into the lives of his two children. That worked to distract and occupy him for awhile. When his children were 17 and 18, however, it became apparent that they would be leaving home. Deciding that he did not want to be alone forever, he took advantage of that opportunity to look at some of the emotions he had not faced for quite a long time and joined our group.

For you as well, it is possible to avoid dealing with these stages for awhile. But you are only delaying the inevitable. Take a lesson from my client—face the issues now while they are fresh, rather than later when they become embedded in established patterns of behavior.

What You Can Do To Accomplish This Adjustment

There are many ways to deal with this adjustment process. Many people find it helpful to join a group of other persons experiencing divorce at the same time that will walk you through some of these experiences. This will also have the effect of forming a support group of others sharing similar experiences with you, which can be substantially more helpful than relying on your traditional support system, many of whom may never have experienced the loss of a love relationship and can be of limited assistance.

In choosing a group, you want to find one run by a competent therapist. Pay attention to your gut reaction to the person who will be facilitating the group. This will give you some good information. We often intuitively pick up information about people, but are not immediately aware of why we either like or feel uneasy about someone. The more you can give credence to this reaction, the better you will be serving yourself.

The therapist should also ascertain that your spouse will not be attending the same group. Even if the two of you are on the best of terms, this would inhibit open and honest sharing of emotions and reactions for both of you. You would both be better off in another group.

Other persons find that they prefer individual counseling to working in a group. You can accomplish much the same thing individually, in terms of working through the issues, but are then deprived of the benefit of a support group.

Many people do fine adjusting to divorce with no outside assistance. Some people pick up self-help books, such as this one or *Rebuilding* (Impact, 1981). I have always been a firm believer in self-help reading. I think we can learn many things from reading a book, most importantly a new approach to a problem or challenge we are facing. Take and use what seems to fit you; leave what does not.

Whether you choose to seek help, in terms of a group, a therapist or a book, *do* take the time and trouble to express those emotions now, or you will be facing them again later and often with greater pain and complications.

"If we really want to love, we must learn how to forgive."

~Anonymous

How to Know When You Are Ready for a New Relationship

Before even considering another long term relationship, you

want to be free of all emotional reactivity toward your former partner. If your spouse can still "push your buttons", you are still reactive and attached to him. This is a good indicator of whether or not it is too soon for a new relationship.

Almost without fail, anyone in the process of a divorce is not ready for another meaningful relationship. Give yourself time to grieve and work through the emotions above before taking on another challenge.

Another way to gauge this is to read through the discussion above. If you can, in all honesty, say that you are no longer affected by any of these emotions or reactions, you may be ready. But, be honest. Don't just convince yourself of what you want to be true. Take the time to really examine your feelings and reactions or you will pay the price later—perhaps with a second or third divorce.

Most people take a year or more to achieve a true readiness for another relationship. If you are leaving your marriage, and you have been contemplating this for the past five years, you will be farther along in the adjustment process than someone who was surprised by divorce papers yesterday. But both of you still probably have some work to do to truly be ready for another healthy significant relationship.

"The cart before the horse is neither beautiful nor useful."

~Henry David Thoreau

Why Kids React to Parents, Dating Behavior

There are a number of reasons children react to the dating behaviors of their parents. If this behavior occurs during the divorce process, most children are still in the throes of their own adjustment process. They want and need you to be focusing on them, both now and for a good while. Many parents erroneously ask these suffering children to share them with a new love interest, so that the children are left to tag along while these newly infatuated parents are doting on a new partner. Talk about a recipe for disaster. Hand the child the biggest jolt of his life, then virtually ignore him to fawn over a new love. This is the quickest way to a sabotaged relationship that I am aware of.

Another reason that children react to dating behavior is that during the divorce process, it feels disloyal to their other parent. Most kids are well aware that the divorce is not yet final, so to go along with one parent being with someone new means they are not sticking up for their other parent, who may be alone, hurting and emotionally dependent on them. Remember, the child is just adjusting to this new state of the family. Don't push him to accept you with a new partner before he comes to terms with the end of the marriage.

The third most common reason for kids, reactions to parents dating behavior is that they are then forced to think of their parents as sexual beings, even if nothing is happening in that realm. In the context of marriage, kids can often pretend this doesn't exist. But when a parent is dressing up to meet a new love interest, the sexual tension is apparent. They may be preening in front of a mirror and trying on different clothes to look their best. All of these behaviors underscore the sexuality that then becomes apparent to the children.

When Is It OK to Introduce Your Kids to a New Partner

There are a number of criteria to determine whether or not you are ready to have a new significant relationship and whether your children are ready to meet this person. A number of these are as follows.

Is Your Divorce Over?

If your divorce is not finalized yet, you are most likely not even ready yourself to be involved in a long term relationship. The exception to this is if you have been contemplating leaving your marriage for five years and have really accomplished many of the goals and worked through many of the emotions mentioned above. Even if this is the case, you most likely could benefit from additional work before jumping into a new commitment. Take your time. There is no hurry.

I can tell you that most persons experiencing divorce do either remarry or become involved in another long term relationship. Even if this new person you have met seems like Ms. or Mr. Right, this will not be your only opportunity for happiness or connection. Take it slowly to make sure you are ready.

Is It A Long Term Relationship?

Many persons experiencing divorce experiment with transitional relationships during and after their breakup. These are relationships where there is never an intention of a long-term commitment; just a mutual meeting of needs and companionship. There is nothing wrong with this type of a relationship, as long as this is the intention of both parties and both of you are open about it.

However, do not even contemplate introducing your children to one of these short term partners. You would just be buying them an additional, preventable loss and more heartache. Keep them out of brief relationships, even if they ask to be a part of them. That kind of request may be an indication that they are not getting enough time or attention from you. Kids also just want you to be happy and may think that they can help facilitate a long term relationship, not understanding that you have already determined it is not possible or desirable with this partner.

Remember, adults process events differently than children—they will not be able to understand these relationships at the same level as you do. Make decisions carefully to protect their fragile emotions.

Are Your Children Still Having Adjustment Problems?

Look back to Chapter One at the list of typical behavioral responses to parental divorce for your child's age group. Think for a minute about any changes in their behavior, even if they are not listed in Chapter One, that you noticed in response to your separation or divorce. Are you still noticing any of these behaviors from your children?

If the answer is yes, they are still in the throes of adjusting to your divorce. Remember the children in a state of chronic stress—the ones whose home lives had not stabilized, but had instead thrown one change after another their way, thereby preventing them from ever adjusting to any change. Prevent this from happening to your children. If they are still reacting, be protective, even if you feel this is a long term relationship. Don't ask them to adapt to any more changes until they show you they have adjusted to the previous ones.

How to Introduce a New Partner to Your Children

When you have worked your way through the stages discussed above, your divorce is final, your children are not suffering from any lingering behaviors or after-effects of your divorce and you have met a wonderful new person who you are sure is going to be a significant, long-term partner in your life, there are some guidelines for introducing that person to your children to set them up for success.

Tell Your Children About the New Partner Yourself

You want your children to trust you to share things with them that will affect their lives, such as the entry of a new focus of your attention. You want them to hear this news from you, rather than from a sibling, a friend, or, worse yet, a stranger or your new partner. When you are sure this relationship will be significant, tell your children you have met a new friend that you sometimes spend time with.

Spend no more than five minutes on this conversation. End the discussion by asking if they have any questions. They most likely will not, but, again, you are leaving the door open for questions later. You are telling them that this is an OK subject to ask you about.

If and when they do have questions, answer them

honestly and briefly. Do not give lengthy dissertations about this person or answer questions they are not asking. You do not want to give them the impression that this person is the most important thing in your life—even if that's how you are feeling at the moment.

And, do not set up the meeting right away. Kids need some time to adjust to the idea of their parents dating and finding a new partner. Let them digest this information for several weeks before having the meeting.

While waiting, watch your children for any signs that they are having difficulty with the information. This would include any of the symptoms in Chapter One about how children are affected by divorce, any changes in them you notice independently and any difficulties they voice to you as you make plenty of opportunities to talk with them about this issue if they choose. Spend sufficient time with your children to determine if they are reacting to this information as well.

If you notice they are struggling with the news, help them to deal with it by engaging in any of the techniques in Chapter Two, putting off the meeting longer than suggested in this chapter, ideally until your children are no longer reacting to this relationship, and continuing to work on stabilizing your home environment as discussed in Chapter Three. Any negative reaction they are having could be related to instability or insecurity they are feeling at home.

Give Them Some Notice of the Meeting

After you've gone through the above steps, several weeks have passed and your children are not showing new symptoms of distress, you may proceed to set up a meeting with this new person. If your partner pressures you to do it sooner, hand her a copy of this book and have her read it for herself.

Just as kids need time to prepare themselves for any changes they will be facing, they need time to prepare for this meeting. Do not be surprised if your children view this person as their future step-parent. Remember, they may see marriage as the only purpose for dating behavior, even if you give them no indication your relationship is at this stage and even if it has not reached that stage for the two of you. Therefore, your children may put a significant amount of weight on this meeting. Make certain you, and they, are prepared for it.

Plan a Short-Term Contact

For this first meeting, I always recommend to parents that they plan a short contact. Planning an all-day activity with someone they don't know at all puts a significant amount of pressure on them, on your new partner and on you. Plan your visit to last about one half hour, just long enough to accomplish the introductions, spend a bit of time together, then move on. Again, your children will need time to digest this experience.

If you are out of ideas as to what to do for this meeting, the following are some of the most typical that seem to do the trick:

❀ Take them to the zoo

❀ Have lunch at McDonald's or a favorite restaurant of *theirs*

❀ Go to a park

❀ Take a drive and get some ice cream

❀ Have a pizza or snacks at home

After the meeting, the new partner should leave or be dropped off somewhere. Do not make the mistake of dropping your children off at a sitter's or at their other parent's home so that you can spend time with your new love interest or they will literally be getting the information they it is they who are being replaced.

Talk with your children after the meeting. Get feedback from them. What did they think? Would they like to see her again in the future? Any thoughts about how they would like to spend time together? Don't be surprised if they now have questions about this relationship. Take this opportunity to spend time with them doing something they enjoy. This can help set the tone for a positive reaction to your new partner and give them the message that they continue to be important in you life.

Maintain Plenty of Contact with Your Children That Does *Not* Involve Your New Partner

Some parents make the mistake, once this meeting has occurred, of involving the new partner in every aspect of their lives. Maintain plenty of contact with your kids in which your new partner is not involved. Give them large doses of your time, attention and affection. Their greatest fear will be that they will cease to matter; that they will lose you to this new partner.

Also, if there are special activities that you have done together, do not automatically include your new partner in them. Get your children's OK to invite her to your Saturday morning basketball game, to come along to Church on Sunday morning, etc. Move very slowly. You want them to feel nurtured and cherished, not invaded by enemy forces.

Maintain All Parenting Responsibilities Yourself; Don't Pass Them Off on Your New Partner

Another significant mistake made by a number of parents is handing over parenting responsibilities to the new partner. Perhaps as a father you were not much involved in the parenting of your children during your marriage and now it all feels a little overwhelming to you. You welcome a new woman in your children's lives who can do some of the motherly tasks like your daughter's hair and your son's homework.

Or, perhaps you are a soon-to-be-single mother who is having some difficulty disciplining her pre-adolescent sons. They are afraid, hurt and angry about the divorce and want you to know it. Now you have a new partner and are relieved to give some of the disciplinary responsibilities over to him because you think they will listen better to a man as he is stricter and has a deeper voice.

Either of these situations is a set-up for disaster. Kids are almost sure to resent a stranger coming into the home and, even with their parent's permission, attempting to enforce rules and discipline them. Your children will act out their displeasure and rightly so.

They are still unsure of their role with you. Now you have abdicated a primary parenting responsibility. It is terrifying for them; they don't know your new partner as well as they know you. They also don't have the bond or connection to this person that they do with you, which is added incentive to act out.

Even in cases of remarriage, most experts suggest continuing to maintain the biological parent as the disciplinarian, with the new stepparent focusing on the role of bonding with the child.[2] It is suggested, at least in the first few years, and much longer if the children are teens when the marriage occurs, that the stepparent take on the role of a caring aunt or uncle, or interested family friend, rather than exerting authority over children.

Over all, your new relationship will be accepted more readily if both you and your children are ready for this to occur and if you follow these few simple guidelines in choreographing these first contacts. A short meeting after a brief discussion, followed by plenty of time alone with the parent is a recipe for a successful transition in this area of your life as well.

Take a look at the overview on the following page to determine how you are doing in setting yourself up for success with your children's new relationship with your new partner.

"You are a living magnet. What you attract into your life is in harmony with your dominant thoughts."

~Brian Tracy

Determining Whether to Introduce a New Partner to Your Children

❀ I feel I have adjusted to the end of my marriage.

❀ I feel I have worked through the following stages of the adjustment process:

___ Denial	___ Anger
___ Loneliness	___ Letting Go
___ Fear	___ Responsibility
___ Grief/Rejection	___ Low Self-Esteem
___ Depression	

❀ I believe I am ready for a new relationship because:

___ My divorce is completed,

___ I have established emotional distance from my children's other parent, i.e. s/he can no longer "push my buttons,"

___ My children seem to have adjusted to the divorce in a positive manner.

❀ I have met someone and have reason to believe the relationship will be a serious and significant one in my life.

❀ I have told my children about this new person and they have responded positively.

❀ I have arranged a short meeting at the following time and location that will be comfortable for my children: _____

❀ I will make certain to spend time with them when my new partner is not present.

❀ I will maintain the parenting responsibilities, while my new partner slowly develops a relationships with my children.

❀ I will monitor my children's reactions to my new partner and talk with them about their reactions to it.

"Love is giving someone your undivided attention."

~Anonymous

CHAPTER 11

FEELINGS AND ACTIONS
ARE NOT THE SAME!

How to Handle Specific Behavior Problems
Your Children May Develop

When his mother and father separated, Sean saw all the
rules change. Thinking it would make things harder on
him if she persisted in imposing the limits they had
always enforced with him, Sean's mother decided to "give him a
break." But to Sean, all of a sudden it didn't matter whether or not he
cleaned his room or unloaded the dishwasher, two tasks that had
previously been required of him. If he didn't do them, his mother
would. Sean gradually did less and less, and eventually decided to test
other limits as well. When he didn't clean his room, nothing
happened. When he got into a fight at school, there were no consequences so Sean kept escalating his actions, looking for something
that would matter to his mother. Sean was crying out for help...and to
be noticed. Only when he was arrested for shoplifting did his mother
begin to re-think her approach.

If children are exhibiting specific behavior problems,
parents are encouraged to look for the underlying cause. In a
divorce, as discussed in Chapter One, the cause is often anger,
appearing secondary to hurt and fear. We have already identified many of the most typical symptoms of distress and

behavior problems in previous chapters and covered some ideas for how to handle them. What follows in this chapter are more specific behavior management and modification techniques parents can use to handle virtually any behavior problem, whether it occurs in the home, at school or in the community.

If Another Authority is Addressing the Behavior, Support It

Some of the problems children create for themselves bring them to the attention of agencies other than the family. Some children become truant or act out in school, or refuse to complete or turn in homework assignments.

Still others act out in the community, shoplifting, violating a community curfew, experimenting with smoking and alcohol. The local police, the school and several other community agencies are likely to attempt to implement a plan to deal with the behavior, once your child has come to their attention.

The school is likely to take some type of disciplinary measures to deal with the problems arising in that setting. Your child may be suspended, expected to serve some detention time or have other consequences imposed on him. He will likely come to you and request that you intervene on his behalf to reduce or eliminate the unfair penalty.

If your child comes to the attention of law enforcement, there are also likely to be consequences. Your child may ask you to intervene on his behalf in this circumstance as well.

Do not do this. What they are receiving is a natural consequence for their behavior that they will be unable to blame on you. You can be supportive of them (hire them an attorney, listen and talk with them), empathize with them ("I understand that you regret your actions; I am sorry you have to go through this experience"), but you cannot and do not want to intervene or attempt to remove the penalty. That way, they will be able to take responsibility for their behavior and to learn from it.

Parents who go through life trying to prevent their children from experiencing the consequences of their actions tend to end up with pretty unruly, irresponsible and unmanageable kids—even as adults. Help your children to take responsibility for their behavior and to learn from their mistakes by not removing the obstacles from their path, but by helping them over and through them with your emotional support.

Be Clear and Consistent in Enforcing Rules at Home

We have already discussed this in Chapter Three. It is important to the stability of your home, which is crucial for your child's long term adjustment to your divorce, for rules and expectations to be clear and consistently enforced.

Even though it may take more energy than you feel you have on a given day as *you* are experiencing this divorce to enforce limits with your child, force yourself to do so. They need to learn that, even though much about your lives together has changed, they can count on you to parent them appropriately.

Never use physical discipline to enforce rules. This models aggressive behavior for children and shows them that is the way to manage frustration. It also gives the message that "might makes right" or, that the biggest or strongest should prevail. It won't be long before they will be as big or tall as you are. Who gets to make the rules then?

Another problem with physical discipline is that it is typically confusing for children. Take, for example, the mother who spanks her child when she runs into the street in front of an oncoming car. She may say, as she is administering the spanking, "Never run in front of a car because I don't want you to get hurt." In the meantime, she, herself, is hurting the child. Talk about a mixed message! What is a child to make of that?

Help Children Talk about Their Feelings

It is normal for your children to have some negative feelings about the divorce. It is positive and healthy if they feel accepted and comfortable enough to share them with you. Honor and respect the trust they are showing you by sharing these painful feelings with you by accepting them.

Do not try to argue them out of their feelings and do not become angry with them for feeling as they do. Feelings aren't right or wrong, they just are. It is a great gift your children are giving you—sharing part of their innermost selves with you. This is behavior you want to encourage, not inhibit.

Encourage them with verbal nudges (un-huh, what happened next...) or with questions that show you are working to understand and accept their painful emotions. To get children started talking, use the techniques outlined in Chapter Two.

Help Your Child Unburden Himself of Some of His Anger

Children's anger is a major cause of behavior problems. Understanding this may enable you to use some of the following techniques to help them relieve some of the anger at its source.

Help Him To Talk About It

It is often obvious to a parent that a child is angry, even if it is not immediately apparent to him. Identify or label his feeling and help him to understand what causes it. Help him to talk about it without trying to talk him out of it.

Be empathic with your children and let them know their anger is normal. This fact, alone, may be a big relief to them. Many children feel guilty for being so angry, especially when anger is directed toward parents.

Alleviate a Problem When You Can

As your children talk with you about their feelings, you may discover ways to relieve part of their anger. You may be able to take some appropriate steps to change some of the things they are angry about. If not spending time with you is making them angry (and the underlying emotion here is obviously hurt), arrange to take more time with them. If they are angry about not seeing their friends anymore because of a move, help them to arrange this.

There may be many things you can do to help alleviate the negative feelings. This does not mean you are responsible for the feelings; only that you can help to make things easier for them once you are aware there is a problem.

Give Them a Break

Work to be more tolerant of children's outbursts than you might ordinarily be. Understand they, too, are going through a difficult adjustment process, with many of the same negative emotions as you are experiencing. Give them a little more leeway than normal due to this added stress.

Do continue to draw a distinction between feelings and behavior, however. It is OK and acceptable to feel angry; it is not OK to throw a book across the room or slap another family member. But the occasional outburst can certainly be forgiven. Remember, just because they are showing their stress now, it doesn't mean this will become a permanent pattern, especially if you help them to talk about their feelings and teach them healthy coping skills to handle them.

Help Them Find Outlets for Their Anger

Work with your children to help them come up with acceptable outlets for their anger in addition to talking about their feelings. Some children find it helpful to act out their feelings through drawing, working with clay or finger painting. Some find that being alone, listening to music or taking a warm bath helps anger to dissipate. Vigorous physical activity (chopping wood, sweeping out the garage, raking the lawn) or sports (running, climbing, throwing balls, biking) is a good release for the extra adrenaline that comes with the anger. Once this is expressed, usually the child feels relieved, calmer and, often, more able to talk about what is bothering him.

Another option is a punching bag, but you want to watch that the use of this technique does not seem to incite more anger, aggression and violent behavior. In some persons, it can be an extremely positive tool to release aggression. In others, it can make them more aggressive and prone to violence. It may be better to encourage some of the other non-violent alternatives discussed above.

Help Children to See WHY They Are Behaving As They Are

Because their brains are undeveloped and do not process information as ours do, children are often unaware of why they are angry and what is upsetting them. Also, most have just not yet learned how, or developed the habit of, looking inward to figure out what is happening to upset them. Reviewing the thinking process explained in Chapter 3 and walking through it with your child, may help this process along. In addition, helping her to talk about what she is feeling may help her to uncover the truth and develop some insight about what is causing these emotions.

Many children also feel quite guilty, not just personalizing the divorce, but for adding to their parents distress by acting out and being angry. They may not be able to articulate this as they most likely do not completely understand it. But it is guiding their actions, just the same.

As discussed in Chapter Two, often just giving them bits of information can help them cope with their emotions. Saying to them, "Many kids feel angry when their parents divorce…" can help to normalize their feelings and help them to feel accepted at the same time. This kind of understanding by a parent, also makes it much easier for a child to acknowledge anger and, thereby, to release it. A little understanding can go a long way

Distinguish Between Feelings and Behavior

We have touched on this briefly, but it is such an important point that I believe it bears repeating. It is not just children that don't get this. I have met many adults in my Men's Anger Management Group that don't understand it, even at 30, 40 or 50 years of age.

Feelings are always OK; behavior may or may not be. One of the most common methods of not taking responsibility for behavior among the men I see with anger problems is to excuse violent behavior with the statement, "I lost my temper." We don't lose our temper; we let it go. The best illustration of how true this is becomes apparent when we ask if the individual has ever become violent at work, in front of a police officer, in church. Even with the most violent offenders, most exert a substantial amount of control in settings in which they realize that it is important not to lose control.

In the few cases where the individual has not identified any setting in which he has not been violent or "lost his temper," I will provoke him in the group to the point where I can see he is frustrated and quite upset. I will tell you I have never been hit because they know there will be consequences if they act out in my setting and they can maintain control because they feel they have to.

Your children can do likewise. They will no doubt be able to come up with a number of settings in which they have never lost control because it was important to them to appear a certain way, either to avoid consequences or to impress someone. This will help them understand the separation between feelings and behavior and that they are able to exercise a substantial amount of choice in how to express their feelings. It can also help many parents feel more comfortable imposing consequences for children's inappropriate actions in the expression of negative emotions.

Teach Them Coping Skills

We don't want to just teach children what not to do. That leaves a vacuum in place of the eliminated behavior. The most natural thing in a time of stress, then, becomes to engage in the old habitual behavior, because we have nothing else to replace it with.

Those of you who have quit smoking know what I mean. If you don't figure out something to chew or suck on, new stress management strategies and something else to do with your hands, you are smoking again before you know it!

Give your children some new ideas for how to handle stress. Suggest they write in a journal, take a hot bath, talk to a friend, listen to music and remove themselves from the upsetting situation when on the verge of losing control. Then, model these coping skills for them when you feel yourself under stress. Any parent knows children follow what we do much more closely than what we say. The old adage, "Do as I say; not as I do," does not apply to parenting. Refer, also, to Chapter Four for a more complete discussion of coping skills which may help your children.

End Conflict With the Other Parent in Your Child's Presence

One of the most upsetting times for children, especially children experiencing divorce, is when their parents are in conflict. They can feel literally torn apart, witnessing the two of you battling with each other over some critical issue such as who gets to spend Christmas Eve with them. They can feel responsible and guilty as well. It is emotionally damaging for children to witness parental conflict and can exacerbate acting out behaviors. The child becomes flooded with emotion while witnessing this battle. His actions are merely the expression of the torment you are imposing on him.

End conflict with the other parent at all costs, at least when your child is around. Consider contacts both in person and over the telephone as in your child's presence, because even if you child only hears your end of a phone conversation or that of the other parent, most children can easily identify who you are speaking with, even if you are handling it appropriately.

Have these telephone calls when you are at work or when you are sure your child is either gone or asleep. If he is just in the other room, be assured he is listening and attentive to your conversation. Kids are vigilant for information about how their lives may change.

Do not make the calls when your child is with the other parent, either. Know that they will try the same techniques on the other end to hear the conversation and have the same reactions. Unless you are sure the child is not at home when you call, wait for another opportunity to resolve the issue.

Be Supportive of Your Children; Realize That Behavior Problems are Symptoms of Their Pain and Distress

It is often helpful for parents to maintain the perspective, especially with a child who is being particularly obnoxious, that any behavior problems are merely symptoms of your child's pain and distress. It is easier to accept them for what they are and to remember that they are time-limited. This, too, shall pass.

Knowing this can also help you to be calm, rather than upset and angry yourself, as you impose an appropriate consequence for an inappropriate action. You will be modeling the very behavior you want your children to practice. The more you can hang in there and be supportive, while teaching your kids positive coping and anger management skills, the more you will be helping them to develop that resilience we all covet for our children.

To help you get a handle on your child's behavior and your own responses, read through the summary sheet on the following page. You may just discover that you are already doing many of the right things! Those that you are not currently practicing should give you some good ideas for new options and directions when you are most at your wit's end. Good Luck!

"Treat people as if they were what they ought to be and you help them become what they are capable of being."

~Goethe

I am helping my child handle behavior problems by:

❀ Supporting other authorities addressing the behavior so my child learns to take responsibility for his actions.

❀ Clearly and consistently enforcing rules at home.

❀ Helping my child talk about his feelings and working at understanding them.

❀ Helping my child to learn how to express anger appropriately by:

~ Helping him talk about it

~ Alleviating a problem when I can

~ Giving him a break when appropriate

~ Helping him find positive outlets for his anger

❀ Helping my child to learn to understand why he is behaving the way he is.

❀ Teaching him to distinguish between feelings and behavior (i.e. I can feel angry and not hit or yell…)

❀ Teaching him coping skills: journaling, exercise, sports, deep breathing, listening to music, etc.

❀ Ending conflict with the other parent in my child's presence.

❀ Being supportive of my children and realizing behavior problems are symptoms of their pain and distress.

CHAPTER 12

REBUILDING YOUR CHILDREN'S SELF-ESTEEM

· *How to Help Your Children Feel Better About Themselves*

Shannon's parents divorced when she was eleven. While she had previously felt like the apple of her parents, eyes, all of a sudden it felt like she didn't matter anymore. Her parents were always preoccupied, either bickering with each other or hashing out the terms of the divorce with lawyers and friends. Both started to be away from home more often, working longer hours and socializing more frequently. They just weren't around when she needed them the most. Suddenly, Shannon began to feel less sure of herself both in school and with her friends. Questions that had once seemed so easy to her suddenly seemed harder to answer, more difficult to figure out. She started to hold back more, both in school and with her friends. At home, she felt safest and most secure alone in her room. While her parents and teachers noticed that she seemed a little quieter than usual, what no one realized was that a deep-seated insecurity was taking root as a result of the emotional damage to her fragile ego.

Virtually anyone, and most often everyone, in a family that is experiencing divorce can use some work on their self-esteem. As a marriage is breaking up, taking the family along with it, things are said and done that are damaging to us emotionally. What follows in this chapter are some suggestions for things parents can do to help rebuild children's fragile self-esteem when it has most likely been damaged by events occurring within the family. While these techniques are designed to help you help your child, be aware that carrying them out may also have the effect of helping you to feel better about yourself, your life and your parenting as well!

Treat Your Child with Respect

The best way to teach a child respect is to treat a child *with* respect. Yes, we are all human and kids know exactly how to push our buttons. But if the majority of the time you speak to your children courteously and respectfully, saying "Please" and "Thank you," you are teaching them to use these behaviors as well.

When kids are struggling with self-esteem issues, they often feel undeserving of respect. A parent, who chooses that moment to order the child around or demand that she do something, feeds into this belief about herself. Help her break out of that pit by showing her that she deserves the same respect and courtesy you reserve for others. She might just believe you!

Offer Praise and Encouragement Liberally

A person struggling with low self-esteem has a difficult time seeing her own positive attributes, even if they are readily apparent and quite obvious to others. I have had many adult clients in this predicament. My favorite technique is to give them the task of creating a list of 25 positive qualities about themselves. For those with true self-esteem issues, this is difficult and most come up with fewer than 10. We work on this together in sessions and they then have a comprehensive list they can refer to whenever they are being hard on themselves. They can often refer back to the session in which the list was created to help themselves feel better as well.

Helping your children build such a list can help them to feel better about themselves as well. It is important that the positive qualities and comments be genuine. Otherwise, they are too easy to dismiss. It's much harder to argue with truth than with exaggeration.

Offer genuine praise and encouragement to your children. Help them build that list in their minds so they can refer to it even when you are not there. As you may know, from your own experience, we tend to carry our parent's voices in our heads throughout our lives; make yours say something positive and encouraging.

When your child does something positive, offer liberal appreciation. Do not make it excessive or it will be dismissed. For instance, if your child unloads the dishwasher when asked and you tell him 12 times how much you appreciate it, he will learn to dismiss your positive comments as inaccurate. Tell him once and let it go. Accompany it with a hug and a smile for maximum effect. Make your comments accurate and appropriate to the deed or event accomplished.

Accentuate the Positives

Focus on the positive attributes and behaviors of your child and downplay the negatives. For instance, when your daughter brings home a report card with six A,s and B,s and one C, complement her on her hard work and good grades. Later you can have a discussion about what she feels she needs to do to raise the C. But spend the majority of your time and attention on the positives, the higher grades.

Children who are faced with much negative feedback tend to internalize this and beat themselves up with it. A little of this is good to motivate a child; but to a child struggling with a major family change and low self-esteem, it can be devastating. Unfortunately, I am only too aware of teens committing suicide over grades after internalizing too much negativity about themselves. Set your child up for success. Help protect him from himself.

Be gentle and specific with any negative comments you make. In our society, we tend to hear approximately 50 negative comments for every one positive comment about ourselves. Those number can be overwhelming, both to us and to our children, especially during times in increased stress.

Avoid Criticisms and Put-Downs

For the same reasons, you want to avoid criticisms and put-downs at all costs. This is true at all times, not just when kids are struggling with low self-esteem.

As parents, it is our job to build our children up, not tear them down. The negative comment or name we use to describe our daughter today will be the voice she hears tomorrow as she is applying for a job or looking for a life-partner. If she thinks of herself as incompetent or lazy, that is what she will project in her search. Set her up for success—give her the messages she needs to land the job and choose a healthy relationship!

Distinguish Between a Child and His Behavior

When your child acts out, make the distinction between him and his behavior. The action or behavior (i.e. throwing a vase across the room) is unacceptable; the child is not. Avoid the labels "good" and "bad"; they cause children to be judgmental of themselves and others. Saying to a child, "You're a bad boy," can lead to a self-fulfilling prophecy of the child choosing to act out because he believes he is "bad."

Say, "What you did was unacceptable." Set the limit clearly and impose a consequence (sitting in time-out or, for an older child, writing a page about why it was unacceptable). Follow through and insist that the consequence is completed before the child gets any other rewards, i.e. treats, playing a game with the parent, etc.

If any of this is new information for you, please refer to a text on basic parenting skills and techniques that can give a more thorough discussion of these issues. Several are included in the reading list in the Appendix.

Make Your Child Feel Special With the Gift of Time

Make your child feel special with your interest and time. Choosing to spend your precious time with your child, gives her the message that she is important and valuable to you. As parents, we make choices every day about how to spend our 24 hours. If our child sees us consistently choosing to spend our time with friends, at work or doing housework, she may feel that the laundry is more important to you than she is.

As we discussed in Chapter Three, I typically recommend that parents spend individual time with their children each day they are with them. Again, you needn't add hours to your day. Simply keep one child at a time with you as you go through your daily routine. Each child will feel precious and her self-esteem will soar with the individual attention

Spending time doing something the child wants to do is even more beneficial to her fragile ego. Say to your child, "For the next two hours, I'm all yours. What would you like to do?" and watch her face light up.

Provide Opportunities to do Things Your Child Does Well

All people feel more positive and confident about themselves when they are doing something they are skilled at. Anyone suffering with low self-esteem needs only to spend time at something they do well, be it cooking, playing a musical instrument, woodworking or craftwork to feel better. Your children are no exception to this rule. They are more likely to feel better about themselves when exhibiting an area of skill, such as playing basketball, riding a bike or training the dog to do a new trick.

As a parent, aware of this phenomenon, you can arrange for your child to have opportunities to engage in activities he does well. Invite friends over to play basketball or go for a bike ride, or suggest these activities to your child. You will see him feeling better in a short time.

You may even ask him to teach you, a sibling or friend the skill, thereby enhancing the positive feelings and sense of competence. Be genuinely interested in learning what he has to teach, however, or he may end up feeling manipulated and could have difficulty trusting you.

Encourage Learning a New Skill

Learning something new can also give us a feeling of accomplishment and do wonders for our egos. Explore with your child a new skill she would like to learn and help her figure out how to go about it. This should engage her in a positive endeavor and take her focus off feeling bad about herself.

Help Set Realistic Goals

Because you are an adult and you realize learning a new skill can be challenging, help her to set realistic goals for herself. Rather than, "I'm going to make a seven course meal and exotic dessert for the family this weekend," suggest, "Why don't you try one or two items to start with."

Kids tend to throw themselves into new activities with gusto. While you don't want to destroy their enthusiasm, helping them to temper it with a bit of realism will be more likely to set them on a course for success than letting them overextend themselves and be disappointed in the outcome.

Increase Challenges in Small, Achievable Steps

Help your child build a list of progressively more challenging goals. Encourage him to start out with something relatively simple and help him imagine, as you create the list together, the most difficult piece of the task. Together you can fill in the middle section of intermediate goals. Aside from building a realistic approach to learning a new skill, you are spending quality time together discussing something important to your child. As he learns, accomplishes and completes each step, his confidence will build, until he doesn't need you to do it for him anymore, but only to provide emotional support.

Avoid Taking Over

Many parents make the mistake of stepping into an activity with their child, only to find that they have completely taken over the process. This behavior only reinforces the child's certainty that he is incompetent to handle even the simplest of tasks. By taking over you are sending your child the message that he cannot handle it without you.

If you participate in the task with your child, be cautious about your role. Let him take the lead and set the course. Often, an effective way to guide him to make good decisions and choices is by asking him questions about the next step in the process. Even if you already know the answer, you may be helping him think through the process ahead of time, increasing his chances of success.

Help Your Child Help Someone Else

When we are down, one of the best ways to feel better about ourselves is to step out of our own reality and help someone else. Many of my clients who are suffering from depression find great satisfaction and relief in this manner. I often recommend that they volunteer at a nursing home, a hospital, the humane society, or any other organization that reaches out to others. The amazing result that typically happens is that they realize that they don't have it so bad after all; others often have it much worse. And many have a more positive attitude.

The other benefit that occurs with this task is that when we do something nice or helpful for others, we end up feel good about ourselves. We feel a sense of accomplishment that most of us carry throughout the rest of our day or week.

Your children can benefit from this technique as much as my adult clients. Suggest that your daughter call a less popular classmate and spend time with her. Or ask your son to mow the lawn for an elderly neighbor who will most likely shower him with compliments and, perhaps cookies and milk as well.

There are many opportunities for this as our society becomes more fragmented. Many of the support systems we had in place in the past have disintegrated. This creates many opportunities for your children to lend a hand which will, in turn, help them as well.

Assign Age-Appropriate Chores

While you want to guard against leaning too heavily on children as discussed in Chapter Three, assigning them age-appropriate chores can set them up for success. When able to successfully complete a chore, the child's self-esteem soars, especially if he is made aware of his contribution to the family. This can help him to feel valuable and important to the group, which can't help but improve how he feels about himself.

An important component to this, however, is something many parents forget to add. When your child completes the task, show your appreciation for his contribution to the family. Appreciation need not be monetary, though that can help. A sincere "Thank you", a warm hug or a plate of cookies can get the message across just as effectively.

Examine Your Expectations to Make Sure They Are Realistic and Age-Appropriate

As you are helping your child to focus on tasks both of you want him to accomplish, take stock of your own expectations. Do a reality check to determine if your expectations are realistic and appropriate for your child's age-group. If you don't have a good sense of this, talk to other parents about what their similarly-aged children can accomplish.

This is an important concept because when children are assigned or take on a task that they cannot possibly accomplish, they feel even more negative about themselves and often give up trying to please you or themselves. In these cases, their self-esteem plummets and you end up doing more harm than good.

If you are unsure whether your expectations are reasonable, check out the recommendations in a child development text. Refer to the reading list in the Appendix for some suggestions on this.

To take stock of where you are at helping your child rebuild his self-esteem, read through the summary on the following page and respond to the comments. Please remember if you are using a library copy of this book to photocopy the page before noting your responses, but do complete the work. This should give you a handle on where you stand and some direction and other ideas for helping your child.

I am helping my child to rebuild her self-esteem by:

❁ *Treating my child with respect. Changes I have made include:*

_____

_____

❁ *Offering genuine praise and encouragement. Some of my favorites are:*_____

_____

❁ *Identifying and commenting on her positive qualities and accomplishments, such as:*_____

_____

_____

❁ *Avoiding criticism and put-downs*

❁ *Distinguishing between my child and her behavior*

❁ *Spending time with my child. These are some of my favorite ways to do this:*

_____

_____

_____

❁ *Providing opportunities to do things my child does well, such as:*

_____

_____

_____

❁ *Encouraging my child to learn a new skill, such as:*_____

_____

_____

_____

❀ *Giving her control over some of the activities we do together and avoiding taking over them.*_____

_____

_____

❀ *Helping my child to help someone else, such as:* _____

_____

_____

❀ *Assigning her age-appropriate chores, such as:* _____

_____

_____

❀ *Keeping my own expectations appropriate and realistic. Areas I need to focus on include:* _____

_____

_____

"Nothing is as strong as gentleness. Nothing is so gentle as real strength."

~Saint Francis de Sales

CHAPTER 13

LIVING HAPPILY EVER AFTER

How to Let Go and Move On

When Samantha's parents divorced, she and her mother were forced to move from their home in an exclusive suburb to a small apartment in the city. While Samantha didn't like the apartment, her mother incorporated several new rituals into their daily routine, such as a walk to the Dairy Queen in their new neighborhood after dinner, in an attempt to make the transition easier for her daughter. Samantha observed her mother fulfilling her responsibilities to both Sam and herself. She saw her go to work regularly, but also make it a point to be at home and available to Sam in case she had questions or just to spend time with her.

Sam saw her mother taking care of herself as well, talking with a therapist about negative feelings left over from the break-up and making sure there was adequate time in her schedule for leisure activities with other adults. While Sam sometimes questioned this, and occasionally resented it, she understood how much better her mother seemed to feel after she was able to be with grown-ups for awhile, concluding that this was probably a good thing after all. Most of all, she appreciated not being put in the middle, by not having to listen to her mother's negative comments about being left by her father.

Successful adjustment to divorce can leave children more independent and emotionally stronger than before. I always tell my Parenting Through Divorce classes that, while I am certainly not recommending divorce as a parenting technique, it is by no means the end of the world for children, even if it feels that way to them at times.

We want to think about this in terms of that resilience that we, as parents, attempt to instill and develop in our children. If parents are emotionally and financially supportive to children during the divorce and strive to stabilize the home as quickly as possible on the heels of any major change, the stress imposed on children can be moderate enough to challenge the children, but not overwhelm them. You have, thus, taught them more about how to handle stress, a life skill that will serve them always.

This helps them develop the resilience they need to manage stress successfully as adults. In this way, parental divorce, while continuing to affect children for the remainder of their lives by helping to create the persons they become, can strengthen and empower them to achieve more than may otherwise be possible. But it does not need to affect them in a lifelong negative way, such as defining who they are for the next 40 years (i.e. I am a child of divorce).

Parents can also assist their children in coming to terms with and letting go of the family the way it was. Children typically are able to make this shift as quickly as their parents do. The more quickly parents move on, the faster children will adjust as well. Talk to your child about the changes you are making and why you are doing so, as Samantha's mother in the example did. Explain the importance of caring for yourself. Again, you are teaching life skills, so that when she is a parent, your daughter will feel no guilt about taking care of herself, understanding as you now do that this is essential to her well-being.

From time to time, as you continue your path forward through divorce and its aftermath, you will often be faced by choices that will affect the lives of your children. If you can routinely get in the habit of asking yourself that magic question, "What is in my child's best interest?" you will make decisions that are positive and forward focused.

When confused about which choice to make, read over some of the key sections of this book. Focus specifically on Chapters One, Three, Six and Nine, especially because, even if they are not specifically on point with regard to the choices you need to make, those chapters convey an approach and attitude that you want to capture in your post-divorce relationship with your children and their other parent. Using the ideas illustrated in those chapters will best guide you to developing and making the positive choices to which your children will most easily adapt.

The more you focus and concentrate on your new life and being the parent you want to be, the more positively you will handle whatever changes life, or your divorce, will throw at you. When I was a single parent, I came across a saying by an anonymous author that I have referred to many times, both personally and professionally, in the succeeding 14 years. It reads as follows:

*"Many things may be sad and unpleasant, but the only thing that's the end of the world is **the end of the world!**"*

The translation is that even though experiencing divorce is a pain, single parenting can be difficult, getting into a step-family (down the road) can be challenging (trust me on this!), none of these things is the end of the world. Take these challenges one day at a time, sometimes one minute at a time, and this, too, shall pass.

As human beings, we have almost a natural tendency to "awfulize" situations we are facing, giving them even more power than they deserve to affect our lives and make us miserable. This gets us nowhere.

Work on minimizing the awfulness of the situations you are facing. Nothing is insurmountable, given the right attitude. We all know of people who are facing the worst of tragedies, but who seem to be able to maintain a positive outlook in spite of the difficulties they face. They keep looking forward and seem to be able to handle anything. In fact, these people often do. Attitude makes all the difference in the world.

Another important part of moving on is forgiveness. You may not be ready for this, yet, especially if you were the partner who was left, or hurt when your spouse had an affair, as I was. But the only person you hurt by hanging onto your resentment, anger and bitterness, is you.

The other person is not affected. Oh, you may make their lives difficult for awhile, but eventually they will learn to work around you. You may make your children miserable for awhile, but in the end, this hurts you, as well, when you realize what you have done.

My favorite saying about forgiveness is one I saw on the outside billboard advertising a small Baptist church in northeastern Wisconsin. It was a simple but powerful statement that I have incorporated into my work with my divorce adjustment group. It reads as follows:

"Forgiveness is giving up my right to hurt you for hurting me."

What a wonderful, empowering statement! What a profound thought. The person I hurt is myself by hanging on to old hurts: I tie up my energy and resentment being angry with you and that paralyzes me to move beyond my hurt.

Work on letting go of your hurt so that you can emerge on the other side of it healthy, happy and well adjusted! There are some terrific books on this issue (see the Reading List in the Appendix), or you may prefer to work with a therapist who can help you on a more individual and personal basis.

Remember, you will be happier for it and your children are watching every move you make, and learning from it.

A generous man forgets what he gives and remembers what he receives."

~Old Proverb

I am working on letting go and moving on in the following ways:

❀ *These are some of the positive new changes I have made in my life that I feel good about:* _____

_____

_____

❀ *These are some of the positive choices I have made regarding my children that I feel good about:* _____

_____

_____

❀ *I am working on developing a more positive attitude in the following ways:* _____

_____

_____

❀ *I am working to forgive my children's other parent for any wounds sustained during the divorce or during our relationship.*

❀ *The hurts I have already forgiven include:* _____

_____

_____

❀ *The hurts I am still working to forgive include:*_____

_____

_____

❀ *This is what I am doing to achieve this forgiveness:*

_____

_____

"All life is an experiment."

~Ralph Waldo Emerson

PARENTING THROUGH DIVORCE
The End Result Is Worth the Effort!

R yan and Sean, discussed previously in this book, truly made a remarkable adjustment to their parents, divorce. Several years after the divorce, Sean graduated from high school and his entire family gathered to celebrate the occasion. When Ryan graduated two years later, the celebration included two step-parents who both boys welcomed into the family, having witnessed the joy these other adults brought to their parents. Both boys completed college and established themselves in fulfilling careers. While neither is yet married, both are involved in committed relationships and have regular and supportive contact with both parents.

I have attempted to share both positive and negative examples with you that are similar, but not identical for reasons of confidentiality, to examples I have witnessed in families and couples that I have worked with. I believe both types of examples are crucial to understanding what is harmful and what is possible. Often, we are unaware of how our loved ones are affected by our behavior until we stand back and witness someone else acted as we do and observe our own and other's reactions. Often, as well, we do our greatest learning from positive examples others share with us, either in written or behavioral form.

I offer these examples not to shame, but to teach. Please take a good look at the scenes described here and do some soul-searching to determine whether you have some work to do in these areas. Learn by these examples.

If you identify with the negative examples, follow the ideas suggested to change the effect you are likely having on your children. If you identify with the positive examples, give your self a pat on the back. You have accomplished great things and the information in this book can validate that for you. Just look at all you're doing right!

Parents tend to be their own worst enemies. No one is harder on you than yourself. Appreciate all the good you do, all the sacrifices you have made for your children, all the times you bite your tongue when there are mouthfuls you could share about their other parent, all the times you swallow your pride and make a request of the other parent because it is important to your children. You are doing a great job! Just accept that.

I also make the offer to all of my Parenting Through Divorce classes to be available for questions regarding any of the material I have presented to them in the class. I tell them I am impossible to reach at the office, because I am always either in session with a client, facilitating a group or teaching a class. But I also commit to always return my phone calls, though it may take me a day or two. There is no charge for this follow-up service.

I make this offer to my readers as well. If you have questions about any of the material in this book, or would like to contact me about the book, I have listed in the Appendix telephone and fax numbers and an email address at which I can be reached. Do not hesitate to contact me if you would like to. I have also listed this information on my website, *www.bluewaterspublications.com*, in the event you misplace the book. Email is probably the best way to get the quickest response, as I am often responding to email late into the evening when it would not be appropriate to make a phone call.

I have also included in the Appendix a Feedback Form

that I would appreciate any interested readers completing and sending back to me. I view this book as a work in progress, much the same as the class, which has evolved over time to become what it is today. Some of the most positive and helpful changes came from class members, suggestions that were incorporated into the program, such as the *How to Re-Structure Your Relationship with Your Children's Other Parent* section. That is a crucial piece of the material I provide, but was only added after feedback from participants. Also, if there is any other subject or issue that you would like to see the subject of a book or article, feel free to share that with me as well. If I have something on the subject I think I can offer, I may send it on to you free of charge, in appreciation of the inspiration.

I want to leave you with the good news. Divorce has been around for many years. Years ago, parents had no idea how children were affected or what to do about it.

Today, we understand a great deal about how divorce affects our children and many ideas of what we can do about it. Their parents, response is proving to be the most powerful factor in determining children's response to divorce. What an opportunity this is for you! Do make the most of it!

"The highest result of education is tolerance."

~Helen Keller

Appendix A

Bill of Rights
for Children in a Divorce Action

I did not write this Bill of Rights, but I give it to all of the parents attending my class. I do not specifically discuss it, but refer to it as espousing some basic principles I ascribe to in the information that I do give them. I believe it helps to set a positive tone for the class and my suggestions. It states that children in a divorce are entitled to the following:

❀ The right to be treated as important human beings, with unique feelings, ideas and desires and not as a source of conflict between parents.

❀ The right to a continuing relationship with both parents and the freedom to receive love from and express love for both.

❀ The right to express love and affection for each parent without having to stifle that love because of fear of disapproval by the other parent.

❀ The right to know that their parent's decision to divorce is not their responsibility and that they will live with one parent and will visit the other parent. *

❀ The right to continuing care and guidance from both parents.

❀ The right to honest answers to questions about the changing family relationships.

❀ The right to know and appreciate what is good in each parent without one parent degrading the other.

❀ The right to have a relaxed secure relationship with both parents without being placed in a position to manipulate one parent against the other.

❀ The right to have the custodial parent not undermine visitation by suggesting tempting alternatives or by threatening to withhold visitation as a punishment for the children's wrongdoing.*

❀ The right to be able to experience regular and consistent visitation and the right to know the reason for a cancelled visit.*

❀ The right to minimal disruption of their lives and activities. The divorce is the decision of the parents.

The language used in this bill of rights is a bit dated and reflects the former use of legal custody and visitation terminology that many states have outgrown, rather than the more typical shared parenting arrangements. The sentiments presented, however, are easily transferable to the newer co-parenting arrangements.

Appendix B ~ Reading List for Adults

Divorce Related Materials:

Co-Parenting After Divorce—How to Raise Happy Healthy Children in Two Home Families, by Diana Shulman (Winnspeed Press, 1997).

Creative Divorce: A New Opportunity for Personal Growth, by Mel Krantzler (Signet Books, 1973).

Divorce and New Beginnings, by Genevieve Clapp (John Wiley & Sons, Inc., 1992).

Divorce Busting, by Michele Weiner-Davis, MSW, (Simon & Schuster, 1992).

Getting Divorced Without Ruining Your Life: A Reasoned Practical Guide to the Legal, Emotional and Financial Ins and Outs of Negotiating a Divorce Settlement, by Sam Margulies, PhD., J.D. (Simon & Schuster, 1992).

The Good Divorce: Keeping Your Family Together When Your Marriage Comes Apart, by Constance Ahrons, Ph.D, (Harper Collins Publishers, 1994).

Healthy Divorce, by Craig A. Everett & Sandra Volgy Everett (Jossey-Bass Publishers, 1994).

Helping Your Kids Cope with Divorce the Sand Castles Way, by M. Gary Newman (Times Books, 1998).

How to Survive the Loss of a Love, by Melba Colgrove, Ph.D, Harold Bloomfield, M. D. & Peter McWilliams (Prelude Press, 1976, 1991).

Mom's House, Dad's House: Making Shared Custody Work, by Isolina Ricci. (Macmillan, 1980).

ReBuilding by Bruce Fisher (Impact Publishers, 1982).

Second Chances: Men, Women, and Children a Decade after Divorce, Who Wins, Who Loses and Why, by Judith S. Wallerstein and Sandra Blakeslee. (Ticknor & Fields, 1990).

The Unexpected Legacy of Divorce, by Judith Wallerstein
(Hyperion Press, 2000)

Other Issues:

The Dance of Anger, by Harriet Goldhor Lerner, Ph.D (Harper
& Row, 1985).

*The Dance of Intimacy: A Woman's Guide to Courageous Acts of
Change in Key Relationships*, by Harriet Goldhor Lerner,
Ph.D. (Harper & Row, 1989)

Feeling Good: The New Mood Therapy, by David D. Burns, M.D.
(Signet Books, 1980).

Getting the Love You Want: A Guide for Couples, by Harville
Hendrix, PhD. (Henry Holt and Company, 1988).

*Necessary Losses: The Loves, Illusions, Dependencies and
Impossible Expectations That All of Us Have to Give Up in
Order to Grow*, by Judith Viorst. (Ballentine, 1986).

When Anger Hurts: Quieting the Storm Within, by Matthew
McKay, Ph.D, Peter D. Rogers, Ph.D & Judith McKay,
R.N. (New Harbinger Publications, Inc., 1989).

You Just Don't Understand: Women and Men in Conversation, by
Deborah Tannen, Ph.D. (Ballentine Books, 1991).

Appendix C ~ Reading List for Children

These are some of the resources available for children regarding divorce. Where there is a recommended age or age range, that information is provided after the publisher.

All About Change, by Kathy Kage-Taylor and Donna Marmer. (Beech Acres, 1990). Early elementary School age.

Boys & Girls, Book About Divorce, by R. A. Gardner (Bantam, 1971). Ages 8-12.

Boys & Girls, Book About One-Parent Families, by R. A. Gardner (Bantam, 1978) Ages 7-12.

Boys & Girls, Book About Stepfamilies, by R. A. Gardner (Bantam, 1982). Ages 7-12.

Changing Families, by David Fassler, M.D., Michele Lash, M.Ed. and Sally Ives, Ph.D. (Waterfront Books, 1988). Preschoolers and School Age Children.

Dinosaurs Divorce, by L. K. Brown and M. Brown (Atlantic Monthly, 1986). Preschool-Early Elementary School.

Dear Mr. Henshaw, by Beverly Cleary. (Morrow, 1983). School Age Children and Preteens.

The Divorce Express, by P. Danziger (Delacorte, 1982). Teens. (Fiction).

Divorce Is a Grown-up Problem, by Janet Sinberg. (Avon, 1978). Preschoolers and School Age Children.

The Divorce Workbook, by David Fassler, M.D., Michele Lash, M.Ed. and Sally Ives, Ph.D. (Waterfront Books, 1985). Preschoolers and School Age Children.

Footsteps on the Stairs, by C. S. Adler (Delacorte, 1982).

How Does it Feel When Your Parents Get Divorced? by T.Berger (Julian Messner, 1977). Elementary School Age.

How It Feels When Parents Divorce, by Jill Krementz. (Knopf, 1984). Teens.

It's Not the End of the World, by Judy Blume. (Bradbury Press, 1972). School age and pre-teen children.

Let's Talk—Early Separation & Divorce Activity Book, By Jim & Joan Boulder (Boulder Publishing, 1991).

My Story—Divorce & Remarriage Activity Book, by Jim & Joan Boulder (Boulder Publishing, 1991).

Please Come Home—A Child's Book About Divorce, by Doris Sanford and Graci Evans (Multnomah Press, 1985).

Stepfamilies: New Patterns of Harmony, by L. Craven (Simon & Schuster, 1982). Ages: 11+.

The Story of May, by Mordecai Gerstein. (HarperCollins, 1993). Preschoolers and School Age Children.

Surviving Your Parents, Divorce, by C. Boeckman (Franklin Watts, 1980). Teens.

Appendix D ~ Parenting Plan Form

The form that follows is similar to that used by the Manitowoc County Family Court system to address the various parenting issues involved in a divorce or other family law action. Feel free to use this form to record or outline parenting arrangements reached regarding your children.

In re the marriage of: Parenting Plan

Case #_____

_____, Petitioner

and

_____, Respondent

NOTE: *Any party who does not file this form by the time of the pretrial conference gives up the right to object to the Parenting Plan filed by the other party.*

This plan is submitted by: _____

The minor children and their dates of birth are: _____

_____

_____

The legal custody or physical placement provisions I am seeking are: _____

_____

_____

I currently reside at: _____

Within the next 2 years I intend to live at:

_____

(Note: if there is evidence of interspousal battery, residence and employment information need not be specifically provided)

I work at the following places and have the following hours of employment:

Employer: _____ Hours: _____

Employer: _____ Hours: _____

The following person(s) will provide any necessary child care when I cannot be with my child(ren):

_____

The cost of this care will be paid by:

_____

The child(ren) will attend school as follows:

_____

_____

Medical care for the child(ren) will be provided by the following doctor/facility:

_____

_____

Medical expenses will be paid by:

_____

_____

The child(ren) will participate in the following church/religion:

_____

_____

The following person(s) will make decisions about the child(ren)'s education, medical care, choice of child care providers and extracurricular activities:

_____

_____

The holidays will be divided as follows:

_____

_____

The child(ren)'s summer schedule will be as follows:

_____

_____

_____

The child(ren) will be able to have contact with the other parent when they are with me at the following time(s) and in the following manner(s):

_____

_____

_____

Disagreements related to matters over which the court orders joint decision making will be resolved in the following manner:

_____

_____

_____

Child support, family support, maintenance or other income transfer will be as follows:

_____

_____

_____

The child(ren) will be transferred between parents for the exercise of physical placement as follows?

_____

_____

(Respond to this item only if there is evidence that either party engaged in interspousal battery or domestic abuse) The following safety measures will be in place to ensure the safety of the child(ren) and the parties during transfers of placement?

Are there any other issues, specific to your family that you would like to include as part of this Parenting Plan?

1.Issue:_____

_____

Ideas for
Resolution:_____

_____

_____

2.Issue: _____

_____

_____

Ideas for Resolution: _____

_____

_____

3.Issue: _____

_____

_____

Ideas for Resolution: _____

_____

_____

Appendix E ~ Feedback Form

In my continuing effort to provide accurate, up to date material, please take a few minutes to complete the following feedback form. This will help me update and improve the material presented. Your assistance and your time are greatly appreciated!

1. Please rate the following on a scale of 1 to 5:

(1= poor; 5= excellent)

a. Content presented	1 2 3 4 5
b. Examples used	1 2 3 4 5
c. Techniques suggested	1 2 3 4 5
d. Chapter summaries	1 2 3 4 5
e. Resources provided	1 2 3 4 5
f. Appendices	1 2 3 4 5

2. What is your overall reaction to the book?

3. What did you most enjoy or find helpful in the book?

4. Do you have suggestions or ideas to be included in further editions of this book?

5. Do have suggestions for other topics that would be of interest to you?

6. How did you learn about this book?

7. OPTIONAL: Please add my name to your mailing list to receive information about future books:

Name: _____

Address: _____

Please send the completed Feedback Form to:
Blue Waters Publications
P. O. Box 411-F
Manitowoc, WI 54221-0411

Appendix F

How to Contact the Author and Publisher

Please feel free to contact me in the following manner:

By US Mail:

Diane M. Berry

Blue Waters Publications

P. O. Box 411

Manitowoc, WI 54221-0411

By Fax:

(920) 683-9624

By Telephone:

(920) 683-3963

By E-mail:

bluewaterspublications@lakefield.net

Please also check out our websites:

www.bluewaterspublications.com
(for books and other materials available for sale)

and

www.bluewatersfc.com
(the clinic—Blue Waters Family Counseling, S. C.)

Notes

Introduction

1. United States Census Bureau (1990).

Chapter One

1. Krementz, J., *How It Feels When Parents Divorce* (Knopf, 1984)

2. Wallerstein, J. & Blakeslee, S., *Second Chances: Men, Women and Children a Decade After Divorce* (Ticknor & Fields, 1989).

3. Wallerstein, J., Lewis, J. and Blakeslee, S., *The Unexpected Legacy of Divorce* (Hyperion, 2000).

4. Wallerstein, J. & Blakeslee, S., *Second Chances.*

Chapter 3

1. Bavolek, S., and Comstock, C., *Nurturing Program* (Family Development Resources, Inc., 1985).

2. Beck, A., Rush, J., Shaw, B. and Emery, G., *The Cognitive Therapy of Depression* (Guilford Press, 1979); Ellis, A. and Harper, R., *A New Guide to Rational Living* (Prentice-Hall, 1975).

3. Wallerstein, J., Lewis, J. and Blakeslee, S., *The Unexpected Legacy of Divorce.*

Chapter 4

1. Benson, H., *The Relaxation Response* (William Morrow, 1975).

Chapter 5

1. Folberg, J. and Milne, A., editors, *Divorce Mediation Theory and Practice* (Guilford Press, 1991).

Chapter 6

1. Wallerstein, J., Lewis, J. and Blakeslee, S., *Second Chances.*

2. Berry, D., *Bonding and Attachment: A Story of Love and Relationship* (An Unpublished Thesis in Partial Fulfillment of the Requirements for the Degree of Master of Social Work, 1994).

3. Boernboom, R. *Self Mastery Workshop: Domestic Violence Treatment and Prevention*, (Rose Mary Boerboom, 2001).

4. Kovacs, D., *When Is Saturday?* (Sesame Street), (Golden Pr. Audio, 1986).

Chapter 7

1. Singer, J. L. and Singer, D. G., *Television Imagination and Aggression: A Study of Pre-Schoolers*, Play (Two studies, 1980).

Chapter 8

1. Boernboom, R., *Self Mastery Workshop*.

2. Ch. DWD 40, Wis. Admin Code.

Chapter 10

1. American Psychiatric Association, *Diagnostic and Statistical Manual of Mental Disorders*, Fourth Edition (American Psychiatric Association, 1994).

2. Visher, E. and Visher, J., *Therapy With Stepfamilies*, (Brunner/Mazel, 1996).

Index

Quick Order Form

Postal Orders: Mail completed form and check to:
Blue Waters Publications, LLC
P. O. Box 411
Manitowoc, WI 54221-0411

E-mail and Credit Card Orders: Please visit our website
www.bluewaterspublications.com

Questions: Telephone:(920) 683-3963
Fax:(920) 683-9624

Please send me the following books and articles:

I understand I may return any of them for a full refund—for any reason with no questions asked.

____Child-Friendly Divorce $17.95

____Positively Managing Your Stress! $5.95

____Soothing the Self $3.95

____Other: _____

Please send me free information on:

_____ Other Books _____ Seminars _____ Consulting

Name: _____

Address: _____

City: _____ State: ____ Zip: _____

Telephone_____

Email Address: _____

Sales Tax: *Please add 5% for products shipped to Wisconsin addresses.*

Shipping: Please add $4.00 for the first book and $2.00 for each additional book or article shipped.

*If you wish to pay by credit card, please visit our website (www.bluewaterspublications.com) at which that option is available. Thank you